David Hume's Theory of Mind

Daniel E. Flage

London and New York

First published 1990
by Routledge
11 New Fetter Lane, London EC4P 4EE

Simultaneously published in the USA and Canada
by Routledge
a division of Routledge, Chapman and Hall, Inc.
29 West 35th Street, New York, NY 10001

© 1990 Daniel E. Flage

Typeset by Columns of Reading
Printed in Great Britain by
T.J. Press (Padstow) Ltd,
Padstow, Cornwall

British Library Cataloguing in Publication Data
Flage, Daniel E.
David Hume's theory of mind.
1. Scottish philosophy. Hume, David, 1711–1776: Treatise
of human nature
I. Title
192

Library of Congress Cataloging in Publication Data
Flage, Daniel E.
David Hume's theory of mind/Daniel E. Flage.
p. cm.
Includes bibliographical references.
1. Hume, David, 1711–1776—Contributions in philosophy of mind.
2. Philosophy of mind. I. Title
B1499.M47F55 1990
128'.2'092—dc20   89–27518
CIP

ISBN 0–415–02138–3

Jacket picture reproduced courtesy of the
Hulton - Deutsch Collection

To my parents

What experience can tell us is that there is something wrong some-where in the system; but we can make our choice as to which part of the system we consider to be at fault.

R. B. Braithwaite, *Scientific Explanation*

Contents

v

Acknowledgements

In working on this study, I have benefited greatly from discussions and comments from a large number of friends and colleagues. I particularly wish to thank Phillip Cummins, Edwin Allaire, Herbert Hochberg, A. P. Martinich, Frederick Kronz, Sarah Broadie, Frederick Broadie, Ronald J. Glass, Kenneth Merrill, Donald W. Livingston, and Jane McIntyre.

Research for this book was supported by a Fellowship for University Teachers from the National Endowment for the Humanities and a Faculty Research Appointment from the University Research Institute of the University of Texas at Austin. I wish to thank both organizations for their encouragement and support.

Some of the early research for *David Hume's Theory of Mind* was presented in articles. I wish to thank the editor of *Noûs* for permission to reprint a revised version of 'Hume's Dualism' (Flage 1982a); the editor of *Hume Studies* for permission to reprint portions of 'Hume's Relative Ideas' (Flage 1981a), 'Hume on Memory and Causation' (Flage 1985b), and 'The Minds of David Hume' (Flage 1987b); the editor of *The Southern Journal of Philosophy* for permission to reprint portions of 'Hume on Denotation and Connotation' (Flage 1986b); the editor of *The Southern Journal of Philosophy* and Ronald J. Glass for permission to reprint portions of 'Hume on the Cartesian Theory of Substance' (Flage and Glass 1984); and the editor of *The Modern Schoolman* for permission to reprint a revised version of 'Hume's Identity Crisis' (Flage 1980).

I wish to thank Oxford University Press for permission to quote passages from the Selby-Bigge and Nidditch editions of Hume's *A Treatise of Human Nature* (Hume 1978) and the *Enquiries concerning the Human Understanding and concerning the Principles of Morals* (Hume 1975), the Nidditch edition of Locke's *An Essay concerning Human Understanding* (Locke 1975), and the Greig edition of *The Letters of David Hume* (Hume 1932).

I wish to thank Clarence Bonnen for guiding me through various labyrinths on the University of Texas mainframe.

Finally I wish to thank my wife, Dana, for her encouragement and patience throughout the research and writing of this book.

D.E.F.
Austin, Texas

A Note on Abbreviations

The following abbreviations will be used throughout the book. References to Hume's writings will be made parenthetically within the text of the book.

T x, *A Treatise of Human Nature* (Hume 1978), page x.
EHU x, *An Enquiry concerning Human Understanding* (in Hume 1975), page x.
EPM x, *An Enquiry concerning the Principles of Morals* (in Hume 1975), page x.
NHR x, *The Natural History of Religion* (Hume 1956), page x.
D x, *Dialogues concerning Natural Religion* (Hume 1947), page x.
Letters x:y, *The Letters of David Hume* (Hume 1932) volume x:page y.
LGFE x, *A Letter from a Gentleman to his Friend in Edinburgh* (Hume 1967), page x.
GG x:y, *The Philosophical Works* (Hume 1886), volume x:page y.
Descartes, *CSM* x:y, *The Philosophical Writings of Descartes* (Descartes 1984-5), volume x:page y.
Descartes, *Principles* X, y, *The Principles of Philosophy* (Descartes 1984-5: 1:179-291), Part X, section y.
Locke, *Essay*, x.y.z, *An Essay concerning Human Understanding* (Locke 1975), Book x.Chapter y.Section z.
Berkeley, *PHK*, X, y, George Berkeley, *A Treatise on the Principles of Human Knowledge* (in Berkeley 1948-57: 2:19-113), Part X, Section y.

All quotations in this book will follow the originals unless duly indicated. Modifications in wording will employ square brackets. Omissions will be indicated by ellipsis points. Changes in emphasis will be indicated by 'my emphasis' or 'emphasis added'.

INTRODUCTION

Anyone who reads David Hume's *Treatise of Human Nature* cannot but be struck by the diversity of philosophical issues Hume addresses, his shifts in emphasis, and his tendency either to ignore traditional philosophical issues or to provide nonphilosophical answers to philosophical questions. In the first book of the *Treatise* alone, Hume discusses such apparently diverse issues as the nature of thought (*T* 1-15), the meanings of words (*T* 17-25), space and time (*T* 26-65), the nature of knowledge (*T* 69-73), causal reasoning (*T* 73-176), the reach of reason (*T* 180-7), material substance (*T* 219-25), immaterial substance (*T* 232-251), and personal identity (*T* 251-63). It is understandable that one might claim the *Treatise* 'lack[s] . . . a clearly defined subject-matter' (Boring 1950: 186) or that 'Hume . . . was a philosophical puppy-dog, picking up and worrying one problem after another, always leaving his teeth-marks in it, but casting it aside when it threatened to become wearisome' (Passmore 1980: 87-8).

Further, Hume's treatment of philosophical issues is anything but what one would expect from a philosopher. Hume was an epistemologist, but his discussions of memory pay little or no attention to the epistemic question of the nature and extent of knowledge based upon memory (cf. *T* 8-10 and 84-86). Hume was a sceptic, but although one of his most famous sceptical discussions shows that one's knowledge of causal connections is severely limited, he provides numerous *causal* explanations of beliefs. Indeed, while he discusses such philosophical issues as our knowledge of the external world and the problem of personal identity, his apparent 'solution' to those problems consists of nothing more than explanations of those beliefs.

In this book I show that, contrary to initial appearances, there is an overriding theme that unites the several issues Hume examines in the first book of the *Treatise*. I argue that Hume's concern throughout the first book was with the nature of the mind, in so far as that nature can be 'known' on the basis of 'the experimental method'. Nor should this be surprising. The very subtitle of the *Treatise* indicates that it is 'An Attempt to introduce the experimental Method of Reasoning into Moral Subjects'. Further, in the Introduction to the *Treatise* Hume extols the advances in natural philosophy (physics) since Bacon (*T* xvii), commenting that "Tis no astonishing reflection to consider, that the application of experimental philosophy to moral subjects should come after that to natural at the distance of above a whole century' (*T* xvi). He then remarks:

> For to me it seems evident, that the essence of the mind being equally unknown to us with that of external bodies, it must be equally impossible to form any notion of its powers and qualities otherwise than from careful and exact experiments, and the observations of its different circumstances and situations. And tho' we must endeavour to render all our principles as universal as possible, by tracing up our experiments to the utmost, and explaining all effects from the simplest and fewest causes, 'tis still certain we cannot go beyond experience; and any hypothesis, that pretends to discover the ultimate original qualities of human nature, ought at first to be rejected as presumptuous and chimerical. (*T* xvii)

His objective is 'to explain the principles of human nature' (*T* xiv), to develop a theory of the nature of the mind along lines similar to those used in physics to develop a theory of the nature of the body, and he proceeds by 'glean[ing] up our experiments in this science from a cautious observation of human life' (*T* xix). I show that much of the first book of the *Treatise* is an attempt to establish that the mind 'is nothing but a heap or collection of different perceptions, united together by certain relations, and suppos'd, tho' falsely, to be endow'd with a perfect simplicity and identity' (*T* 207).

In Chapter 1 I examine Hume's method of inquiry. I show that the Hume of the *Treatise* was committed to accepting whichever theory provides the 'best explanation' of a phenomenon of a certain kind and that he provided three criteria for judging what makes a theory best. First, all theoretical terms must be definable in terms of observable properties. Second, a theory must be explanatorily complete, that is, it must explain all phenomena of a certain kind. Finally, one should always choose the 'simplest' theory, that is, in so far as two or more theories are explanatorily complete, one should choose that theory which commits one to the fewest distinct kinds of entities and explanatory laws. To show that a theory is the most plausible of the available alternatives, one must examine particularly problematic cases and show that one's theory will allow one consistently to explain those phenomena. In Hume's case, the problematic cases are cases of persistent beliefs that are unwarranted by empirical evidence. I argue that the primary function of Hume's sceptical arguments--many of which were anything but original with Hume--is to show that certain beliefs are evidentially problematic, and it is on the basis of his theoretical explanation of these beliefs that Hume initially deemed his theory of mind adequate.

In Chapter 2 I examine the fundamental elements of Hume's theory, viz., his theory of perceptions, his theory of relations, and his theory of linguistic meaning. I show that perceptions were taken to be nothing more than the fundamental elements of Hume's theory and that the principles of the association of ideas were principles that, on the face of it, appear to explain all mental phenomena. This is nothing more than a preliminary examination of his theory; the adequacy of the theory founded on these elements is to be judged on the basis of its explanatory completeness.

In Chapter 3 I examine Hume's account of thought. I argue that, in its most primitive sense, an idea is an 'image', but that Hume also countenanced nonimagistic ideas, what he called 'relative ideas'. Relative ideas play an important role in Hume's account of one's thoughts of imperceptible objects. I conclude by arguing that Humean thoughts are complex cognitive states often composed of both impressions and ideas: they are intentional acts, and every thought has an idea as its intentional object.

In Chapter 4 I examine Hume's attack on the doctrine of substance. This is the first example of what I call Hume's method of 'doxastic pathology', which is a combination of a critical examination of a belief and an explanation of that belief on the basis of the principles of the association of ideas. I show that this pattern is found in his discussion 'Of the Antient Philosophy'. I then turn to 'Of the Immateriality of the Soul' and argue that Hume's primary objective in that section was to call the Cartesian theory of substance into doubt. I argue that even his seemingly satirical charge of Spinozism against the substance theorists is significant, for in so far as the Cartesian theory of substance can be made intelligible, absurd consequences follow from it. While Hume's attacks on the doctrine of substance are inconclusive to the extent that they do not show that the term 'substance' is and must be meaningless, they at least pave the way for a bundle theory of mind.

In Chapter 5 I examine Hume's discussions of induction and necessary connection. I begin by showing that Shaftesbury held that necessary connections unite objects in a system. Since Hume was well aware of Shaftesbury's works (cf. *T* 254n), the attack on necessary connections was needed to show that perceptions, the fundamental entities in Hume's theory of mind, are independent entities. I show that his discussions of induction and necessary connection parallel his discussions of substance in so far as they are studies in doxastic pathology.

In Chapter 6 I examine Hume's accounts of mind and body. I show that the method of doxastic pathology comes to the fore in 'Of Scepticism with Regard to the Senses', and that while Hume might not have been a representational realist in so far as he was sceptical of the claim that external objects 'resemble' one's perceptions, he held that positing the existence of material objects--whatever their nature might be-- provides the best explanation of perceptions. I conclude the chapter by arguing that Hume drew a distinction among perceptions on the basis of their susceptibility to spatial relations and that it is reasonable to suggest that he distinguished mental systems (minds) from physical systems (bodies) on the basis of the susceptibility of entities in each system to spatial relations: all entities in a physical system are susceptible to spatial relations, while not all entities in a mental system are susceptible to spatial relations.

In Chapter 7 I examine Hume's discussion of personal identity. I show that, for Hume, the belief in personal identity is the belief in the substantiality of the mind, that is, the belief in the perfect simplicity and identity of the mind. After arguing that he finds no empirical evidence for such a belief, he explains the belief in the identity of the mind and suggests that the same explanation holds, *mutatis mutandis*, for the belief in simplicity. But, as Hume tells us in the Appendix to the *Treatise*, the account of personal identity failed, although his explanation of *why* it failed is notoriously opaque. I show that Hume's two 'inconsistent' principles (*T* 636) are inconsistent with the belief in the simplicity of the mind, and I argue that the principles of the association of ideas will not allow him to explain the belief in mental simplicity. I show that this failure is sufficient to generate a veritable labyrinth of contradictions, difficulties sufficient to call the very foundations of Hume's theory of mind into doubt.

In Chapter 8 I turn to the first *Enquiry*, asking whether Hume was able to refurbish the theory of the *Treatise* in such a way that he could overcome the difficulties he had uncovered. I argue that he made no attempt to refurbish the theory, rather, he changed his objectives. While he provides an 'account of mind', that 'account' is nothing more than a lawful description of the mind, and as such, its adequacy is compatible with virtually any theory of the *nature* of the mind. I conclude by arguing that a nonstylistic ground for Hume's disavowal of the *Treatise* is found in the inadequacy of the theory of mind he had

4

developed in that early work and show that in this respect alone the disavowal of the *Treatise* constitutes 'a complete Answer to Dr Reid and to that bigotted silly Fellow, Beattie' (*Letters* 2:301).

I conclude the work with an appendix on force and vivacity. I show that Hume was not wholly satisfied with the account of force and vivacity in the *Treatise* and that there is some evidence that in the first *Enquiry* he construed force and vivacity as impressions of reflection that 'accompany' other perceptions.

Before turning to the *Treatise*, one further point should be made. The current work is a historical study. As such, my objective is to construct a clear account of Hume's theory of mind on the basis of the textual evidence, not to enumerate the philosophical shortcomings of Hume's work. Hence, if my remarks seem uncritical in that regard, I take it to be a function of the type of study in which I am engaged.

1

Hume's Method

Hume tells us that the *Treatise of Human Nature* is '*an Attempt to introduce the experimental Method of Reasoning into Moral Subjects*' (*T* xi), yet he devoted little space to the meta-theoretical constraints he assumed in constructing a theory. In this chapter I attempt to reconstruct Hume's account of the adequacy of theories. I begin by examining those passages in which Hume alludes to the meta-theoretical constraints he uses in constructing a theory. Next I examine Hume's discussion of 'realities' and argue that he considered it a normal human activity to construct 'theories' in the sense of schemes for interpreting empirical data. Finally, I briefly examine the strategy Hume used in defending his theory of mind. If my argument is sound, it shows that Hume accepted whichever theory in a particular subject area provides the 'best explanation' of a certain range of phenomena, and he provides various normative strictures for determining which explanation is 'best'.[1]

Meta-Theory

Hume's meta-theoretical principles are of three kinds: principles governing the acceptability of theoretical terms, a principle of parsimony, and a principle of explanatory completeness. As we shall see, each of these kinds of principle is relevant to considerations of the acceptability and epistemic status of scientific theories.

It is clear that Hume accepted an empiricist theory of meaning, and, therefore, that any theoretical term one employs in a scientific or philosophical theory must have its meaning assigned on the basis of experience (cf. *T* 17-25 and *EHU* 21-2).[2] This is a minimal condition for the intelligibility of a theory. Although a commitment to an empiricist theory of meaning does not entail that one must be directly acquainted with theoretical objects, it does place several constraints upon the theoretical terms one uses. In his discussion of Spinozism Hume spelled out some of these constraints. In his words:

> I say then, that since we may suppose, but never conceive a specific difference betwixt an object and impression; any conclusion we form concerning the connexion and repugnance of impressions, will not be known certainly to be applicable to objects; but that on the other hand, whatever conclusions of this kind we form concerning objects will, most certainly be applicable to impressions. The reason is not difficult. As an object is suppos'd to be different from an impression, we cannot be sure, that the circumstance, upon which we found our reasoning, is common to both, supposing we form the reasoning upon the impression. 'Tis still possible, that the object may differ from it in that particular. But when we first form our reasoning concerning the object, 'tis beyond doubt, that the same reasoning must extend to the impression: And that because the quality of the object, upon which the argument is founded, must at least be conceiv'd by the mind; and cou'd not be conceiv'd, unless it were common to the impression; since we have no idea but what is deriv'd from that origin. Thus we may establish it as a certain maxim, that we can never, by any principle, but by an irregular kind of reasoning from experience, discover a connection or repugnance betwixt objects, which extends not to impressions; tho' the inverse proposition may not be equally true, that all the discoverable relations of impressions are common to objects. (*T* 241-2; cf. *T* 29)

Hume's empiricist theory of meaning places constraints upon the descriptions one can offer of theoretical objects. Although the objects in one's theory need not be immediately observable, they cannot be 'specifically different' (different in kind) from impressions, that is, the characteristics assignable to theoretical objects must be characteristics of the same species or kind as one assigns to impressions.[3] Thus, properties such as motion or spin can be applied to theoretical objects, since such terms obtain their meaning in the domain of impressions. On the other hand, terms allegedly denoting nonempirical properties are unintelligible. But the passage is not concerned solely with the delimitation of the properties of theoretical objects to the empirically observable. It also raises issues regarding the construction and evaluation of a theory.

Hume claimed that, in constructing a theory, one cannot simply draw inferences from the properties of impressions to the properties of objects, since ''Tis still possible, that the object may differ from it in that particular.' On the other hand, 'when we first form our reasoning concerning the object, 'tis beyond doubt, that the same reasoning must extend to the impression' (*T* 242), that is, if one begins by constructing a theoretical description of objects, one's reasonings regarding objects must extend to one's reasonings concerning impressions, since it is on the basis of impressions that one assigns meanings to theoretical terms. Given an empiricist theory of meaning, an intelligible, and therefore minimally plausible, theory must (1) draw all its concepts from experience and (2) reach conclusions that are consistent with those empirical concepts. What I shall call 'Hume's principle of theoretical objects' allows one to examine the consistency of one's theoretical descriptions: if a claim is absurd with respect to the domain of impressions, the same claim is absurd with respect to the domain of theoretical objects, since the meaning of a theoretical term is derived from the domain of impressions.[4]

Finally, the passage suggests that Hume, like Locke and Bacon (Locke, *Essay* 4.12.13; Bacon 1960: 121-272; cf. Urbach 1987), recognized a distinction between three phases of a theoretical investigation. Although one might begin with observation, at a certain point one constructs an explanatory theory (hypothesis), and one then proceeds to examine the evidence in an attempt to confirm or refute that theory.

In addition to his principle of theoretical objects, Hume accepted a version of the principle of parsimony, contending that 'it is an inviolable maxim in philosophy, that where any particular cause is sufficient for an effect, we ought to rest satisfied with it, and ought not multiply causes without necessity' (*T* 578). Thus, in one's theory, one should attempt to discover the smallest number of different kinds of theoretical entities and natural laws that are sufficient to explain a certain domain of phenomena.

Finally, Hume held that a theory must be explanatorily complete. The search for natural laws occurs at the level of observable phenomena: it follows the inductive principles sketched in the 'Rules by which to Judge of Causes and Effects' (*T* 173-6). But if the theory is complete, it must explain all phenomena of a particular kind, and, as we shall see, particularly the problematic cases. Since Hume took Newtonian mechanics as a paradigm of a theory that is explanatorily complete (*EHU* 14-15), an adequate theory of mind must provide a similarly complete explanation of mental phenomena.[5]

Evidence that Hume actually considered these the proper grounds for accepting a theory can be drawn from the *Natural History of Religion*. Commenting on the origins of polytheism, Hume indicates that primitive peoples posited a multiplicity of gods as the unknown causes of events. Contrasting this with the corpuscular hypothesis, he wrote:

> Could men anatomize nature, according to the most probable, at least the most intelligible philosophy, they would find, that these causes are nothing but the particular fabric and structure of the minute parts of their own bodies and of external objects; and that, by a regular and constant machinery, all the events are produced, about which they are so much concerned. But this philosophy exceeds the comprehension of the ignorant multitude, who can only conceive the unknown causes in a general and confused manner; though their imagination, perpetually employed on the same subject, must labour to form some particular and distinct idea of them. The more they consider these causes themselves, and the uncertainty of their operation, the less satisfaction do they meet with in their researches; and, however unwilling, they must at last have abandoned so arduous an attempt, were it not for a propensity in human nature, which leads into a system, and gives them some satisfaction. (*NHR* 29)

There are four reasons why the corpuscular hypothesis is superior to polytheism. (1) The theoretical entities (corpuscles) are wholly describable on the basis of the properties of impressions. The corpuscular hypothesis is consistent with both an empiricist theory of meaning and Hume's principle of theoretical objects. (2) The corpuscular hypothesis is simpler than the religious hypothesis, since it allows one to explain physical events solely on the basis of objects that are themselves physical. (3) The movements of the corpuscles can be explained on the basis of a limited number of natural laws, namely, the principles of Newtonian mechanics. (4) Assuming that the thesis of determinism is true (cf. *T* 406, *EHU* 92-3, and 108-16), such theoretical explanations would be complete.

One point should be noted regarding the passage from the *Natural History of Religion*. Although Hume suggested that the corpuscular hypothesis is 'the most probable, at least the most intelligible philosophy' (*NHR* 29), he did not claim that the theory could be known to be true. But, as he indicates in his letter to John Stewart, the absence of intuitive or demonstrative certainty does not detract from either the truth of a belief (theory) or its certainty, although the kind of certainty differs from that of intuition or demonstration (*Letters*, 1:187). This suggests that the most Hume would claim in favor of a theory is moral certainty,[6] that, in accordance with his meta-theoretical strictures, the theory in question provides the best explanation of a certain domain of phenomena and it is, therefore, the most plausible theory.[7]

While an adequate theory must provide the best explanation of *all* phenomena within a certain domain, does this imply that all explanations are of equal value in providing evidence for the acceptability of a theory? Hume's answer seems to be negative, and he seems to be in agreement with some recent proponents of theoretical justification on the basis of the best explanation who suggest that acceptability of a theory rests primarily upon its ability to explain puzzling phenomena or anomalies.[8] The Hume of the *Enquiries* alludes to the '*experimentum crucis*, or that experiment which points out the right way in any doubt or ambiguity' (*EPM* 219). But which are these crucial experiments or crucial explanations? As we shall see when we turn to the theory of mind in the *Treatise*, the anomalous cases seem to be those in which one has a belief that is shown to be unwarranted by various sceptical arguments, and yet the belief remains.[9] How can there be such an unwarranted belief? If Hume's psychological theory can explain how such unwarranted beliefs are generated, and if, consistent with his own meta-theoretical constraints, his theory provides a better explanation than any known alternative theory, he has good grounds for accepting his theory until such a time as some alternative theory provides an even better explanation.

If my suggestion is correct, Hume's sceptical arguments are presented neither for their own sake nor, as in the case of the classical sceptics, to obtain mental tranquillity (cf. Sextus Empiricus 1985: 41). While convinced that the sceptical arguments are sound, the Hume of the *Treatise* sets them forth merely as a starting point for an explanatory program. I shall call Hume's two-stage discussion of beliefs, that is, his sceptical objections to a particular belief followed by an explanation of why one holds the belief in spite of its lack of evidential foundations, 'doxastic pathology', and we shall see that doxastic pathology is Hume's fundamental approach to philosophical problems in the first book of the *Treatise*. Further, and consistent with this objective, most of Hume's sceptical arguments are anything but original: many are anticipated in the works of both the classical and the sixteenth- and seventeenth-century sceptics.

If my sketch of Hume's method is correct, then judgements of theoretical adequacy are based primarily on questions of intelligibility and coherence. In turning to Hume's discussion of 'realities', that is, the informal interpretive schema all persons construct, we shall see that it is questions of evidential coherence that play a primary role in even the lowest forms of theoretical inquiry.

Realities

There can be little question that Hume deemed the coherence and consistency of one's claims (beliefs) to be of primary importance in both one's theoretical undertakings and in common life. Hume the sceptic was never willing to *assume* that one's impressions of sensation are caused by or resemble external objects (*T* 84). Hence, the question of the 'truth' of one's impressions, ideas or theoretical claims, that is, their correspondence with external objects (cf. *T* 448 and 458), was an issue he generally left open as indeterminable (cf. *T* 272; cf. *T* 121). Nonetheless, he held that 'We may draw inferences from the coherence of our perceptions, whether they be true or false; whether they represent nature justly or be mere illusions of the senses' (*T* 84).[10] As we shall see, Hume's notion of coherence involves considerations of (1) causal relations, (2) relations of resemblance, (3) relations of contiguity, and (4) logical consistency.[11] It is on the basis of coherence that human beings construct 'realities'.

Hume's discussion of realities in *Treatise* I.iii.9 is a response to an objection to his associationist account of belief, an objection to the effect that it is possible that all beliefs arise solely on the basis of causal relations. He wrote:

> 'Tis evident, that whatever is present to the memory, striking upon the mind with a vivacity, which resembles an immediate impression, must become of considerable moment in all the operations of the mind, and must easily distinguish itself above the mere fictions of the imagination. Of these impressions or ideas of the memory we form a kind of system, comprehending whatever we remember to have been present, either to our internal perception or senses; and every particular of that system, joined to the present impressions, we are pleased to call a *reality*. But the mind stops not here. For finding, that with this system of perceptions, there is another connected by custom, or if you will, by the relation of cause or effect, it proceeds to the consideration of their ideas; and as it feels that 'tis in a manner necessarily determin'd to view these particular ideas, and that the custom or relation, by which it is determin'd, admits not of the least change, it forms them into a new system, which it likewise dignifies with the title of *realities*. The first of these systems is the object of the memory and senses; the second of the judgment. (*T* 107-8)

Human beings have a natural tendency to organize experience into systems of objects, that is, realities.[12] In this paragraph Hume is concerned with the commonsense division between one's own mind or person and the world of ordinary objects. Each is believed to be a distinct reality. Assuming a Lockean account of personhood (Locke, *Essay* 2.27.9-17; cf. *T* 261-2), Hume notes that the ideas of the memory form a system of objects that one deems a reality. Memory, of course, rests upon resemblance (*T* 8-9; 85), which shows that causation alone is not involved in the formation of a belief. But as Hume goes on to show, causation can claim the lion's share in the construction of one's beliefs, since it is on the basis of the presumption that the perceptions constituting one's self are causally related to other objects that one constructs a second reality, or system of realities, namely, a system of beliefs regarding the external world. This system is the object of judgement.

The passage above provides only barest outline of what is involved in and the significance of those systems of realities that are the objects of judgement, although it is worthy of notice that Hume uses the plural '*realities*'. Why does he use the plural? A plausible reason is that the external world is composed of a system of interrelated systems of objects. Each *ordinary* object would constitute one system in the larger system. For example, each *ordinary* object has its own history and is distinct from every other ordinary object. Yet each is a part of a larger systematic whole.

In continuing his discussion Hume tends to confirm this account of the external world, the realm of judgement, as a system or systems of objects, each system or reality being itself an epistemic construct. Hume continues:

> 'Tis this latter principle [judgement], which peoples the world, and brings us acquainted with such existences, as by their removal in time and place, lie beyond the reach of the senses and memory. By means of it I paint the universe in my imagination, and fix my attention on any part of it I please. I form an idea of ROME, which I neither see nor remember; but which is connected with such impressions as I remember to have received from the conversation and books of travellers and historians. The idea of *Rome* I place in a certain situation on the idea of an object I call the globe. I join to it the conception of a particular government, and religion, and manners. I look backward and consider its first foundation; its several revolutions, successes, and misfortunes. All this, and every thing else, which I believe, are nothing but ideas; tho' by their force and settled order, arising from custom and the relation of cause and effect, they distinguish themselves from the other ideas, which are merely the offspring of the imagination. (*T* 108)

In constructing systems of realities, the judgement correlates ideas with ideas and, indeed, systems of ideas with systems of ideas. Rome is one such reality. One constructs one's idea of Rome on the basis of the verbal, written, and pictorial testimony of travelers and historians. As one gains more and more information, one's idea of Rome becomes increasingly rich. First, the word 'Rome' might be associated with nothing more than an idea of a point on the globe, that is, it might be deemed a proper part of a more general reality. Later the word 'Rome' might be associated with a certain style or styles of architecture, a certain series of historical events, certain governmental forms, certain religious traditions, and so forth. Each of the additional presumed facts that one adds to one's constructed idea of Rome is based upon the testimony of others, and, if one's construction is to be deemed plausible, this testimony itself must be subject to critical evaluation based upon one's wider experiences (cf. *T* 113). For example, at some point in one's construction of one's idea of Rome, one might include the legendary claim that the city was founded by Romulus and Remus, two men who had been raised by a she-wolf. At a later point in time one might reject this claim because (1) one's experience indicates that she-wolves do not raise children or (2) one might discover an alternative account of the founding of Rome that is more consistent with the general dictates of one's experience.[13]

One's idea of Rome is a construct, and in deeming it a 'reality', Hume's discussion smacks of phenomenalism, if not idealism.[14] This appearance is reinforced by the fact that Hume held that 'Whatever we conceive, we conceive to be existent' (*T* 67), which entails that one can conceive of something as an existent but not as a real thing (cf. Berkeley, *PHK*, I, 29-34), a point that seems to be entailed by Hume's discussion of the Elysian Fields (*T* 109). Does this mean that Hume should be subject to the same kinds of criticisms G. E. Moore raised against Berkeley and Bradley, namely, that the existence/reality distinction is unintelligible (Moore 1922: 75-8 and 197-219)? Perhaps, but there is another plausible interpretation of Hume available.

The construction of a reality is comparable to Locke's account of the construction of an abstract idea of gold. In his discussion of the nominal essence of gold, Locke claimed that the idea is slowly constructed as one's experience increases. As Locke wrote:

> What then are we to do for the improvement of our *Knowledge in substantial Beings*? . . . *Experience here must teach me*, what reason cannot: and 'tis by trying alone, that I can certainly know, what other Qualities co-exist with those of my complex *Idea*, *v.g.* whether that *yellow, heavy, fusible* Body, I call *Gold*, be *malleable*, or no; which Experience (which way ever it prove, in

that particular Body, I examine) make me not certain, that it is so, in all, or any other *yellow, heavy, fusible* Bodies, but which I have tried. Because it is no Consequence one way or t'other from my complex *Idea*; the Necessity or Inconsistence of *Malleability*, hath no visible connexion with the Combination of that *Colour, Weight*, and *Fusibility* in any body. What I have said here of the nominal Essence of *Gold*, supposed to consist of a body of such a determinate *Colour, Weight*, and *Fusibility*, will hold true, if *Malleableness, Fixedness*, and *Solubility* in *Aqua Regia* be added to it. (Locke, *Essay* 4.12.9)

Hume *appears* to take Locke's account of the nominal essence of gold over into his own account of concept formation (*T* 16),[15] and the formation of one's idea of gold and one's idea of Rome differs only in so far as temporal considerations play no role in the construction of an idea of what gold is--gold presumably possesses the same qualities at all points in time--while temporal considerations play a significant role in the construction of a 'reality' such as Rome. Hume's notion of a reality is a theoretical account of what something is. Like all theoretical accounts, it is based upon observation, testimony, considerations of internal consistency, and consistency with the remainder of one's experience. It is on the basis of the latter that one would discount the claim that Romulus and Remus were raised by a she-wolf. Further, in the case of a limited but spatially and temporally complex reality such as Rome, it must be locatable within a more general scheme of spatial-temporal realities.

I do not wish to suggest that there are no differences between explanatory theories and Lockean abstract ideas, for differences there certainly are. For example, an explanatory theory can provide grounds for claiming that there are unobservable things having certain properties. Yet there are significant similarities. Both are constructed on the basis of experience. Both support counter-factual conditionals. Both are subject to revision or modification on the basis of experience that is contrary to the claims of the abstract idea or theory. Finally, both general abstract ideas and general theories in principle can be subsumed under abstract ideas or theories of greater generality. Because there are these similarities between abstract ideas, theories, and Humean realities, I believe it is reasonable to consider a Humean reality such as Rome a kind of 'theory', although it is a 'theory' constructed without recourse to the meta-theoretical strictures Hume deemed germane to proper theory construction.

Although Hume's example of Rome as a reality is little more than a Lockean abstract idea of a spatially and temporally complex object, his comment that Rome as a reality is itself located within a more complex reality--'the idea of *Rome* I place in a certain situation on the idea of an object, which I call a globe' (*T* 108)--indicates that realities can be very complex and very general. Virtually any system of beliefs can be treated as a reality or theory, and, as such, it can be evaluated in terms of the meta-theoretical strictures Hume employs. As we shall see in subsequent chapters, Hume's critical discussions of mental and physical substance, theories of perception, and the primary/secondary qualities distinction all might be placed under the heading of 'realities', and some of his criticisms of each of these theories follow the strictures of his meta-theory: many of his arguments go beyond the standard sceptical claims that a certain theoretical belief is unwarranted by the empirical evidence or that there are counter-balancing arguments both for and against a point.

Hume's Strategies

How did Hume use his meta-theoretical principles in constructing his theory of mind? How did he introduce the fundamental entities in this theory? What are the fundamental explanatory principles in his theory, and how does he justify them?

As we shall see in the following chapters, Hume's theoretical moves are of two sorts. In so far as he was attempting to provide the *best* explanation of mental phenomena as the basis for deeming his bundle theory of mind plausible, it was incumbent upon him to show that his own theory of mind was more plausible than any other. To do so, Hume devoted a significant amount of space to the refutation of the major competitor to a bundle theory of mind, namely, a substance theory. According to Descartes, Locke, Berkeley, and most philosophers of the modern period, a mind is a substance or substratum in which ideas inhere. If such a theory is at all plausible, the term 'substance' must be intelligible, that is, one must be able to provide a definition of the term that is based upon data available to experience. Hume argued time and again that this cannot be done. Hence, the substratum theory of mental substance must be rejected strictly on grounds of intelligibility. As we shall see, Hume argued that one has no idea of substance *qua* substratum, and in so far as one attempts to intelligibly provide content to the notion of a substratum, one becomes entangled in a web of absurdities.

Although the substratum theory of substance was the primary substance theory current in the early eighteenth century, there was an alternative theory of substance set forth by Lord Shaftesbury and others according to which a substance is a complex of ideas necessarily connected with one another (cf. Shaftesbury 1964: 2: 64, 99-100). Hume spends little time explicitly discussing this theory (cf. *T* 254-5), although he almost certainly had it in mind when discussing the alleged necessary connection in a causal relation, and we shall see that the theory is of some importance in finding our way through that 'labyrinth of contradictions' to which Hume alludes in the discussion of personal identity in the Appendix to the *Treatise*.

Although it is incumbent upon Hume to discredit alternative theories of mind, the bulk of the first book of the *Treatise* is devoted to developing his positive account of mind, namely, the bundle theory. The first part of Book I is devoted primarily to the introduction of the fundamental entities in his theory of the mind (perceptions), the basic laws or principles that describe how these entities are related in the mind (the relations of the association of ideas) and some *initial* inductive arguments to show that the principles in question are operative in the mind. The confirmation or disconfirmation of these principles occurs primarily in the third and fourth parts of Book I. There Hume engages in doxastic pathology; he argues that various beliefs are unwarranted and explains how it is possible to have those beliefs on the basis of the principles of the association of ideas.[16] If his explanations succeed, they show it is plausible to claim the mind is nothing but a collection of perceptions and, since such a theory is simpler and more intelligible than any version of the substance theory of mind, it is reasonable to contend that 'what we call a *mind*, is nothing but a heap or collection of different perceptions, united together by certain relations, and suppos'd, tho' falsely, to be endow'd with a perfect simplicity and identity' (*T* 207).

So let us turn to the first part of Book I of the *Treatise*, where Hume introduces the fundamental elements of his theory of mind and provides some initial arguments to show that there is an inductive basis for his explanatory principles.

Notes

[1]J. P. Monteiro has anticipated some of my remarks on Hume's method (see Monteiro 1981). Nonetheless, the interpretation I develop differs from Monteiro's on several fronts. First, I shall focus almost exclusively on the method in the *Treatise*, since I shall argue later that Hume's objective in the *Enquiry concerning Human Understanding* was significantly different from

that in the *Treatise*. Monteiro seems to hold that the method is the same in both works. Second, I emphasize the role of sceptical arguments in setting the problems to be explained, a claim that is absent from Monteiro's account. Nonetheless, like Monteiro, I shall show that the notions of intelligibility and plausibility play a much larger role in Hume's theory than does the notion of truth.

[2]I discuss Hume's theory of meaning in Chapter 2.

[3]There is some disagreement in the literature regarding Hume's use of 'specifically different'. On the basis of his claim at *T* 68 that 'The farthest we can go towards a conception of external objects, when supposed specifically different from our perceptions, is to form a relative idea of them without pretending to comprehend the related objects', some commentators have contended that Hume's notion of specific difference is a difference in ontological kind. (See, for example, Butchvarov 1959: 106; Yolton 1984: 149-50; Fogelin 1985: 67.) But this certainly is not adequate as a general account of the notion of 'specific difference'. Already in his discussion 'Of Relations' Hume used a much broader notion of 'specific difference' than is suggested by Butchvarov, Yolton, and Fogelin. He wrote, 'Difference is of two kinds as oppos'd either to identity or resemblance. The first kind is call'd a difference in *number*; the other of *kind*' (*T* 15). Since in his discussion of abstraction he divides the world into kinds on the basis of resemblances, this at least shows that the limitation of 'specific difference' to ontological differences is too broad. Further, Hume's clearest discussion of the distinction between numerical and specific identity--and therefore between numerical and specific difference--is found at *T* 257-8, and there he indicates that claims of specific identity are based upon resemblance among either impressions or objects (cf. Anderson 1975). Whether or not Butchvarov, Yolton, and Fogelin are correct in claiming that one of Hume's uses of 'specific difference' concerns difference in ontological kind, it is clear that one of his uses of that term is concerned with the more mundane differences based upon resemblances, for example, differences between tables and chairs. We shall see that it is this second sense of 'specific difference' that is germane to the passage under consideration.

[4]Ronald Glass and I have discussed this in detail in Flage and Glass 1984.

[5]As many scholars have noticed, Hume's meta-theoretical principles are consistent with and quite probably drawn from Newton's 'Rules of Reasoning in Philosophy' (Newton 1966: 2:398-400; cf. Passmore, 1980: 43; Smith 1941: 57; Hendel 1963: 366; Flew 1961: 18; Gardiner 1963: 41; Jessop 1952: 35-52; Noxon 1973; Capaldi 1975: especially 49-70; cf. Jones 1982: 11-19; Force 1987: 166-216.) Nor should one be surprised that Hume was at least broadly a Newtonian, since by the mid-eighteenth century the expression 'the experimental method' denoted Newton's method (Schlereth 1977: 26). Nonetheless, to claim that Hume was a Newtonian tells one relatively little regarding the precise method he employed, for there is some scholarly controversy regarding the method Newton himself employed. Some suggest that Newton assumed a straightforward hypothetical-deductive model for the justification of his theory (cf. Bergmann 1957: 84-91; Braithwaite 1959: 12-21).

Others have argued that a hypothetical-deductive model does not fit Newton's arguments (cf. Glymour 1980: 203-26). Still others have argued that Newton accepted an account very much like the one I find in Hume (cf. Hanson 1958: 1079-89).

[6]On 'moral certainty' cf. *T* 404, and see Ferreira 1986: 211-22.

[7]For discussions of justification by the best explanation, see Harman 1973: 158-61; and Thagard 1978: 76-92; Hanson 1961: 85-90; and Hanson 1971: 63-7; cf. Annas and Barnes 1985: 108-9.

[8]Cf. Hanson 1958; Hanson 1961: 86; and Hanson 1971: 65-6.

[9]That Hume considered these to be cases common to virtually all beliefs attacked by the sceptics can be discerned from the fact that he deemed it characteristic of sceptical arguments that '*they admit of no answer and produce no conviction*' (*EHU* 155n).

[10]Notice that this is consistent with some of the standard views on theory construction. In constructing a theory it is the question of coherence that plays the primary role. It is a necessary condition for the plausibility of a theory that the theoretical claims are mutually consistent and that the predictions of observable phenomena made by the theory are consistent with the phenomena observed. It is commonly claimed that if a theory can meet both of these conditions, then the theory might be an accurate description of the facts.

[11]Notice, I am suggesting that Hume generally uses the term 'coherence' more broadly than at *T* 194, where he ties the notion of coherence exclusively to causal considerations.

[12]On systems, cf. Shaftesbury 1964: 1:245.

[13]While Hume was willing to deem only such systems of objects based upon experience 'realities', it is clear that he applied the same principles of coherence in fictitious contexts. See *T* 121-2.

[14]This point has not been wholly overlooked in the literature. See Passmore 1980: 100-1.

[15]As we shall see in Chapter 2, there also appear to be significant differences between Locke's account of one's idea of gold and Hume's account, but both agree at least to the extent that one learns over a period of time what qualities are constantly conjoined in learning what a thing of a kind is.

[16]This is not to say the explanatory program is absent in the second part of Book I (cf. *T* 55-62) but merely that it comes to the fore after his discussion of belief (*T* 94-8).

2
Fundamentals

In Book I, Part I of the *Treatise* Hume introduces the fundamental elements of his theory of mind. In this chapter I examine the several issues Hume discusses there, showing how these issues are related to his meta-theoretical constraints. In the next chapter I provide a more detailed examination of Humean perceptions. I begin by discussing Hume's initial account of impressions and ideas. I focus on his principle that ideas are caused by and exactly resemble impressions and on his initial defense of that principle. Next I examine Hume's contention that all relations are reducible to seven general headings and his initial arguments for the principles of the association of ideas. Finally, I examine Hume's discussions of the ideas of mode and substance and his discussion of abstract ideas.

Perceptions as Fundamental Entities

Hume begins the *Treatise* by drawing a distinction between impressions and ideas. He wrote:

All the perceptions of the human mind resolve themselves into two distinct kinds, which I shall call IMPRESSIONS and IDEAS. The difference betwixt these consists in the degrees of force and liveliness, with which they strike upon the mind, and make their way into our thought or consciousness. Those perceptions, which enter with the most force and violence, we may call *impressions*; and under this name I comprehend all our sensations, passions, and emotions, as they make their first appearance in the soul. By *ideas* I mean the faint images of these in thinking and reasoning; such as, for instance, are all the perceptions excited by the present discourse, excepting only, those which arise from the sight and

> touch, and excepting the immediate pleasure or uneasiness it may occasion. I believe it will not be very necessary to employ many words in explaining this distinction. Every one of himself will readily perceive the difference betwixt feeling and thinking. The common degrees of these are easily distinguished; tho' it is not impossible but in particular instances they may very nearly approach to each other. Thus in sleep, in a fever, in madness, or in any very violent emotions of soul, our ideas may approach to our impressions: As on the other hand it sometimes happens that our impressions are so faint and low, that we cannot distinguish them from our ideas. But notwithstanding this near resemblance in a few instances, they are in general so very different, that no-one can make a scruple to rank them under distinct heads, and assign to each a peculiar name to mark the difference. (*T* 1-2)

In this paragraph, Hume introduces the fundamental entities in his theory, namely, perceptions. Notice that Hume provides no positive characterization of the nature of perceptions as such, nor should this be surprising. It is characteristic of a theoretical primitive that it cannot be described within the theory of which it is a part: if it could be described within the theory, it would not be a primitive. This meta-theoretical fact was widely utilized if not explicitly acknowledged. In traditional substance theories, there is no positive characterization given of the substance or substratum itself: it is simply the thing--whatever its positive nature might be--that fulfills a particular function, for example, that provides the basis for identity claims through time, that is the subject that has properties, and so forth (cf. Aristotle 1941: 9; Descartes, CSM 2:124; Locke, *Essay* 2.13.19; Butler 1906: 257-63). Much the same may be said regarding the fundamental entities in the corpuscular hypothesis characterized as things having all and only the primary qualities. Presumably a corpuscle is something over and above the properties it has, although whatever more it might be is of no consequence to the theory.[1] Unlike substances and corpuscles, however, perceptions are immediate objects of consciousness. Therefore, to posit the existence of perceptions as the fundamental elements of a theory of mind is consistent with the strictures of empiricism.

Hume divides the class of perceptions into impressions and ideas on the basis of the greater 'force and liveliness' of the former relative to the latter. But consideration of the degrees of 'force and liveliness' of these two kinds of perceptions is, at best, nebulous and 'unphilosophical' (cf. *T* 629, *EHU* 49). Early in the paragraph he claims that 'Those perceptions, which enter with the most force and violence we may name *impressions*' while ideas are 'the faint images of [impressions' in thinking and reasoning]. But late in the paragraph he acknowledges that force and vivacity do not provide conclusive grounds for the impressions/ideas distinction. On the one hand, the degree of force and vivacity of ideas in dreams, hallucinations, and 'any very violent emotions of the soul' often is indistinguishable from that of impressions (*T* 2). On the other hand, 'it sometimes happens, that our impressions are so faint and low, that we cannot distinguish them from ideas' (*T* 2). Hence, degrees of force and vivacity are not reliable grounds for distinguishing between impressions and ideas.

Does this inadequate distinction imply that Hume's philosophical project is doomed from the outset? No. There are two ways in which one might attempt to defend Hume. First, one might argue that Hume is working within a particular philosophical tradition and that the kind of distinction Hume is making was commonly made along similar lines within that tradition. For example, while the distinction between impressions and ideas is nominally Hume's,[2] a similar distinction is found in George Berkeley's *Principles of Human Knowledge*. In distinguishing between ideas of the sense and ideas of the imagination, Berkeley claimed that 'The ideas of sense are more strong, lively, and distinct than those of the imagination' (Berkeley, *PHK* I, 30). Since Hume himself was later to distinguish between ideas of the memory and ideas of the imagination in terms of their differing degrees of force and vivacity (*T* 9, 85), it is not *prima facie* unreasonable to suggest that he was attempting to build upon something like Berkeley's phenomenal criterion.[3] Notice that while this might explain why Hume distinguished between impressions and ideas on the basis of their respective degrees of 'force and violence', it does not avoid the contention that the criterion is inadequate.

There is a second line of interpretation that might avoid the charge of inadequacy. If Hume is attempting to construct a theory of the mind, then perceptions, however one might attempt to positively characterize them, are primarily nothing more than the fundamental elements of that theory. Although one way he characterizes the division of perceptions into impressions and ideas is in terms of the greater 'force and liveliness' of impressions *vis-à-vis* ideas, he states that 'under this name ['impressions'] I comprehend all our sensations, passions and emotions, *as they make the first appearance in the soul*. By *ideas* I mean the faint images of these in thinking and reasoning' (*T* 1; emphasis added). It is primarily on the basis of the priority of impressions to ideas that Hume divides the class of perceptions into impressions and ideas. Force and vivacity, then, are nothing more than characteristics by which one can generally distinguish between impressions and ideas: the phenomenal criterion provides nothing more than a rule of thumb for drawing the distinction.[4]

In his initial characterization of the impressions/ideas distinction, the kind of priority germane to the distinction initially is left open. As he continues his discussion, however, Hume shows that he is concerned is causal priority. After drawing a distinction between simple and compound perceptions (*T* 2), Hume claims, 'After the most accurate examination, of which I am capable, I venture to affirm, . . . that every simple idea has a simple impression, which resembles it; and every simple impression a correspondent idea' (*T* 3). His basis for this claim is inductive, and he challenges his reader to provide a counter-example (*T* 4). He then states his conclusions, conclusions which show that he was concerned with the causal priority of impressions to ideas. In his words:

> Thus we find, that all simple ideas and impressions resemble each other; and as the complex are formed from them, we may affirm in general, that these two species of perception are exactly correspondent. Having discover'd this relation, which requires no further examination, I am curious to find some other of their qualities. Let us consider how they stand with regard to their existence, and which of the impressions and ideas are causes and which effects.

> The *full* examination of this question is the subject of the present treatise; and therefore we shall here content ourselves with establishing one general proposition, *That all our simple ideas in their first appearance are deriv'd from simple impressions, which are correspondent to them, and which they exactly represent.* (*T* 4)

This passage shows us two things. First, it shows that Hume took impressions to be *causally* prior to ideas. Second, it shows that the priority of an impression to a corresponding idea is not an analytic claim; it is a causal hypothesis, a hypothesis that will tend to be confirmed or refuted by the considerations in the remainder of the *Treatise*. Following tradition, I shall call Hume's first general principle 'the copy theory of ideas'.

Hume continues by providing some initial evidence for the copy theory of ideas. He wrote:

> In seeking for phenomena to prove this proposition, I find only two kinds; but in each kind the phenomena are obvious, numerous, and conclusive. I first make myself certain, by a new

review, of what I have already asserted, that every simple impression is attended with a correspondent idea, and every simple idea with a correspondent impression. From this constant conjunction of resembling perceptions I immediately conclude, that there is a great connection betwixt our correspondent impressions and ideas, and that the existence of one has a considerable influence upon that of the other. Such a constant conjunction, in an infinite number of instances, can never arise from chance; but clearly proves a dependence of the impressions on the ideas, or of the ideas on the impressions. That I may know on which side this dependence lies, I consider the order of the *first appearance*; and find by constant experience, that the simple impressions always take precedence of their corresponding ideas, but never appear in the contrary order. To give a child an idea of scarlet or orange, of sweet or bitter, I present the objects, or in other words, convey to him these impressions; but proceed not so absurdly, as to endeavour to produce the impressions by exciting the ideas. Our ideas upon their appearance produce not their correspondent impressions, nor do we perceive any colour, or feel any sensation merely upon thinking of them. On the other hand we find, that any impression either of the mind or body is constantly followed by an idea, which resembles it, and is only different in the degrees of force and liveliness. The constant conjunction of our resembling perceptions, is a convincing proof, that the one are the causes of the other; and this priority of the impressions is an equal proof, that our impressions are the causes of our ideas, not our ideas of our impressions. (*T* 4-5)

Hume here provides an inductive argument to show that impressions are causally prior to ideas. He assumes that it is possible to distinguish between impressions and ideas independently of questions of the priority, that is, he assumes that the distinction based upon force and vivacity is adequate. Assuming this independent basis for the distinction, Hume can well turn to the constant conjunction between impressions and ideas and ask which is the cause and which the effect. He claims experience teaches that impressions always are followed by their correspondent ideas, but ideas do not produce their corresponding impressions. Hence, (simple) impressions cause (simple) ideas.

Hume continues by providing additional examples that support his claim that impressions are causally prior to ideas. He wrote:

To confirm this I consider another plain and convincing phenomenon; which is, that where-ever by any accident the faculties, which give rise to any impressions, are obstructed in their operations, as when one is born blind or deaf; not only the impressions are lost, but also their correspondent ideas; so that there never appear in the mind the least traces of either of them. Nor is this only true, where the organs of sensation are entirely destroy'd, but likewise where they have never been put in action to produce a particular impression. We cannot form to ourselves a just idea of the taste of pine-apple, without having actually tasted it. (*T 5*)

Following the common assumption that impressions of sensation are produced by objects impressing upon the organs of sense, Hume here notes that when the organ that is the presumptive cause of a certain kind of impression of sensation is dysfunctional, one has neither the impressions nor the ideas corresponding to that sense. Similarly, even if all one's sense organs are functional but one has never had the occasion to have a particular kind of impression, for example, if one has never tasted pineapple, one will have neither an impression nor an idea of the taste of pineapple (cf. Locke, *Essay* 2.1.6).

Do Hume's arguments establish that all ideas are causally dependent upon impressions? No. While they provide some inductive evidence for the copy theory of ideas, the evidence is inconclusive. Since his arguments are inductive, they are subject to disconfirmation on the basis of a single counter-instance. It is for this reason that the 'missing shade of blue' (*T* 5-6), seems to be a glaring counter-example to his general principle.[5] But even apart from the missing shade of blue, there are things of which one might claim to think, but of which one can have no impression, for example, substance as such (cf. Descartes, CSM 2:124; Locke, *Essay* 2.13.19; Berkeley, *PHK* I, 27). Hence, it was incumbent upon Hume to explain how one can form ideas of things for which one has had no corresponding impression and why one believes one has ideas of things of which one could not have had an impression. These are among the tasks of his explanatory program.

Relations and Associations

Up to this point we have examined the fundamental entities in Hume's theory of mind, namely, impressions and ideas. If Hume can provide an account of mind solely on the basis of these entities, his account will be ontologically simpler than its foremost competitor, the substratum theory, and therein fulfill one of the requirements for the adequacy of a theory. But Hume's penchant for simplicity is not limited to a concern with fundamental entities. His discussion of relations also reflects an attempt to attain theoretical simplicity. It is to his discussions of relations and the principles of the association of ideas, the explanatory principles of Hume's theory, that we now turn.

In 'Of Relations', Hume distinguishes between two senses of the term 'relation'. In one sense, a relation is 'that particular circumstance, in which, even upon arbitrary union of two ideas in the fancy, we may think proper to compare them' (*T* 13; cf. Locke, *Essay* 2.25.1). In the other sense, a relation is 'that quality, by which together in the imagination, one naturally introduces the other' (*T* 13). The first class is the broader of the two. Since ''tis only in philosophy, that we extend [the word 'relation'] to mean any particular subject of comparison, without a connecting principle' (*T* 13-14), Hume calls those relations 'philosophical relations'. The second class, the 'relations of the association of ideas' or 'natural relations' (*T* 11, 15) is a subclass of the first.

Hume's discussion of relations is a prime example of his drive toward theoretical simplicity. He claims that all philosophical relations can be reduced to seven general categories. These are:

1. Resemblance (also a natural relation)
2. Identity
3. Space and Time (contiguity is a natural relation)
4. Quantity and Number
5. Degrees of a Quality
6. Contrariety
7. Cause and Effect (also a natural relation)

If all relations can be reduced to these seven general headings, then it is incumbent upon Hume to provide the relevant reductions. If he can do this and his explanatory program is successful, then Hume has grounds for claiming that any supposedly irreducible relation is merely a pseudo-relation. As we shall see below, Hume's first such reduction is the reduction of the meaning relation to the causal relation, a reduction that is sufficient to cast doubt on the scholastic contention that meaning is fundamental (cf. Sergeant 1697: 33). Since it is on his relations of association (natural relations) that his theory of mind stands or falls, it is to these relations that we shall now turn.

Hume begins his discussion 'Of the connexion or association of ideas' by noting that 'As all simple ideas may be separated by the imagination, and may be united again in what form it pleases, nothing wou'd be more unaccountable than the operations of that faculty, were it not guided by some universal principles, which render it, in some measure, uniform with itself in all times and places' (*T* 10). Simple ideas are inherently separable from one another (*T* 2), but since the mind exhibits a certain amount of uniformity in its operations, there must be certain relations that unite--but do not inseparably connect--the perceptions in the mind. Hume accounts for this 'gentle force, which commonly prevails' (*T* 10) in terms of relations of 'RESEMBLANCE, CONTIGUITY in time or place, and CAUSE and EFFECT' (*T* 11).

Hume provides a brief argument in *Treatise* I.i.4 to show that these relations, and only these relations, unite ideas in the mind. He wrote:

> I believe it will not be very necessary to prove, that these qualities produce an association among ideas, and upon appearance of one idea naturally introduce another. 'Tis plain, that in the course of our thinking, and in the constant revolution of our ideas, our imagination runs easily from one idea to any other that *resembles* it, and that this alone is to the fancy a sufficient bond and association. 'Tis likewise evident, that as the senses, in changing their objects, are necessitated to change them regularly, and take them as they lie *contiguous* to each other, the imagination must by long custom acquire the same method of thinking, and run along the parts of space and time in conceiving its objects. As to the connection that is made by the relation of *cause and effect*, we shall have occasion afterwards to examine it to the bottom, and therefore shall not at present insist upon it. 'Tis sufficient to observe, that there is no relation, which produces a stronger connection in the fancy, and makes one idea more recall another, than the relation of cause and effect betwixt their objects. (*T* 11)

Hume's argument consists of nothing more than observations of what he takes to be apparent in experience. The argument is inductive, and even if one grants that his appeals to what ''tis plain' or ''tis evident' provide grounds for claiming that *at least* the relations of resemblance, contiguity in space and time, and causation associate ideas in the mind, it shows nothing more than that. Nor should one find this surprising. Hume is doing nothing more here than providing preliminary evidence that the three relations of association are among the relations by which 'two ideas are connected together in the imagination, and the one naturally introduces the other' (*T* 13), that is, they provide the weak 'connections' that unite the mind into one thing.[6] As he proceeds, it is incumbent upon him to provide additional arguments to show that one actually can explain all psychological phenomena on the basis of these relations. Thus, when he introduces his account of belief, he provides similar inductive arguments to show that resemblance, contiguity, and causation are operative in the formation of beliefs (*T* 99-100; cf. *T* 110-11). Yet these inductive arguments show nothing more than that the relations of association are *among* the relations that are found in the mind; it does not show that they are the only such relations. The plausibility of his claim that they are the *only* relations among perceptions rests upon the success of his explanatory program. If Hume can explain all one's most empirically problematic beliefs, that is, those beliefs that cannot be based directly on experience, on the basis of the principles of the association and the copy theory of ideas, then, given the principle of parsimony, he has grounds for claiming that the relations of association alone constitute the 'connections' among perceptions in the mind.

Abstraction and Meaning

We have now briefly examined the fundamental entities in Hume's theory of mind and the fundamental laws governing those entities. We have noticed that Hume provides nothing more than very limited inductive evidence for both his copy theory of ideas and his principles of the association of ideas. We also have noticed that Hume claimed that all philosophical relations can be subsumed under seven general headings, a claim that commits Hume to providing reductive explanations of the several putative relations that do not immediately fit under those headings. His first such explanation is found in 'Of Abstract Ideas', where he attempts to reduce the relation of linguistic meaning to the causal relation. It is to that endeavor we now turn.

Hume's discussion of abstract ideas is a critical discussion of the common (Lockean) account of abstraction and linguistic meaning. According to the common view, 'our abstract ideas have been suppos'd to represent no particular degree either of quantity or quality' (*T* 18), since, given the finite capacity of the mind, it is assumed that no determinate idea can represent 'all possible sizes and qualities' of all things of a kind (*T* 18; cf. Locke, *Essay*, 3.3.2). In examining the Lockean position, Hume focuses on two questions: (1) Is it possible to conceive of determinable but indeterminate qualities? and (2) How can one explain the meaning of sortal terms?[7] Hume answered these questions in 'Of Abstract Ideas'.

Hume provides three arguments to show '*that the mind cannot form any notion of quality or quantity without forming a precise notion of the degrees of each*' (*T* 18), that is, that any idea that is the object of thought is determinate in quantity and quality. I shall examine the first of these arguments and briefly comment on the second and third.

Hume's first argument reads as follows:

First, We have observ'd, that whatever objects are different are distinguishable, and whatever objects are distinguishable are separable by the thought and imagination. And we may here add, that these propositions are equally true in the *inverse*, and that whatever objects are separable are also distinguishable, and that whatever objects are distinguishable are also different. For how is it possible we can separate what is not distinguishable, or distinguish what is not different? In order therefore to know, whether abstraction implies a separation, we need only consider it in this view, and examine whether all the circumstances, which we abstract from in our general ideas, be such as are distinguishable and different from those, which we retain as essential parts of them. But 'tis evident at first sight, that the precise length of a line is not different nor distinguishable from the line itself; nor the precise degree of any quality from the quality. These ideas, therefore, admit no more of separation than they do of distinction and difference. They are consequently conjoined with each other in the conception; and the general idea of a line, notwithstanding all our abstractions and refinements, has in its appearance in the mind a precise degree of quantity and quality; however it may be made to represent others, which have different degrees of both. (*T* 18-19)

If such abstractionists as Locke are correct, it should be possible to form an idea of a quality *simpliciter*, that is, an idea of a quality that is indeterminate in degree. But the degree of a quality is neither distinguishable nor separable from the quality of which it is a degree. Hence, the degree of a quality is inseparable from the quality itself, and it is impossible to form an abstract idea of an indeterminate quality. As Hume indicates, the same argument applies, *mutatis mutandis*, with respect to the determinateness of one's conception of quantity. Thus, in so far as it is possible to form an abstract idea (an idea of a kind of thing), the idea formed must be determinate in quantity and quality.

Hume's second and third arguments support the same conclusion. The second argument is based upon considerations of the copy theory of ideas. Since all impressions are determinate in degrees of quantity and quality and ideas are copies of impressions, they also must be determinate in degrees of quantity and quality. Hence, on the basis of the copy theory of ideas, it is impossible for an idea to be indeterminate in degrees of quantity or quality (*T* 19).

The third argument is based upon two widely accepted philosophical principles. The first principle is that all existents are individuals (cf. Locke, *Essay* 3.3.1), that is, objects having determinate properties, and that it is impossible for a thing to exist with indeterminate properties. The second principle is that whatever is impossible is inconceivable (cf. *T* 32). From these two principles it follows that it is impossible to conceive (form an idea) of an object with indeterminate properties (*T* 19-20).

Given these arguments, Hume reached the conclusion that, in so far as it is possible to form an abstract idea, that idea must be determinate in quantity and quality. In his words:

> Abstract ideas are therefore in themselves individual, however they may become general in their representation. The image in the mind is only of a particular object, tho' the application of it in our reason be the same, as if it were universal. (*T* 20)

Abstract ideas are determinate in quantity and quality. An abstract idea of a cup is as determinate as the impression I presently have of the cup on my desk. Abstract ideas differ only in function from ideas of particulars. The idea I have when I think of the cup on my desk also can function as an abstract idea in so far as I take it as my paradigm of a cup. As an abstract idea, my determinate idea of the cup will allow me to classify other objects as cups in so far as those objects resemble that idea. As abstract ideas, determinate ideas are applied 'beyond their nature' and are taken to represent all things of a kind (*T* 20).

After completing his argument for the determinate nature of abstract ideas, Hume indicates that a sortal term denotes each of the objects of a sort, that is, he indicates that the meaning of sortal terms is fundamentally denotational. He wrote:

> When we have found a resemblance among several objects, that often occur to us, we apply the same name to all of them, whatever differences we may observe in the degrees of their quantity or quality, and whatever other differences appear among them. (*T* 20)

Hume suggests that first we find that there are several resembling objects, and once we have noticed this resemblance, we apply the same name to all those objects. Unlike Locke, who contended that sortal terms denote objects only through the mediation of abstract ideas (cf. Locke, *Essay* 3.10.14), Hume contended that the sortal term applies directly to each of the resembling objects. Hume's theory of meaning is denotational: a particular object (or idea) provides the meaning of a term.[8] In proposing a denotational theory of the meaning of sortal terms, Hume suggests that one takes one's (determinate) abstract idea as a paradigm of a thing of a kind and that the sortal term denotes all things of that kind.

But since some deemed such a position untenable (*T* 18), it was incumbent upon Hume to explain how a finite mind can apply a sortal term to an indefinitely large number of determinate objects, even though one has no acquaintance with the overwhelming majority of objects of any kind. To explain this, Hume discusses the psychological mechanisms that are operative in assigning the meaning to a sortal term, and, in so doing, he reduces the meaning relation to the causal relation. As he wrote:

> After we have acquired a custom of this kind [the application of a general word to a number of resembling objects], the hearing of the same name revives the idea of one of these objects, and makes the imagination conceive it with all its particular circumstances and proportions. But as the same word is suppos'd to have been previously applied to other individuals, that are different in many respects from that idea, which is immediately present to the mind; the word not being able to revive the idea of all these individuals, only touches the soul, if I may be allow'd so to speak, and revives that custom, which we have acquir'd by surveying them. They are not really and in fact present to the mind, but only in power; nor do we draw them all out distinctly in the imagination, but keep ourselves in readiness to survey any of them, as we may be prompted by a present design or necessity. The word raises up an individual idea, along with a certain custom; and that custom produces any other individual one, for which we may have occasion. But as the production of all the ideas, to which the name may be apply'd, is in most cases impossible, we abridge that work by a more partial consideration, and find but few inconveniences to arise in our reasoning from this abridgment. (*T* 20-1)

The meaningful use of a sortal term involves a habitual association between a word and a set of ideas. Once this habit is developed, the hearing of a word causes one to think of one's paradigm of a thing of a kind, and in so far as the circumstances in which one uses a word might require the consideration of an idea that differs from one's paradigm, one will substitute some other idea of that kind (an idea that resembles one's paradigm) for one's paradigmatic idea.[9] Hume avoids objections to his account based upon the finite capacity of the mind by suggesting that all ideas of a kind are 'present to the mind . . . in power', that is, the mind has the ability (habit) to call up various ideas of the kind as needed and to recognize that the things of which one becomes aware are things of certain kinds. Abstract ideas (paradigm cases) actually play only a small role in his theory of meaning. A sortal term denotes *all* objects of a kind, and one's abstract idea (paradigm) merely provides a subjective standard to which one might compare other things when classifying them as things of a certain kind.

Since an 'abstract idea' is merely what one takes to be a paradigm of a thing of a kind, Hume suggests that 'the very same idea may be annext to several different words' (*T* 21), that is, qualitatively identical ideas at various times may be used as paradigms of different kinds of things, and it is the custom that associates the word and the abstract idea that accounts for the alternative substitutions that might be germane to the situation in which one uses a word. As Hume wrote:

> Thus, the idea of an equilateral triangle of an inch perpendicular may serve us in talking of a figure, of a rectilinear figure, of a regular figure, of a triangle, and of an equilateral triangle. All these terms, therefore, are in the case attended with the same idea; but as they are wont to be apply'd in a greater or lesser compass, they excite their particular habits, and thereby keep the mind in a readiness to observe, that no conclusion be form'd contrary to the ideas, which are usually compriz'd under them. (*T* 21-2)

Although one idea might be one's paradigm of things of several kinds, it is fundamentally the ability to recognize other particular complex objects as objects of a certain kind (apply the right word) that provides the basis for meaningful discourse (cf. *T* 22, *EHU* 158n).

While Hume's discussion of linguistic meaning in 'Of Abstract Ideas' suggests that he reduced the meaning relation to the causal relation and championed a purely denotative theory of meaning, one might suggest that in 'Of Modes and Substances' he writes as if he were a proponent of a Lockean (connotative) account of linguistic meaning. By examining Hume's description of the idea of substance, we shall see how Hume's account of the meaning of sortal terms can be extended to comply with complex states of affairs.

In 'Of Modes and Substances' Hume wrote:

> The idea of substance as well as that of a mode, is nothing but a collection of simple ideas, that are united by the imagination, and have a particular name assigned them, by which we are able to recall, either to ourselves or others that collection. But the difference betwixt these ideas consists in this, that the particular qualities, which form a substance, are commonly refer'd to an unknown *something*, in which they are supposed to inhere; or granting this fiction should not take place, are at least supposed to be closely and inseparably connected by the relations of contiguity and causation. The effect of this is, that whatever new simple quality we discover to have the same connexion with the rest, we

immediately comprehend among them, even tho' it did not enter into our first conception of the substance. Thus our idea of gold may at first be a yellow colour, malleableness, fusibility; but upon the discovery of its dissolubility in *aqua regia*, we join that to the other qualities, and suppose it to belong to the substance as much as if its idea had from the beginning made a part of the compound one. The principle of union being regarded as the chief part of the complex idea, gives entrance to whatever quality afterwards occurs, and is equally comprehended by it, as are the others, which first presented themselves. (*T* 16)

There are several things to notice here. First, what Hume here calls an 'idea of substance' appears to be a construct of the imagination, rather than an arbitrarily chosen complex idea drawn from memory. Second, there is no concern with the determinate nature of the qualities that are included in one's idea of a substance. It appears to be weight, malleability and fusibility *in general* that are included in one's idea of gold and not a determinate degree of any one of these qualities. Third, a name (sortal term) is applied to this general idea, and Hume seems to suggest that it is this general idea that provides the meaning of the sortal term. Finally, the number of qualities in one's idea of a substance can change with an increase in one's experience, which suggests that the meaning one assigns to a sortal term can become richer in *intensional* content, while the most one might expect a person proposing a denotational theory of meaning to claim is that experience increases one's awareness of the number of objects in the extension of a term.

These features of Hume's account of the idea of substance become even more striking when one compares it with Locke's description of the nominal essence of gold. A Lockean nominal essence is an abstract general idea that provides the basis for classifying objects as objects of a certain kind (cf. Locke, *Essay* 3.3.18-19). Notice what Locke wrote regarding the nominal essence of gold:

What then are we to do for the improvement of our *Knowledge in substantial Beings?* . . . *Experience here must teach me*, what Reason cannot: and 'tis by trying alone, that I can certainly know, what other Qualities co-exist with those in my complex *Idea*, *v.g.* whether that *yellow*, *heavy*, *fusible* Body, I call *Gold*, be *malleable*, or no; which Experience (which way ever it prove, in that particular Body, I examine) makes me not certain, that it is so, in all, or any other *yellow*, *heavy*, *fusible* Bodies, but that which I have tried. Because it is no Consequence one way or t'other from my complex *Idea*; the Necessity or Inconsistence of *Malleability*, hath no visible connexion with the Combination of that *Colour*, *Weight*, and *Fusibility* in any body. What I have said here of the nominal Essence of *Gold*, supposed to consist of a Body of such determinate *Colour*, *Weight*, and *Fusibility*, will hold true, if *Malleableness*, *Fixedness*, and Solubility in *Aqua Regia* be added to it. (Locke, *Essay* 4.12.9)

Both Hume's idea of gold and Locke's nominal essence of gold are collections of qualities to which 'a particular name [is] assigned . . . by which we are able to recall, either to ourselves or others, that collection' (*T* 16). Both are ideas of particular *kinds* of substances. Both can be expanded on the basis of additional experience. Both Locke and the Hume of 'Of Modes and Substances' seem to accept a *connotative* theory of meaning. But a nominal essence is a Lockean abstract idea, and this is precisely the kind of idea against which Hume inveighed in his discussion of abstract ideas.

What is one to conclude? Is one to conclude that in 'Of Modes and Substances' Hume implicitly accepted both a theory of abstract general ideas and a connotative theory of the meaning of sortal terms, only to reject both in the following section? Or is there a coherent account of the relationship between the two sections? In the remainder of this chapter I hope to show (1) that in so far as 'Of Abstract Ideas' is construed, in part, as a continuation of 'Of Modes and Substances', Hume's arguments against abstract general ideas show that it is impossible to have any (positive) idea of substance,[10] and (2) that even though Hume's discussion of the 'idea of substance' might be an accurate description of how one comes to know the several properties of a thing of a kind, it is more properly construed as providing a criterion for classification than as an idea, and, given such a construal, it is consistent with a denotational theory of meaning. So let us continue by turning again to 'Of Modes and Substances'.

In 'Of Modes and Substances', Hume examines the nature and source of one's idea of substance. Like Locke (*Essay* 2.23.1-2), he notes that one's idea of substance is a simple idea of neither sense nor reflection (*T* 15-16). In so far as one can have an idea of substance, this is 'nothing but a collection of simple ideas, which are united by the imagination, and have a particular name assigned them' (*T* 16). As his discussions in *Treatise* I.iv show,[11] Hume was a strenuous opponent of the doctrine of substance, and consequently, if he could show that it is impossible to have a (positive) idea of substance *in any sense of that term*, one would expect him to provide an argument to establish that claim. By reading 'Of Modes and Substances' in conjunction with 'Of Abstract Ideas', the following argument is suggested:

1. If it is possible to form a (positive) idea of substance, that idea corresponds to what Locke called a nominal essence, that is, it is an abstract general idea.
2. But it is impossible to form abstract general ideas.
3. Therefore, it is impossible to form a (positive) idea of substance.

Hume never stated this argument, but it is reasonable to claim that it is implicit in the *Treatise*. As we shall see when we turn to Hume's most serious criticisms of the doctrine in Book I, Part iv, Section 5 of the *Treatise*, those criticisms are theory-specific: they are directed primarily against the Cartesian theory of substance. The argument I have constructed also is directed against a specific account of one's idea of substance, and it shows that, even though such an idea is consistent with the general strictures of empiricism, it is impossible to have such an idea of substance. Given the juxtaposition of his discussion of one's idea of substance and his discussion of abstract general ideas, Hume probably believed the perceptive reader would recognize that the arguments he advanced show it is impossible to form even a Lockean (positive) idea of substance.

If my account is correct, Hume's 'idea of substance' in *Treatise* I.i.6 is not properly an idea at all.[12] Nonetheless, Locke and Hume were certainly correct in claiming that as one becomes more familiar with objects of a certain kind, one attributes a greater number of distinct properties to the objects of that kind and the intensional content of a connotative definition increases. Is such a fact consistent with Hume's claims that the meaning of a sortal term is primarily denotative? I believe it is. To understand why, let us turn again to 'Of Abstract Ideas'.

We have seen that in 'Of Abstract Ideas' Hume championed a denotative theory of meaning, devoting the bulk of that discussion to a consideration of the psychological mechanisms that make such a theory of meaning plausible, and in the course of this explanation he reduced the meaning relation to the causal relation. In so far as one's determinate idea is taken to be a paradigm of a thing of a kind, this provides one with the psychological basis for classifying other resembling objects as objects of the same kind. Hume's contention that 'the very same idea may be annext to several different words' (*T* 21), that is, that the same idea (or object) can be one's paradigm of objects of several kinds, indicates that he recognized the multiple classifiability of objects. Hence, my idea of my wedding ring might be my 'abstract idea' of both gold (things) and round (things). Now let us assume that for some reason I become terribly interested in gold things. I might first recognize that all things I classify as gold are yellow in color. But as I examine these things further, I also might notice that they are heavy relative to their size, that they are malleable, that they are fusible, that they are dissolvable in *aqua regia* and so forth. In each of these cases I am doing nothing more than classifying objects in different ways. Eventually I might form the hypothesis that everything I classify as gold I also would classify as something that is yellow, heavy, malleable, fusible and dissolvable in *aqua regia*, although not all things having any one or a limited combination of the latter properties are things I would classify as gold. Notice, what I am doing is providing a multiple classification of things that are gold that is analogous to the construction of a Humean 'idea of substance', although there is no presumption that I am constructing anything like a mental image. If I conclude that everything that is gold is yellow, heavy, malleable, fusible and dissolvable in *aqua regia*, I am providing a criterion for classifying objects as pieces of gold. Further, in so far as this is merely a criterion, that is, a list of the several classes into which all golden things fall, it is consistent with a denotative theory of meaning: it is consistent with the claim that the word 'gold' denotes all and only those determinate things that are made of gold, and each of the sortal terms used in stating the criterion denotes all those things in the relevant class. Understood in this way, a Humean 'idea of substance' is nothing more than a general description or connotative definition that functions as a criterion for classifying objects as objects of a certain kind. If I am correct in this, Hume took the connotation of a term to be epistemically dependent upon the denotation of a term.

There are two consequences of understanding a Humean 'idea of substance' as a criterion for classifying objects. First, such an 'idea' need not--and based on Hume's principles in 'Of Abstract Ideas'-- cannot be a Humean (positive) idea. It need be taken as nothing more than a linguistic enumeration of the several classes of objects into which a thing of a certain kind falls. Second, it allows one to account for the relationship between Hume's subjective account of meaning in 'Of Abstract Ideas' and his contention that the meaning of sortal terms is based upon linguistic conventions (*T* 490; cf. *T* 10). Linguistic conventions are laws governing the use of a word in a language, and, in so far as such conventions are stated, statements of a convention (lexical definitions) are themselves composed of general terms. A statement of a convention governing the meaning of a sortal term is a criterion for picking out those objects conventionally included in the extension of a term. In so far as the convention is expressed linguistically, it allows one to assess the correctness of one's linguistic usage:

it allows one to determine whether the objects one includes in the extension of a term are consistent with those that lexicologists include. But notice that, consistent with a denotative theory of meaning, such a criterion is nothing more than alternative classifications of a thing of a kind: if the criterion is adequate, it will pick out all and only things of a certain kind.[13]

Thus, we have seen that Hume's account in 'Of Abstract Ideas' explains (1) how the meaning relation is reduced to the causal relation, (2) how general words obtain meanings, and (3) how it is possible for the intensional content of a term to increase on the basis of experience, even though Hume provided an extensional (denotative) theory of meaning. Further, if I am correct in contending that one should read 'Of Modes and Substances' in conjunction with 'Of Abstract Ideas', there is an implicit argument showing that it is impossible to form a positive idea of substance.

Conclusions

In this chapter I have examined the arguments Hume provided for his copy theory of ideas and his principles of the association of ideas. I have shown that the arguments are inductive and anything but conclusive. I have argued that his initial arguments are intended to show no more than the plausibility of the principles and that Hume recognized that the plausibility of the principles ultimately rests upon the success of his explanatory program. I also have mentioned Hume's claim that all relations can be reduced to seven general headings and have examined his arguments to reduce the meaning relation to the causal relation.

There are several issues that must be examined in greater detail. To this point I have taken Humean perceptions to be nothing more than the fundamental elements of his theory of mind. We must ask whether it is possible to provide a positive characterization of them. In particular, we must ask whether, and if so, in what sense ideas are 'images' of impressions. Further, since Book I, Part i of the *Treatise* provides the fundamental elements of Hume's philosophy (*T* 13), we also should ask how his extensive discussion of linguistic meaning is germane to that theory. I attempt to answer these questions in the next chapter.

Notes

[1]Such a limited characterization of an entity is also found in Wolfgang Pauli's initial characterization of the neutrino as a thing that has all and only the characteristics needed to balance certain physical formuli. See Gale 1979: 278-85, especially 278-9.

[2]This is not to say either that earlier philosophers had not used the term 'impression' or that none had used it in a fashion similar to Hume's. While in eighteenth-century parlance the term 'impression' connoted an occurrence on an organ of sense (cf. Crousaz 1724: 1:14 and 38; Reid 1969b: 21-27) and Hume noted that he was using 'impression' 'in a sense different from what is usual' (*T* 2n), Cummins has shown that Locke occasionally used 'impression' in a sense that anticipates Hume's (Cummins 1973b: 297-301).

[3]I cite Berkeley for purposes of illustration only, and I do not wish to enter into the debate regarding Hume's familiarity with Berkeley's works. On Berkeley's phenomenal criterion see Flage 1987a: 69-74.

[4]This is not to say that Hume himself downplayed the role of force and vivacity, for he certainly did not. Notice that he claimed the difference between force and vivacity is the only difference between impressions and ideas that 'strikes my eye' (*T* 2), and, as we shall see shortly, he needs some such distinction for the plausibility of his inductive arguments for the causal priority of impressions to ideas. While I shall follow the Hume of the *Treatise* and treat the notions of force and vivacity as primitive and unproblematic, in the Appendix to this book I argue that Hume eventually was aware of the problems with his characterization of 'force and vivacity' and that there seems to be a subtle change in his characterization of these notions in the move from the *Treatise* to the first *Enquiry*.

[5]We will consider this in some detail in the next chapter.

[6]The word 'connections' is placed in quotation marks to distinguish it from Hume's typical opposition between a real or necessary connection and a relation.

[7]While Hume acknowledges his intellectual debt to Berkeley (*T* 17), it is arguable that Berkeley's arguments focused on the first of these questions and the question whether it is possible to conceive of the simple or complex sensible qualities of objects in isolation from those objects of which they are qualities (unexemplified qualities). On this see Flage 1986a: 483-501 or Flage 1987a: 13-53.

[8]Notice that at *T* 20 Hume wrote, 'But to form the idea of an object, and to form an idea simply is the same thing; the reference of the idea to an object being an extraneous denomination, of which in itself it bears no mark or character.' Hence, it makes little difference whether one suggests that Hume includes ideas or both ideas and objects in the extension of a term.

[9]Cf. Hume's example of such a substitution with respect to one's idea of a triangle, *T* 21.

[10]As we shall see in the next chapter, Hume, like Locke, recognized a distinction between positive and relative ideas. A 'positive idea' is a direct

conception of the content of a sensory or reflective state; such an idea might reasonably be construed as a mental image (cf. Locke, *Essay* 2.8.1-7 and 2.25.6). A relative idea, on the other hand, allows one to single out an object, but it provides one with no knowledge of the object's implicit nature. Locke held that one has only 'An obscure and relative *Idea* of Substance in general' (*Essay* 2.23.3), and in his *Letter to the Right Reverend Edward, Lord Bishop of Worcester* he provides an account of the nature of such a relative idea (Locke 1823: 4:21).

[11]See particularly *T* 219-25, 232-4, 240-6, and 251-2. I examine these passages in Chapter 4.

[12]Here it makes no difference how one construes the term 'idea' in Hume's works, that is, whether or not the term 'idea' is taken to denote a mental image. In whatever sense the term 'idea' is used in 'Of Abstract Ideas', it is impossible to form an idea of a substance (or a kind of substance).

[13]If my account of Hume's theory of meaning is correct, it can be shown that the intellectual debt to Berkeley that Hume acknowledged at the beginning of 'Of Abstract Ideas' is a genuine debt. Berkeley also proposed a denotational theory of the meaning of sortal terms (cf. Berkeley, *PHK*, Introduction, Sections 11-12 and 16). Further, just as Hume proposed an 'idea of substance', that is, a criterion for classifying objects as objects of a certain kind, Berkeley's concern with the 'explication of the meaning of a term' (*PHK*, Part i, Section 49) consists of such a criterion. However, to provide an extensive examination of the similarities between the denotative accounts of meaning in Berkeley and Hume is beyond the scope of this work.

3
Thought

In this chapter I examine Hume's account of thought. I argue that Humean thoughts are intentional acts. My paradigm of a Humean thought will be an abstract idea. I begin by sketching the standard interpretation of Humean thought and argue that even though simple ideas are fundamentally 'images' of qualities, there are things of which Hume claims to have ideas that cannot be images in anything like a pictorial sense. I show that Hume acknowledged a distinction that was common in the intellectual milieu of the eighteenth century, a distinction between positive ideas (images) and relative ideas. I argue that relative ideas function in the 'way of ideas' in the same way that definite descriptions function in the linguistic realm. Finally, I suggest that had Hume provided a discussion of the nature of thoughts, he would have suggested that they are intentional acts in which a causal relation joins a cognitive content with an intentional object.[1]

Ideas

The standard interpretation of Hume's views on thought goes something like this. The fundamental elements in Hume's theory are impressions (sense data and introspective data) and ideas (images of impressions). Although simple impressions are causally prior to simple ideas, the only inherent difference between an idea and an impression is the greater 'force and vivacity' of an impression *vis-à-vis* its corresponding idea.[2] The standard interpretation has been the subject of considerable philosophical and historical criticism, ranging from the sophomoric objection that 'image' properly pertains only to visual ideas,[3] to Yolton's attempt to effect a thorough re-examination of perception in the early modern period (Yolton 1984).

The standard interpretation takes ideas to be images of sensory or reflective qualities. While we shall see that Hume uses the word 'idea' in circumstances that are incompatible with a purely imagistic interpretation of ideas, there are good reasons to suggest that Hume's most fundamental sense of 'idea' is imagistic. First, Hume's most common characterization of ideas is as images (cf. *T* 1, 6, 20, 27, 111, 119, 134, 135, 141, 192, 239, 265; *Abstract*, *T* 647). Second, in the philosophical parlance of the time, ideas often were described as images or as very similar to images.[4] Third, Hume occasionally attributes properties to ideas that reasonably can be attributed to images but cannot reasonably be attributed to nonimagistic states. For example, he claims that ideas of extension are extended (*T* 240).[5] Finally, even in those cases in which an idea is not to be construed wholly as an image, there is an imagistic element in it.

To claim that an idea is an image, however, does not provide an exhaustive description of even the fundamental sense of 'idea'. Whatever else they are, they are among the fundamental components of the mind (*T* 1, 207, 252), and, as his discussions of belief show (cf. *T* 96, 97, 105-6, 119-20), they are often the objects of thought.[6] In this section I explore the relationship between the idea as image and the idea as object of thought. I begin with a brief discussion of simple ideas.

After dividing the class of perceptions into impressions and ideas, Hume introduces a second distinction that cuts across the class of perceptions, namely, the distinction between simple and complex perceptions. He wrote:

> There is another division of our perceptions, which it will be convenient to observe, and which extends itself both to our impressions and ideas. The division is into SIMPLE and COMPLEX. Simple perceptions or impressions and ideas are such as admit of no distinction nor separation. The complex are the contrary of these, and may be distinguished into parts. Tho' a particular colour, taste, and smell are qualities all united together in this apple, 'tis easy to perceive they are not the same, but are at least distinguishable from each other. (*T* 2)

Simple ideas are those 'parts' of a complex idea that are neither distinguishable nor separable. Hume's reference to the several qualities of the apple suggests that the relevant notion of simplicity is qualitative simplicity, and his remarks on the missing shade of blue (*T* 5-6) seem to bear this out.[7] But the case of the apple is ambiguous. One's complex idea of an apple is composed of ideas derived from various perceptual modes, and what he *might* be claiming is that one can 'distinguish and separate' the ideas of the several perceptual modes from one another, but one cannot distinguish and separate 'parts' within ideas of a given perceptual mode. For example, one might distinguish and conceive of the taste of an apple apart from its other qualities, but one might not be able to distinguish and separate the visual color and shape of an apple.[8]

There is some evidence to support this latter rendering of the notion of simplicity. In 'Of Abstract Ideas' Hume devotes several pages to the notion of distinctions of reason. Within that context, he seems to claim that the simplicity of an idea is not to be identified with qualitative simplicity. He wrote:

> 'Tis certain that the mind wou'd never have dream'd of distinguishing a figure from the body figur'd, as being in reality neither distinguishable, nor different, nor separable; did it not observe, that even in this simplicity there might be contain'd many different resemblances and relations. Thus when a globe of white marble is presented, we receive only the impression of a white colour dispos'd in a certain form, nor are we able to separate the colour from the form. But observing afterwards a globe of black marble and a cube of white, and comparing them with our former object, we find two separate resemblances, in what formerly seem'd, and really is, perfectly inseparable. After a little more practice of this kind, we begin to distinguish the figure from the colour by a *distinction of reason*; that is, we consider the figure and colour together, since they are in effect the same and undistinguishable; but still view them in different aspects, according to the resemblances, of which they are susceptible. (*T* 25)

This passage might be taken to show that the notion of simplicity cannot be identified with qualitative simplicity. Since the mark of simplicity is indistinguishability and inseparability, and since the color and the (visual) shape of a globe of white marble are 'in reality neither distinguishable, nor different, nor separable', this passage might be taken to indicate that simple ideas are qualitatively complex (cf. Butler 1976; Tweyman 1974a). But there are several things that speak against such an interpretation. First, Hume claims that color and shape are not '*in reality*' distinguishable or separable. What does this mean? Surely at least part of it is this: one cannot, as a matter of fact, form an idea of *any* color apart from *some* shape, and consequently, there are no grounds for claiming that it is possible for a color to exist apart from a shape (cf. *T* 32). Hence in any reality one would pair every color with some shape, and vice versa. This, of course, does not mean that color and shape are utterly indistinguishable, as seems required by Hume's initial discussion of simple perceptions (*T* 2). Second, there is a sense in which Hume must grant that color and shape are separable: apart from this his account of the imagination is unintelligible. Assume that the only fuchsia-colored thing I have ever seen is my wife's swimming suit. This does not mean that I cannot imagine what it would be like for my typewriter to be colored fuchsia. Since, for Hume, ideas of the imagination are based upon a recombination of simple ideas (cf. *T* 3), the fact that I can imagine a fuchsia-colored typewriter seems to imply that a particular shade of color must be considered a simple idea, and, more generally, that simple ideas are qualitatively simple.[9]

If simplicity is qualitative, then it is reasonable to suggest that ideas are imagistic. But to claim that there are images--whether impressions or ideas--passing in one's mind is far from giving an adequate phenomenal description of thought. On the one hand, there are things of which Hume claims one has ideas that cannot plausibly be construed as images. Among these are the notorious missing shade of blue (*T* 5-6; cf. Butler 1976; Cummins 1978), the ideas of the thousandth and ten-thousandth part of a grain of sand (*T* 22-3), and, if it is possible to have such, the idea of a substance as substratum. On the other hand, one typically thinks of a thing as a thing of a kind, that is, typically thought involves abstraction. In the remainder of the chapter I shall examine the implications of these two facts.

In the next section I argue that Hume countenanced nonimagistic ideas, what he occasionally called relative ideas. Such ideas allow one to single out an object without knowledge of the nature of the thing singled out. They provide one with what Russell called 'knowledge by description' (Russell 1912: 46-59).

Relative Ideas

A distinction was commonly drawn in the 'way of ideas' between positive ideas and relative ideas. A *positive idea* represents an entity as it is, and such ideas were commonly described in terms of images. A *relative idea*--what Berkeley often called a relative notion (Berkeley, *PHK*, I, 27, 89, 142; cf. Flage 1987a: 133-72)--singles out an unperceived entity on the basis of its relations to a perceived entity, that is, a positive idea. Since virtually all philosophers prior to Hume were substance theorists and agreed that substance itself is imperceptible,[10] there was general agreement among the empiricists that one has no positive idea of substance *per se*. Both Locke and Berkeley were explicit on this point. For example, Locke wrote:

We have no such *clear Idea* at all, and therefore signify nothing by the word *Substance*, but only a certain supposition of we know not what; (*i.e.* of something whereof we have no particular distinct positive) *Idea*, which we take to be the *substratum*, or support of those *Ideas* we do know. (Locke, *Essay* 1.4.18)

One has only an 'obscure and relative *Idea* of Substance in general' (Locke, *Essay* 2.23.3), indeed, 'we have no *Idea* of what it [substance] is, but only a confused and obscure one of what it does' (Locke, *Essay* 2.13.19; cf. 3.23.1-3 and 2.31.6; Locke 1823: 4:7-8; Ammerman 1965; Flage 1981b). On this point Berkeley was at one with Locke. Regarding one's putative ideas of material substance, he wrote:

Now I desire that you would explain what is meant by matter's *supporting* extension: say you, I have no idea of matter, and therefore cannot explain it. I answer, though you have no positive, yet if you have any meaning at all, you must have at least a relative idea of matter; though you know not what it is, yet you must be supposed to know what relation it bears to accidents and what is meant by its supporting them. (Berkeley, *PHK*, I, 16; cf. I, 17, 26, 27, 142).

Notice that in the writings of both Locke and Berkeley one's idea of substance is not a positive idea: one has no idea that represents substance as it is in itself. The most one can claim to have is a relative idea of substance, that is, an idea that singles out an entity on the basis of the relations in which that entity stands to a positive idea. As Berkeley's discussions indicate, if one claims to have a relative idea of an entity, the relations involved in that idea must be clearly known. It is Berkeley's contention that the relation of support cannot be elucidated in the case of material substance (Berkeley, *PHK*, I, 8-18), while it can be elucidated in the case of immaterial substance (Berkeley, *PHK*, I, 138), that accounts for his rejection of the doctrine of material substance and his adherence to the doctrine of immaterial substance.[11]

Although his allusions to relative ideas are brief and few in number, they are sufficient to show that Hume also acknowledged a distinction between positive ideas (images) and relative ideas. It is in terms of positive ideas that the overwhelming majority of his discussions are couched. Nonetheless, in his discussions of the limits of ideational thought in Book I, Part ii, Section 6 of the *Treatise*, after concluding that ''tis impossible for us so much as to conceive or form an idea [that is, a positive idea] of anything specifically different from ideas and impressions' (*T* 67), he went on to claim that it is possible to form a relative idea of an external object as a thing specifically different from a perception. As he wrote, 'The farthest we can go towards a conception of external objects, when supppos'd *specifically* different from our perceptions, is to form a relative idea of them, without pretending to comprehend the related objects' (*T* 68). As Hume's discussion of the philosophical belief in the external world indicates, 'to conceive an external object merely as a relation without a relative' (*T* 241) assumes that the relation of causation (or the relations of resemblance and causation) obtains between a given perception of which one is aware and some external object.[12]

Hume also alludes to relative ideas in a footnote to his discussion 'Of the Necessary Connection' in the first *Enquiry*. There he claimed one has a relative idea of power as the unknown quality of an object that causes (is constantly conjoined with) a known effect. He wrote:

> According to these explications and definitions, the idea of *power* is relative as much as that of *cause*; and both have a reference to an effect, or some other event constantly conjoined with the former. When we consider the *unknown* circumstance of an object, by which the degree or quantity of its effect is fixed and determined, we call that its power: And accordingly, it is allowed by all philosophers, that the effect is the measure of the power. But if they had any idea of power, as it is itself, why could not they Measure it in itself? (*EHU* 77n)

As in the case of one's idea of an external object as something specifically different from a perception, one's idea of power as the quality that causes a particular effect is a relative idea. One has no idea of the power itself; one can merely conceive of power as the property that causes (is constantly conjoined with) an observable effect.

These passages show that Hume recognized the distinction between positive and relative ideas. The contexts in which he drew this distinction also provide one with significant clues to the correct model for understanding relative ideas. If relative ideas provide the foundation within the 'way of ideas' for a representational theory of perception, one's relative idea of a material object must single out exactly one entity that causes a known perception and is not itself a perception. Similarly, to claim that one has a relative idea of power as an unknown quality or type of quality that is causally related to a particular effect, one's relative idea of power must single out a particular quality or type of quality that is causally related to the particular effect or type of effect one perceives. Since Hume's paradigm cases of relative ideas appear to be cases that involve a uniqueness requirement, it is reasonable to suggest that relative ideas function within the 'way of ideas' in a fashion analogous to that of definite descriptions in the linguistic realm. Hence, one may linguistically express the intent of one's relative idea of a material object (although not describe the relative idea itself) by the definite description, 'the entity that causes a and is not itself a perception', where a is a perception of which one is aware, one's relative idea succeeds in singling out a material object just in case it is true that there is exactly one thing x that causes a and x is not a perception. Similarly, the intent of one's relative idea of power can be expressed by the definite description, 'the property that causes (is constantly conjoined with) b', where b is an observed event, that is, one's relative idea succeeds in singling out a power just in case it is true that exactly one property Φ is the cause of b. My suggestion that Hume's relative ideas should be understood on the model of definite descriptions accounts for the uniqueness claims that are implicit both in a representational theory of perception that holds that perceptions are specifically different from objects and in Hume's discussion of the relative idea of power. The doctrine of relative ideas, therefore, can provide an ideational foundation for a distinction between knowledge by acquaintance and knowledge by description in Hume's philosophy. As we shall see later, even though Hume did not allow that one can claim to know that all the putative entities singled out by relative ideas exist, the theory of relative ideas at least accounts for the intelligibility of various concepts.

Although definite descriptions seem to provide a reasonable model for understanding relative ideas, and therefore a basis for claiming that the criteria for the adequacy of a contextual definition of definite descriptions apply to relative ideas, someone might object that this model is anachronistic. In reply to such an objection, I shall show that the logical theory of the late seventeenth and early eighteenth centuries was sufficiently sophisticated to provide such a model to Hume. I shall first consider the type of complex linguistic expression Arnauld called a 'determination', since one type of determination is what we now call a definite description. I shall then turn to the criteria for the adequacy of a real definition and argue that these criteria apply, *mutatis mutandis*, to the question of the adequacy of relative ideas.

In his discussion of linguistic expressions, Arnauld indicates that a determination is a complex linguistic expression in which 'the extension of a complex term is less than the extension of the idea expressed by the principal word' (Arnauld 1964: 60). Although any noun modified by an adjective is an example of a determination, Arnauld indicates that some determinations have only one individual in their extensions. These determinations are what we now call definite descriptions. Of these Arnauld wrote:

Some determinations are proper names: A general word may be joined with other words in such a way that the idea expressed has in its extension but a single individual. When, for example, I form the complex expression 'the present Pope,' I have determined the general word 'pope' in such a way that the complex expression applies to no other person than to Alexander VII. (Arnauld 1964: 60)

One finds the same point made even more succinctly in the writings of the eighteenth-century logician Isaac Watts. Watts wrote:

Note in the *third* place, That any *common* name whatsoever is made *proper* by terms of particularity added to it, as the common words *pope, king, horse, garden, book, knife,* &c. are designed to signify a particular idea, when we say, the *present pope*; *the king of Great Britain*; *the horse that won the last plate at Newmarket*; *the royal garden at Kensington*; *this book, that knife,* &c. (Watts 1806: 50)

These passages show that by the early eighteenth century there was an awareness of the uniqueness claim made by a denoting phrase. Since it is undeniable that Hume was acquainted with Arnauld's *The Art of Thinking* (*T* 43n), and since it is probable that he was acquainted with Watts,[13] it is reasonable to understand the uniqueness claim of a relative idea on the model of a definite description.

If it is proper to construe Hume's relative ideas on the model of a definite description, the truth conditions for a statement that a definite description is fulfilled should apply to a relative idea, namely, it must pick at least and at most one thing (Russell 1918: 249). There are several reasons why I consider this proper. First, the Russellian analysis specifies uniqueness conditions, and it is clear that there is a uniqueness claim implicit in a Humean relative idea. Second, if one can allow that a relative idea might single out a type as well as a token, thereby grounding the meaning of a general term as well as a proper name--a move that is consistent with both the Russellian analysis of definite descriptions and Hume's discussion of linguistic meaning (Russell 1918: 243; Chapter 2 above)--the criteria for the adequacy of a real definition are applicable to words denoting objects known mediately. Since Arnauld allowed that a real definition can be relative, that is, a word can be defined 'by identifying the cause, or the matter, or the form, or the purpose of any referent of the defined word' (Arnauld 1964: 165), a relative idea can provide the foundation within the 'way of ideas' for a real definition. Further, by examining the criteria for the adequacy of a real definition, we shall come to understand why the theory of relative ideas is consistent with empiricism and why it may *seem* one has a relative idea of something while, in fact, one does not have such an idea.

Arnauld stated three criteria for the adequacy of a real definition. He wrote:

1. A definition must be exhaustive, that is, the defined words must refer to all those things to which the defining words refer.
2. A definition must be proper, that is, the defining words must refer to only those things to which the defined word can refer.
3. A definition must be informative--that is, the defining words must express a clearer, more distinct idea than the defined word. (Arnauld 1964: 165-6; cf. Watts 1806: 85-8)

Since the first two criteria demand that the *definiens* refer to all and only those things in the extension of the *definiendum*, they comply with the conditions under which a statement that a definite description is fulfilled is true. Just as a statement that a definite description is fulfilled is true just in case the description picks out at least and at most one thing, in an analogous way, if one employs a relative idea to provide the basis in the 'way of ideas' for the meaning of the term 'material object', it must single out exactly one type of thing. The third criterion is also instructive, for its application to relative ideas demands that one's ideas of the known *relatum* and the relation in which it stands to the unknown *relatum* be clear. Since Hume held that ideas are clear just in case they are copies of impressions (*T* 72-3), the application of the third criterion to relative ideas can be understood as demanding that one have positive ideas of the relation and the known *relatum* in a relative idea (cf. *T* 243). When understood in this way, the third criterion complies with Russell's 'fundamental principle in the analysis of propositions containing descriptions' that '*Every proposition which we can understand must be composed wholly of constituents with which we are acquainted*' (Russell 1912: 58). As we shall see in the next chapter, this principle provides the basis for one of Hume's criticisms of the doctrine of substance.

If my interpretation of Hume's position on relative ideas is correct, it explains both why Hume seemed to hold that the missing shade of blue posed no serious problem for the copy theory of ideas and how it is possible to think of very large and very small numbers, even though one has no clear and adequate (positive) ideas of them. Furthermore, the theory of relative ideas is consistent with Hume's scepticism: Hume did not allow that one could know that all putative things singled out on the basis of a relative idea complying with the three criteria are existents, although he did allow that it is possible that anything of which one has an adequate relative idea could exist. To allow a claim of knowledge by description, to claim to know *that* there is a thing singled out by one's relative idea, Hume required that it be possible to have a positive idea of an entity of at least the same categorial kind as that singled out by the relative idea in question. It is for this reason that he could take the relative idea of a material object as a paradigm, while still claiming that the actual existence of material objects as entities specifically different from perceptions is subject to doubt, since 'The only existents of which we are certain, are perceptions', and 'no beings are ever present to the mind but perceptions' (*T* 212).

As we saw earlier, Hume held that some relative ideas single out things or types of things, for example, one's relative idea of power singles out the property that causes a particular effect. We have also noted that if a relative idea is to single out a thing or type of thing, one must have a clear idea of the relevant relation in the relative idea. Since Hume claimed that all genuine relations fall under seven general headings (*T* 13-15), the relation in an adequate relative idea must fall under one of those headings. Recognizing this, we can see how Hume's considerations of the missing shade of blue and the thousandth part of a grain of sand can be subsumed under the theory of relative ideas.

In his discussion of the missing shade of blue, Hume suggests the possibility that one can form an idea of a particular simple shade of blue, even if one has never had an impression of that color. Assuming that a man of thirty has been acquainted with all shades of blue save one, and all the shades of blue with which he has been acquainted were placed before him in a progression from the lightest to the darkest, the man would notice that there is a greater difference between two shades of blue than there is between any others. Hume then suggested that it would be possible for the man to imagine (form an idea of) this simple missing shade of blue, even though he had never had an impression of it (*T* 5-6; *EHU* 21). Hume allowed that we possess ideas of relations of quality, and he included ideas of differences in shades of color among these qualitative relations (*T* 15). This indicates that one can single out the missing shade of blue on the basis of the relative idea corresponding to the definite description, 'the shade of blue that is darker than x and lighter than y', where x and y are the shades of blue flanking the missing shade. If one can allow that one might have a *relative*, rather than a *positive*, idea of the missing shade of blue, this will explain why Hume seemed unconcerned about what would otherwise be a telling counter-example to his copy theory of simple ideas.

Similarly, since Hume allowed that 'All those objects which admit of *quantity*, or *number*, may be compar'd in that particular' (*T* 14-15), one can understand how Hume could claim that one has an idea of the thousandth part of a grain of sand, even though one's mental image of that minute particle differs in no way from that of the grain of sand itself. Notice what Hume wrote:

> When you tell me of the thousandth and ten thousandth part of a grain of sand, I have a distinct idea of these numbers and of their different proportions; but the images which I form in my mind to represent the things themselves, are nothing different from each other, nor inferior to that image, by which I represent the grain of sand itself, which is suppos'd so vastly to exceed them. (*T* 72)

Since one can understand proportions, even though one has a distinct (positive) idea of nothing other than numerals representing large numbers (*T* 22-3), it is reasonable to assume that one's understanding of the thousandth part of something consists of a relative idea of the singular part of a collection of ten times ten times ten things, where one has a clear and positive idea of ten things. It is due to Hume's claim that one has an idea of relations of quantity and number that it is reasonable to understand his discussion of the thousandth part of a grain of sand as the result of the operation of a relative idea on the mental image of a grain of sand.

Thus, the theory of relative ideas allows one to explain how it is possible to form ideas of some objects that either have not been or cannot be perceived. A relative idea is like a definite description in so far as it allows one to single out an object on the basis of a positive idea and a relation. We have seen that this provides Hume with a cognitive basis for a representative theory of perception and an idea of power. We also have seen that it explains how it is possible for Hume to deem the missing shade of blue unproblematic and to account for ideas of the thousandth and ten thousandth part of a grain of sand, even though he claimed one's positive ideas of these minute entities do not differ from one's idea of the grain itself. And the list of problematic entities conceived on the basis of relative ideas might be lengthened. For example, the idea of God as the cause of the universe (*D* 142) is merely a relative idea.

But one need not focus exclusively on the problematic cases to discover relative ideas in Hume. Hume's account of memory also seems to require relative ideas. In his accounts of the distinction between ideas of memory and ideas of the imagination (*T* 8-10 and 85-6), Hume introduces both a phenomenal *cum* doxastic criterion for drawing the distinction, that is, a criterion based on degrees of force and vivacity (cf. Smith 1941: 232-3; Noxon 1976: 273), and an epistemic or formal criterion. Although the phenomenal *cum* doxastic criterion might allow one to distinguish between psychological states, it makes no epistemic guarantees, and consequently, it is not a reliable basis for drawing the distinction. On the one hand, memories 'fade' over time (they lose their force and vivacity). On the other, ideas of the imagination can become so forceful and vivacious that they are taken to be ideas of the memory (*T* 86). Furthermore, it provides no guidance for distinguishing ideas of the memory from beliefs regarding temporally located objects that are not based upon the memory (nonmnemonic beliefs). As we shall see, the formal criterion allows one to do both, and it also shows that the ideas of memory are relative ideas.

Hume states his formal criterion as follows:

> There is another difference betwixt these two kinds of ideas, which is no less evident, namely that tho' neither the ideas of the memory nor imagination, neither the lively nor faint ideas can make their appearance in the mind, unless their correspondent impressions have gone before to prepare the way for them, yet the imagination is not restrain'd to the same order and form with the original impressions; while the memory is in a manner ty'd down in that respect, without any power or variation.

> 'Tis evident, that the memory preserves the original form, in which its objects were presented, and that where-ever we depart from it in recollecting any thing, it proceeds from the same defect or imperfection in that faculty. . . . The chief exercise of the memory is not to preserve the simple ideas, but their order and position. (*T* 9; cf. *T* 85)

The formal criterion is based on the flexibility of the imagination and the inflexibility of the memory with regard to the 'form and order' of its ideas. Ideas of the memory and the imagination are complex (*T* 85). In so far as complex ideas are composed of simple ideas and '*all our simple ideas in their first appearance are deriv'd from* [caused by] *simple impressions*' (*T* 4), ideas of the memory and of the imagination are on a par: both types of idea can trace their ancestries back to simple impressions.[14] The difference between them is found in the 'form and order' or 'order and position' of the simple ideas that compose a complex idea. While the simple ideas composing a complex idea of the imagination might originally have been caused by any number of simple and temporally separated impressions, the causal history of a complex idea of the memory must be traceable back to a single complex impression which exactly (or closely) resembles that idea.[15] The formal criterion is basically a causal thesis: if a particular positive idea (image) is a genuine idea of the memory, then at some point in the past there was a complex impression that was the cause (or the original cause) of and exactly (or closely) resembles the positive ideas as an idea.[16] But the formal criterion is not merely a causal thesis. It also reflects the fact that one conceives of a particular positive idea as representing a particular complex impression. Since Hume took ideas of the memory to be representational, it is reasonable to take ideas of the memory to be relative ideas corresponding to definite descriptions of the following general form: 'the impression that is the (original) cause of and exactly (or closely) resembles m', where 'm' denotes a particular positive idea.[17]

There are three points to notice. (1) It is fundamentally the causal reference in an idea of the memory that distinguishes it from an idea of the imagination, and it is on this that the adequacy of an idea of the memory depends. A complex relative idea of the memory singles out the impression that was the cause of its positive component, and even if there were an idea of the imagination that could trace its causal ancestry back to a single complex positive idea, that idea of the imagination either would be a purely positive idea (image) with no temporal reference, or, if there were a temporal reference, there still would be no reference to the cause of the complex positive idea. (2) The formal criterion is consistent with Hume's scepticism with regard to memory, since although the formal criterion specifies the necessary and sufficient conditions for an idea to be an idea of the memory, and therefore the conditions under which such an idea is 'true' (cf. *T* 448 and 458), one is never in a position to know whether the causal relation obtains. (3) The formal criterion allows one to distinguish memories from nonmnemonic beliefs, since in the case of nonmnemonic beliefs there is no causal relation between the positive component of one's relative idea and the (original) cause of that idea.[18]

Thus, we have seen that Hume drew a positive/relative ideas distinction, that relative ideas will allow him to explain how one can conceive of objects that are not immediately available in experience or of which one's positive idea is indeterminate, and that even his account of memory rests upon relative ideas. As we shall see in subsequent chapters, relative ideas play a significant role in Hume's account of mind.

Intentional Acts

Up to this point I have argued that the most fundamental kind of Humean ideas are images of impressions. Then I argued that Hume recognized a distinction between imagistic or positive ideas and relative ideas. Relative ideas allow one to single out unperceived objects on the basis of their relations to positive ideas. Since we are assuming with the Hume of the *Treatise* that the notions of force and vivacity are primitive and unproblematic, we now have examined the elements of Humean thought. We must now ask how these elements fit together to form thoughts.

In what remains I argue that Humean thoughts are intentional acts. I consider this *prima facie* plausible in so far as Hume often alludes to 'acts' or 'operations of the mind' (*T* 22, 96-7n, 114, 177, 205n), and, given the long history of discussions of intentionality (cf. Hickman 1980; Sergeant 1696: 2; Sergeant 1697: 26-7), it seems implausible to suggest that Hume was unaware of the technical use of 'act'. Further, as Yolton notes, there are various contexts in which Hume's discussions of thoughts do not seem reducible to ideas alone (Yolton 1984: 192-5). I take abstraction to be a paradigm of a Humean intentional act since (1) Hume refers to it as an 'act of the mind' (*T* 22), (2) he deemed it elemental to his philosophy (*T* 13), and (3) the discussion in 'Of Abstract Ideas' explains how it is possible to conceive of a thing as a thing of a kind, which seems essential to human thought. So I begin with a review of the discussion in 'Of Abstract Ideas'. Next, I indicate that the structure of Hume's relation of linguistic meaning is analogous to the intentional relation in many contemporary discussions of intentional acts. Finally, I describe three cases of thinking in accordance with this model of intentional acts.

In 'Of Abstract Ideas' Hume argued that the mind is incapable of forming what Locke called abstract general ideas (*T* 18-20) and provided a psychological explanation of the meaning of general terms. He wrote:

> When we have found a resemblance among several objects, that often occur to us, we apply the same name to all of them, whatever differences we may observe in the degrees of their quantity and quality, and whatever other differences may appear among them. After we have acquired a custom of this kind, the hearing of that name revives the idea of one of these objects, and makes the imagination conceive it with all its particular circumstances and proportions. (*T* 20)

Hume's reduction of the meaning relation to a causal relation consists of construing meaning relations as causal relations. Hearing or seeing a word causes the experienced user of a language to form a determinate idea that functions as the paradigm of a thing of a kind.

But this causal relation between the word and the idea is only half of what might happen. On Hume's account, children learn words by seeing, touching, hearing, smelling, or tasting an object and simultaneously hearing a word. If I want to teach my young daughter what a rose is, for example, I might take her into a garden and say the word 'rose' while she is looking at red roses, yellow roses, and pink roses. She might repeat the word 'rose', and thereby develop the habit of using the word 'rose' when seeing a certain kind of flower. As Hume would put it, having 'found a resemblance among several objects, [she] appl[ies] the same name to all of them' (*T* 20). In this case, seeing the object causes her to think of the word; there is a sense in which the object (impression) 'means' the word.

Hence, in his account of linguistic meaning there are two causal relations.[19] To a competent speaker of a language, an impression of sensation or reflection causes an idea of a word, and an idea of a word causes a paradigmatic idea of a certain kind of thing. Put schematically, where 'I' is an impression of sensation or reflection, 'i_w' is an idea of a word (a sound or a mark), 'i' is an idea of sensation or reflection, and 'C' is a causal relation, the two 'meaning' relations might be represented as follows: ICi_w and i_wCi.

To those familiar with contemporary discussions of intentionality, Hume's discussion of abstraction should strike a familiar chord. Much of the contemporary literature on intentional acts analyzes such acts in terms of a two-place relation cRo, where 'o' is an intentional object and 'c' is a certain cognitive--often propositional--content (Bergmann 1959; Searle 1983: 1-36; but see also Hochberg 1978: 347-413). It is also agreed that the relation 'R', which is often construed as a meaning relation, is asymmetrical: while c is said to mean, or to be about, or to represent o, o does not mean c. While there is this much agreement, there is also considerable controversy regarding the nature of intentional acts. The status of the relation 'R', whether it is necessary (Bergmann 1959; Bergmann 1964: 33; Bergmann 1967: 125-9; cf. Sergeant 1697: 26) or contingent (cf. Searle 1983: 11), is a matter of some dispute, as is the ontological status of intentional objects that do not actually exist (cf. Marras 1972: 3-4).

If Hume's discussion of abstraction and linguistic meaning also is taken as a model of intentionality, the problematic questions can be answered. For Hume the intentional relation is taken to be a causal relation, and as such it is a contingent relation. Further, given that

'There is no impression nor idea of any kind, of which we have any consciousness or memory, that is not conceiv'd as existent' (*T* 66), all intentional objects *qua* ideas are existents, although this does not imply that the ideas are a part of a 'reality'.[20] Finally, one should notice that if one can take the discussion of abstraction and linguistic meaning as Hume's model of intentionality, it differs from recent attempts to reduce the intentional relation to the causal relation. Typically, those who give a causal account of the intentionality of perception claim that the effect, the perceptual belief, is about the cause (cf. Armstrong 1968: 208-44; Swain 1979; Kripke 1980: 59n, 91-7; Searle 1983: 37-78; Boër and Lycan 1986: 126-9). If Hume took his discussion of linguistic meaning as his paradigm of intentionality and construed the intentional relation as a causal relation, the intentional *cum* causal relation is always from cause to effect: the cause means or is about the effect, that is, the cause functions as the cognitive content and the effect as the intentional object. To understand this more clearly, let us consider three examples.

Hume claimed that thought and reasoning in animals are of the same kind as thought and reasoning in human beings (cf. *T* 176-9), and we might begin by considering how the model of intentionality applies in the case of animals. Assume Beauregard is an elderly bear. In his youth, Beauregard narrowly escaped from a forest fire. Through this experience he discovered the correlations between smoke and fire, between fire and burning trees, and between fire and a certain kind of pain, shrieks of pain, and injured or dying animals. In the summer of 1988 Beauregard was living a comfortable life in Yellowstone National Park. One day Beauregard saw smoke in the distance. How would one describe his thoughts? The impression of smoke causes an idea of fire, which causes ideas of burning trees, which causes ideas of pain and shrieks of pain, which causes an idea of dead and badly burned animals. One of these ideas also causes an impression of fear, and Beauregard lumbers off away from the smoke. In each of these causal relations from an impression to an idea or from an idea to an idea, the cause is a 'natural sign' of its effect, and in this sense one might suggest that the cause 'means' the effect. If I am correct in suggesting that Hume reduced the intentional relation to the causal relation, then even animals and prelinguistic children engage in intentional acts.

Many writers on intentionality contend that the content of an intentional act is propositional.[21] While it does not seem that all Humean intentional acts have propositional content, certainly some acts do, and all have content fitting the semantic categories used in propositional thought. Clearly, an idea of a sentence can cause an idea of a state of affairs. Since Hume divided the world into kinds on the basis of semantic categories, it is on the basis of the semantic categories of a particular language that human beings recognize things as things of various kinds, and to give a description of this requires that the 'act' involved be a complex composed of several acts. Consider what is involved in recognizing something as a red rose. I am aware of an impression. This impression causes the linguistic idea 'a red rose'. Given Hume's account of abstract ideas and linguistic meaning, this linguistic idea causes one's paradigmatic idea of a red rose. Hence, an act of recognition is complex. It consists of two intentional acts and may be represented as:

$$ICi_w \ \& \ i_wCi,$$

where 'I' is an impression, 'i_w' is a word, phrase, or sentence, and 'i' is a nonlinguistic idea. This might be deemed a *complete* act of recognition.

There are several things to notice. First, in the case of recognition there seems to be another relation that is essential to the complete act, namely, a relation of resemblance between I and i, and it would seem that such a resemblance relation also is essential to other complex acts in so far as recognition is a necessary condition for those acts. Second, although in some complex acts there is a resemblance relation between the impression I in the first act and the idea i in the second, the intentional *cum* causal relation and the relation of representation are distinct. While Hume sometimes suggests that the relation of representation is based upon resemblance (*T* 233), we have seen that in so far as the case of linguistic meaning provides the paradigm for an intentional act, there need be no resemblance between the impression or idea *qua* cognitive content and the idea *qua* intentional object in the act. This should be clear from the case of animal thought we considered above. In so far as an impression of smoke causes an idea of fire, the impression of smoke might be said to mean or be about fire, but there is no resemblance between the impression and the idea. Thus, although resemblance might be essential to certain kinds of complex acts, it is not essential to simple Humean intentional acts. Third, although all complete acts that include propositional (linguistic) content are complex acts, not all acts that include propositional content are complete. Hume notes that it is 'usual, after the frequent use of terms, which are really significant and intelligible, to omit the idea, which we wou'd express by them, and preserve only the custom, by which we recal the idea at pleasure' (*T* 224). This explains why the competent user of language is generally unaware of the kind of impression-idea duplication that seems to be involved in a complete act. Finally, as the third case indicates, the intentional *cum* causal relation is probabilistic in Hume's sense: there are cases in which an impression or idea will have an effect, and there are others in which it will have none. Infants prior to a significant amount of experience will have nothing more than 'simple apprehensions', that is, awarenesses of impressions without effects following from them. Similarly, adults might be 'preoccupied' while having impressions of various sorts or a visual impression might be so complex that one does not 'notice' all of its details.

Before turning to our final case, a further point should be noticed. If the case of abstraction and linguistic meaning is Hume's paradigm of an intentional act, the intentional object of an act is *always* an idea. In the case of acts with propositional (linguistic) content, this should be clear: an impression can be the cause of an idea of a word and the account of abstraction indicates that an idea of a word causes an abstract idea (paradigm) of a thing of a kind. Were one to suggest that there are Humean intentional acts in which the intentional object is not an idea, these either would be cases in which the intentional object is an impression of reflection or cases in which the intentional object is something other than an occurrent perception. I deal with the latter case below. Regarding the former, one must recognize that there is a causal relation between a perception of sensation and an impression of reflection (*T* 275), but it seems implausible to claim that such a causal relation is to be understood as an intentional relation. While one might claim that smoke means or is about fire and attempt to explain this 'meaning' or 'aboutness' relation in terms of one perception causing another, it is at least odd to claim that if Beauregard the bear has an idea of fire it *means* or *is about* fear, or to claim that if Sherlock Holmes recognizes Moriarity on the streets of London and has an impression of hatred, a certain idea of sensation *means* or *is about* hatred. It is for this reason I consider it plausible to suggest that not all causal relations among perceptions are intentional. If I am correct, then it is only causal relations complying with Hume's second definition of causation (*T* 170, 172) that function as intentional relations, and causal relations between perceptions of sensation and impressions of reflection must be understood in terms of Hume's first definition of causation.[22]

Finally, consider cases of mediate perception or conception (for example, thinking of material objects *as such*)[23] and the case of thinking of the missing shade of blue, cases in which one thinks of things that neither are nor can be a (positive) idea. If the model of Humean intentional acts I have developed is correct, then only an idea can be an object of thought (cf. *T* 67-8). But we have seen that Hume distinguished between positive and relative ideas, and although Hume does not discuss cases of indirect perception or conception in terms of intentional acts, cases of indirect perception can be accommodated by the model of intentionality we have been considering. Consider the thought of the missing shade of blue (*T* 5-6). Seeing the succession of shades of blue with which one has been acquainted would cause one to recognize the gap among the color samples, that is, it would cause one to form an idea whose content is the words 'there is a greater difference between *c* and *d* than there is either between *a* and *b* or *d* and *e*'. This, in turn, might cause either an idea of the definite description 'the blue that is lighter than *d* and darker than *c*', which 'names' a relative idea and causes one to form that idea, or the recognition of the gap might simply cause the relative idea of the missing shade of blue. In this case the relative idea of the missing shade of blue would be the intentional object of an act, and the idea itself singles out an unsensed sensum.[24] Other cases of indirect perception or conception would be analogous, although they would be subject to all the constraints germane to relative ideas, notably the requirement that one have positive ideas of the relation and one relatum.

Conclusions

In this chapter I have discussed Hume's account of thought. First, I argued that Hume's most fundamental sense of 'idea' is imagistic. Second, I showed that Hume acknowledged a distinction between what Locke called positive and relative ideas, and I argued that relative ideas single out unperceived or imperceptible objects on the basis of a positive idea and a relation in much the same way that a definite description allows one to single out an object. Finally, I argued that Humean thoughts are intentional acts that have ideas as their intentional objects.

Notes

[1] Throughout this chapter I follow the Hume of the *Treatise* and treat the notions of 'force and vivacity' as primitive and unproblematic. I return to those notions in the Appendix to this book.
[2] Cf. Russell 1912: 95-6; Broad 1925: 233-4; Laird 1932: 25ff; Price 1940: 4; Smith 1941: 209-10; Basson 1958: 34; Copleston 1959: 68; Zabeeh 1960: 10, 32, 39-40, 46; Broad 1961: 161-76; Flew 1961: 22-3; Anderson 1966:

43-7; Bennett 1971: 222; Sisson 1976: 18-20; Pears 1976: 3-22; Stroud 1977: 26; Ayer 1980: 15; Bricke 1980: 101-8; Passmore 1980: 84-96; Flew 1986: 25ff; Matson 1987: 2:353. Of course, the general tenor of this interpretation is much older than 'sense datum' talk. It seems to have found its original statement in Thomas Reid's *Inquiry into the Human Mind* of 1764 (cf. Reid 1970: 32ff).

[3]Cf. Zabeeh 1960: 72. This kind of objection to the philosophical use of 'idea' during the early modern period also is found in writers prior to Hume (cf. A. (B.) C. 1727: 3).

[4]Cf. Descartes, CSM 2:25; A. (B.) C. 1727: 3; Bolingbroke 1844: 3:76; Locke, *Essay*, 1.1.8. The root of the notion is representation, although the notion of representation is itself understood in different ways. Hume, for example, generally explains representation in terms of resemblance (*T* 233), so Humean ideas might be understood as something like mental photographs. Descartes and Locke, on the other hand, were quite willing to allow that although ideas of secondary qualities 'represent' qualities of objects they bear little or no resemblance to their physical archetypes--and in Descartes's case, even what Locke deemed ideas of primary qualities do not resemble their archetypes. See Descartes, CSM 1:304 and 1:153; Locke, *Essay*, 2.8.8-13.

[5]This should not be taken to mean, as some recent writers have suggested (Anderson 1976; cf. Yolton 1984: 184), that impressions or ideas are physiological entities. Hume drew two kinds of distinctions, a distinction between the properties of perceptions (a material/immaterial distinction) and a distinction between mind and body (a mental/physical distinction), and, consequently, the fact that some impressions and ideas are extended does not show that perceptions are physical objects. I discuss this point in detail in Chapter 6.

[6]This is part of the Lockean tradition; cf. Locke, *Essay* 1.1.8. One might argue that there is a rather opaque allusion to this already at the beginning of the *Treatise*, when Hume claims that ideas are 'the faint images of [impressions] *in* thought and reasoning' (*T* 1, emphasis added). Cf. McRae 1985: 150.

[7]At other points Hume is concerned with geometric simplicity, i.e., indivisibility (cf. *T* 27). Since Hume held that ideas of smells, sounds, and tastes are nonspatial (*T* 235-6; cf. *T* 75, 191, 504n), obviously it cannot be geometrical simplicity to which he here alludes.

[8]There is a sense of 'part' according to which something is a proper part of another thing just in case it is possible for the part to exist independently of the thing of which it is a part (cf. Spinoza 1985: 274). If this were Hume's sense of 'part' then, as we shall see, simple ideas are not qualitatively simple.

[9]Nonetheless, I believe that Butler and Tweyman are on to something. First, they are correct in claiming that there are 'aspects' of simple ideas, and these 'aspects' are known only on the basis of abstraction. Hume claims that simplicity itself is one such aspect (*T* 637, *Letters* 1:39). Second, if I am correct in contending a simple idea is qualitatively simple, they are still correct in claiming that at least some simple ideas can be conceived 'in isolation' only by means of abstraction.

[10]Even Descartes held that substance itself is known only mediately. See Descartes, CSM 2:124.

[11]This type of distinction was not limited to the proponents of the 'way of ideas'. A distinction analogous to the positive/relative ideas distinction was also drawn by Reid (Reid 1969a: 7-10; cf. Segerstedt 1935).

[12]As I argued in a note to Chapter 1, Hume's notion of 'specific difference' is, in the context of *Treatise* I.ii.6, merely the notion of nonresemblance.

[13]Although the fact that Watts's *Logic* went through many editions in the early part of the eighteenth century suggests that Hume was quite probably familiar with Watts's *Logic*, Hume never cites Watts, and I have been unable to find any hard evidence that Hume was familiar with Watts's logical writings. Nonetheless, the fact that both Watts and Arnauld discussed a rudimentary theory of definite descriptions indicates that such a theory was fairly well-known among knowledgeable people in the early eighteenth century, and this strongly suggests that Hume was aware of the theory even if he did not read Watts.

[14]This is what Livingston calls the 'past-entailing' feature of ideas (Livingston 1979: 188-91).

[15]I use the locution 'exactly (or closely)' since there clearly are cases in which one remembers some event, but not all the details of the event. In such a case, the positive idea of the memory only closely resembles the impression.

[16]There are two distinctions one might do well to keep in mind. First, one should distinguish between the cause of an idea as an idea and the cause of a memory. The cause of an idea as an idea is an impression that resembles that idea (cf. *T* 4). The cause of a memory, on the other hand, need not be a resembling impression, that is, the 'circumstance . . . that touches the memory' (*T* 628) might not resemble the positive idea that grounds one's resultant idea of the memory. Second, one might need to distinguish between the cause of an idea as an idea and the original cause of an idea. Since Hume emphasizes that an impression is the cause of a simple idea in its *first appearance* (*T* 4), he seems to have allowed that ideas can be the causes of other ideas after their first appearance. But since the ancestry of any simple idea can be traced back to an impression, I shall use the locution 'the cause of an idea' to refer to the original cause of an idea.

[17]While this case might be the paradigm, it will not account for memories of particular psychological states, for example, memories of dreams. If the account of force and vivacity I develop in the Appendix is correct, memories of psychological states easily can be taken into account. Since the object of thought in a memory of a dream is an idea (cf. *EHU* 153), a particular dream state can be singled out on the basis of a relative idea corresponding to a definite description of the general form, 'the "feeling" (impression of reflection peculiar to dream states) that was associated with some complex idea d_1 and is the cause of a positive idea f that is (now) associated with a positive idea d_2, and d_2 exactly or closely resembles d_1.' With a change in the kind of 'feeling' involved, one also could account for one's memories of imaginings, one's memories of rememberings, one's memories of judgings, and so forth.

[18]Don Garrett recently has argued that Hume's problem with personal identity rests upon an inadequacy in his account of memory, namely, that Hume's account of memory will not allow him to differentiate qualitatively identical remembered perceptions (see Garrett 1981: 352-4). Garrett suggests that if there are two qualitatively identical perceptions occurring at some time t and one remembers one of these at time $t+n$, it is indeterminate which of the two perceptions one remembers, and therefore, which of the two is bundled into oneself. But if I am correct in suggesting that an idea of the memory is a relative idea, then the idea of the memory will single out the relevant impression--whichever one happens to be causally related to the positive component of one's relative idea of the memory--and Hume has no problem of the sort Garrett suggests. But Hume has a related problem. If the idea of the memory occurring at $t+n$ is to single out the relevant impression, it must be 'true', that is, it must be a genuine idea of the memory. Given Hume's scepticism with regard to the memory, however, one may never be able to know that an idea of the memory is 'true'. But this problem differs in kind from that raised by Garrett, and, as we shall see in Chapter 7, any problem Hume might have with memory is the least of his problems with personal identity.

[19]For present purposes we may ignore both the relation of resemblance among the numerous particulars denoted by a sortal term and the ability to substitute other ideas in situations where one's paradigm is inappropriate (cf. *T* 20-1).

[20]On realities, see pp. 11-15 above.

[21]I here use the word 'proposition' very generally to include anything from a sentence to a universal that is the meaning of a declarative sentence, since this is the latitude in which the word is used in the literature. In Hume's case it can be nothing more than a sentence.

[22]This is not to say there are no intentional acts having *ideas* of reflection as objects. Acts of recognition that one is in a state of fear or joy or hatred are examples of such acts, and complete acts of these kinds would include an impression of reflection, a linguistic idea (an idea of sensation), and an idea of reflection.

[23]Cases of conceiving of a material object *as such* should not be confused with cases of misidentifying a perception as a material object or substance. We shall examine Hume's explanations of such misidentifications in the following chapters.

[24]Remember, Hume is willing to countenance unperceived perceptions (*T* 207; cf. *T* 233).

4
Substance

It is part of Hume's legacy that he was the first philosopher to raise a thoroughgoing critique of the doctrine of substance, that he extended Berkeley's criticisms of the doctrine of material substance to the doctrine of immaterial substance.[1] In this chapter I examine Hume's criticisms of the doctrine of substance. If Hume's objective in the first book of the *Treatise* was to defend a bundle theory of mind (cf. *T* 207, 250), this is a necessary step in his program, for some version of the doctrine of substance was accepted by virtually every philosopher from at least Aristotle onward. In the early modern period the doctrine was generally set forth as a substratum theory,[2] and it is primarily against such a doctrine of substance that Hume's criticisms are directed.

In this chapter I begin by examining Hume's extended discussion of substance in 'Of the Antient Philosophy'. As we shall see, Hume's discussion there is a study in doxastic pathology, that is, it is a combination of a critical examination of the belief in substance with an explanation of that belief. Next I turn to the discussions in 'Of the Immateriality of the Soul'. I argue that Hume's criticisms there are focused explicitly on the Cartesian theory of substance and that, in spite of the banterous tone of his charge of Spinozism, these arguments are Hume's most powerful arguments against that theory. I conclude the chapter with some remarks on the nature and force of Hume's arguments.

'Of the Antient Philosophy'

There are certain beliefs that are held universally. Among these are the beliefs in necessary connection, material and immaterial substance, external existence, and personal identity. The universality of these beliefs does not show that they are true. Hume examines these beliefs, shows that each is evidentially suspect but recognizes that, even after critical examination, they persist (cf. *T* 218). These are examples of what Norman Kemp Smith called 'natural beliefs'.[3] In each case Hume argues either that the belief in question involves a misidentification of the kind of idea that is the object of one's belief or it rests upon an alleged relation between a perception and a presumptive object, a relation that cannot be known to obtain. He then provides an explanation of the belief on the basis of the principles of the association of ideas. I call this two-fold procedure 'doxastic pathology'. As in the case of its medical analogy, it consists of both a diagnosis of the 'disease' (arguments to show that the belief is unwarranted) and a causal explanation of the 'diseased' belief.

'Of the Antient Philosophy' is a critical explanation of the beliefs in the existence of material substance, substantial forms, accidents, and occult qualities on the basis of the principles of the association of ideas. It presupposes Hume's earlier discussion in 'Of Modes and Substances'. There Hume argued that it is impossible to have a (positive) idea of substance *qua* substratum, since it can be based upon neither an impression of sensation nor an impression of reflection (*T* 15-16).[4] Given that a belief requires an idea as its object (cf. *T* 96), the claim that there cannot be an idea of substance seems to show that there cannot be a belief in the existence of substance.[5] But there is such a belief. Part of Hume's task, then, is to explain the 'very intimate connection' between the belief in substance and the basic 'principles of human nature' (*T* 219).

Hume begins his account by specifying the nature of one's idea of body and the conflict between this idea and one's beliefs. He wrote:

> 'Tis confest by the most judicious philosophers, that our ideas of bodies are nothing but collections form'd by the mind of the ideas of the several distinct sensible qualities, of which objects are compos'd, and which we find to have a constant union with each other. But however these qualities may in themselves be entirely distinct, 'tis certain we commonly regard the compound, which they form, as ONE thing, and as continuing the SAME under very considerable alterations. The acknowledg'd composition is evidently contrary to this suppos'd *simplicity*, and the variation to the *identity*. It may, therefore, be worth while to consider the *causes*, which make us almost universally fall into such evident contradictions, as well as the *means* by which we endeavour to conceal them. (*T* 219)

Hume makes two points in this paragraph that are crucial to understanding his approach. First, one's idea of a body is that of a collection of the several qualities of which the body is composed. His reason for this claim should be clear. All simple ideas are copies of impressions. Complex ideas are either copies of complex impressions or are compounded by the imagination from simple ideas. Since one's ideas are strictly limited to one's experience, and since one's experiences concerning bodies are limited to impressions of their qualities (cf. *T* 64 and 67-8), one's *idea* of body is limited to the idea of a collection of qualities. This idea of body is recognized by 'the most judicious philosophers', because its content does not exceed the limits of experience.

Hume's second point concerns one's actual beliefs regarding bodies. Although each of the qualities in one's idea is distinct, one generally considers the complex to be one thing. Moreover, one tends to consider it a simple object, that is, one believes that its unity precludes internal diversity. Finally, even though the ideas in a collection vary over a period of time, one believes that these qualities are qualities of the same object. In so far as one believes that an object of experience or thought is a simple thing that retains its identity over time, one believes it to have characteristics traditionally attributed to substance. Thus, one believes that certain objects of *experience* are substances, despite the fact that they are neither unitary nor identical. Nonetheless, one's *idea* of a particular body, for example, an apple, is not an idea of substance, rather it is an idea of a body which is believed, though falsely, to have the distinct characteristics of a substance. Thus, the belief in substance is unwarranted by experience; the sensible idea that is the object of one's belief is misidentified. These are the conclusions reached in the diagnostic phase of the pathology of one's belief in material substance.

Hume continued by inquiring into the causes of the belief. He began by examining the supposition that objects are identical over time. He wrote:

> 'Tis evident, that as the ideas of the several distinct *successive* qualities of objects are united together by a very close relation, the mind, in looking along the succession, must be carry'd from one part of it to another by an easy transition, and will no more perceive the change, than if it contemplated the same unchangeable object. This easy transition is the effect, or rather the essence of relation; and as the imagination readily takes one idea for another, where their influence on the mind is similar; hence it proceeds, that any such succession of related qualities is readily consider'd as one continu'd object, existing without any variation. The

smooth and uninterrupted progress of the thought, being alike in both cases, readily deceives the mind, and makes us ascribe an identity to the changeable succession of connected qualities. (*T* 220)

Hume defined identity in terms of the invariability and uninterruptedness of an object through a supposed variation in time (*T* 201).[6] Thus, the notion of strict identity allows no qualitative change in an object. As a matter of fact, however, objects continually change: colors fade, sharp edges become dull, plants grow, and so forth, but unless a change is rather acute, one does not notice it. This is precisely Hume's point. The successive qualities of an object, those involved in any change, are generally unnoticed. The qualities are 'united by a very close relation'. The relation to which he alludes is resemblance, as is evident from the parallel passage in 'Of Scepticism with Regard to the Senses' (*T* 202-5). Since the successive qualities resemble each other very closely, the mind does not become aware of their differences. The mental state involved in perceiving one quality resembles that in perceiving the other. Furthermore, there is a resemblance between the act of mind in perceiving resembling perceptions and that in perceiving an unchangeable object (cf. *T* 204n-205n). The joint effect of these two resemblances is that one does not distinguish between the resembling qualities, and one ascribes identity to a temporally complex object, that is, a consideration of the successive qualities of an object in the serial order of their appearance causes the mind to assume that an object is identical over time.

But one need not consider the successive qualities of an object in the order of their occurrence. According to Hume, if one does not do so one's supposition of the identity of an object is destroyed. It is the conflict between these two ways of viewing an object that leads to the positing of a new category of entities, namely, unperceived substance. In Hume's words:

But when we alter our method of considering the succession, and instead of tracing it gradually thro' the successive points of time, survey at once any two distinct periods of its duration, and compare the different conditions of the successive qualities; in that case, the variations, which were insensible when they arose gradually, do now appear of consequence, and seem entirely to destroy the identity. By this means there arises a kind of contrariety in our method of thinking, from the different points of view, in which we survey the object, and from the nearness or remoteness of those instances of time, which we compare together. When we gradually follow an object in its successive changes, the smooth progress of the thought makes us ascribe an identity to the succession; because 'tis by a similar act of the mind we consider an unchangeable object. When we compare its situation after a considerable change the progress of the thought is broke; and consequently we are presented with the idea of diversity: In order to reconcile which contradictions the imagination is apt to feign something unknown and invisible, which it supposes to continue the same under all these variations; and the unintelligible something it calls a *substance, or original and first matter.* (*T* 220)

Considered successively, the qualities of an object yield the notion of identity. When one considers the qualities of an object at two separated points in time, the qualities of the object do not resemble, and one does not hold that the two ideas are of the same object. The changes that occur during an interval of time allow one to clearly distinguish the qualities of the object at one time from those at the other. This yields a contrariety based upon one's point of view. To reconcile this inconsistency, 'the imagination is apt to feign something unknown and invisible, which it supposes to continue the same under all these variations', that is, the imagination posits the existence of a new entity which '*has*' those qualities we no longer believe ordinary objects have.

In giving this explanation of one's belief in the identity of objects through time, Hume has explained half of the belief in substance. The other half is the belief that objects are simple, that is, there is an internal unity to qualitatively complex objects at a time. His explanation of this belief is parallel to the explanation of the belief in identity. In his words:

We entertain a like notion with regard to the *simplicity* of substances, and from like causes. Suppose an object perfectly simple and indivisible to be presented, along with another object, whose *co-existent* parts are connected together by a strong relation, 'tis evident the actions of the mind, in considering these objects, are not very different. The imagination conceives the simple object at once, with facility, by single effort of thought, without change or variation. The connexion of parts in the compound object has almost the same effect, and so unites the object within itself, that the fancy feels not the transition in passing from one part to another. Hence, the colour, taste, figure, solidity, and other qualities, combin'd in a peach or melon, are conceiv'd to form *one thing*; which makes them affect the thought in the same manner, as if perfectly uncompounded. But the mind rests not here. Whenever it views the object in another light, it finds that all these qualities are different, and distinguishable, and separable from each other; which view of things being destructive of its primary and more natural notions, obliges the imagination to feign an unknown something, or *original* substance and matter, as a principle of union or cohesion among these qualities, and as what may give the compound object a title to be call'd one thing, notwithstanding its diversity and composition. (*T* 221)

In providing a causal account of one's belief in the simplicity of substance, Hume claimed that, as in the case of identity, this belief is based upon a mental confusion. The state of mind in apprehending a simple object is similar to that in apprehending a complex object in which the qualities are 'connected together by a strong relation'. The similarity of these two states of mind causes one to claim that a particular collection of qualities, such as a melon, is one noncomposite thing, that is, it causes one to believe in the simplicity of objects that are actually complex. But one also can notice the complexity of a complex object, and noticing the complexity destroys the initial belief in the unity of the object. It is the conflict between simplicity of an object and belief in the complexity of an object that causes one to posit the existence of an unknown entity, substance, as a principle of unity among the qualities. It is a surrogate for the object of experience that initially was believed to be simple.

With this, Hume has explained the belief in material substance in accordance with the principles of association. He continues, however, to examine the notions of substantial forms, accidents, and occult qualities, which the ancient (Aristotelian and scholastic) philosophers deemed elements of their general theory of substance. Since the same kinds of distinctions are found in modern (Cartesian) theories of substance, to explain the 'errors' of the ancients completes a general explanation of the philosophical beliefs regarding substance. So let us turn briefly to Hume's subsequent discussions.

On species and substantial forms, Hume wrote:

The peripatetic philosophy asserts the *original* matter to be perfectly homogeneous in all bodies, and considers fire, water, earth, and air, as of the same substance; on account of their gradual revolutions and changes into each other. At the same time it assigns to each of these species of objects a distinct *substantial form*, which it supposes to be the source of all those different qualities they possess, and to be a new foundation of simplicity and identity to each particular species. All depends on our manner of viewing the objects. When we look along the insensible changes of bodies, we suppose all of them to be of the same

substance or essence. When we consider their sensible differences, we attribute to each of them a substantial and essential
difference. And in order to indulge ourselves in both these ways
of considering objects, we suppose all bodies to have at once a
substance and a substantial form. (*T* 221-2)

Hume's earlier explanation of the belief in the existence of material
substance was an explanation of the belief that, at bottom, substance is
one sort of thing. Yet substances generally are divided into kinds: the
peripatetics distinguish among earth, air, fire, and water; the Cartesians
distinguish between mind and body. The peripatetics introduced the
notion of a substantial form (essence) to explain the differences in
kinds of substances and the unity of the species. As his earlier explanation shows, Hume contends that the tendency to look at substance as
one kind of thing arises from the resemblances among the successive
qualities of objects perceived. The division of objects into species
arises from the perceived differences among the objects one perceives
and the *presumption* that there is a causal basis for these differences.[7]
Given his account of the belief in substantial forms, it is only a small
step to the explanation of the belief in accidents and occult qualities.

For having never discover'd any of these sensible qualities
[colors, sounds, tastes, etc.], where, for the reasons above
mention'd, we did not likewise fancy a substance to exist; the
same habit, which makes us infer a connexion betwixt cause and
effect, makes us infer a dependence of every quality on the unknown substance. The custom of imagining dependence has the
same effect as the custom of observing it wou'd have. This con-
ceit, however, is no more reasonable than any of the foregoing.
Every quality being a distinct thing from another, may be
conceiv'd to exist apart, and may exist apart, not only from every
other quality, but from that unintelligible chimera of a substance.
(*T* 222).

Once the belief in the causal dependence of a set of qualities of a
substance has been introduced, the notion of accidents follows
naturally. As a matter of fact, qualities are never perceived to exist
apart from complex objects. Given the presumption that *some* qualities
are causally dependent upon substantial forms and the confusion of
ontological with causal dependence, it is a small step to the belief that
all qualities are (ontologically) dependent upon substance. Hume, of
course, rejects such ontological dependence, that is, dependence based
upon necessary connections among objects.[8]

Thus, Hume argued that the belief in (material) substance rests fundamentally on confusions between resemblance and identity and between a closely related complex of qualities and simplicity. He explained both beliefs, together with the attendant beliefs in substantial forms and accidents, on the basis of his principles of the association of ideas. While Hume ostensibly was concerned with the peripatetic notion of substance, two points should be noted. First, if 'substance' is defined in terms of identity and simplicity, Hume's definition also applies to the Cartesian variants of the doctrine. Although one might argue that a Cartesian essence differs from an Aristotelian substantial form in so far as a Cartesian essence need not be deemed a causal notion, a Lockean *real* essence is a causal notion (cf. Locke *Essay* 3.6.6), and the explanation Hume provides of the belief in a underlying unity that explains the properties one perceives in a thing of a kind applies equally to each variant on a theory of essence. Further, there is merely a nominal difference between 'accidents' and 'modes'.

Second, if to believe in substance is to believe that objects are unities that are identical through time, the belief in substance also was held by the common person (cf. *T* 222-3). In 'Of Scepticism with regard to the Senses', Hume discussed at length the perceptual beliefs of the common person. Since his discussion is couched in terms of objects, that is, 'what any common man means by a hat, or shoe, or stone, or any other impression, convey'd to him by his senses' (*T* 202), it is clear that the assumption of objective unity was a working hypothesis. Further, since common persons believe that these objects retain their identity over time (*T* 202-9), this is sufficient to indicate that the philosopher and the common person share the belief in the existence of substance.

While Hume held that there is a 'natural' belief in substance, one should ask what the idea is that is the object of this belief. In the case of the common person, this is certainly nothing more than a misidentification of a series of complex resembling ideas as a thing that is simple and identical through time. In the case of philosophers who posit an imperceptible substratum, the idea involved must be a relative idea corresponding to a definite description such as 'the thing that is simple and perfectly identical through time' or 'the thing that supports qualities' (cf. Locke, *Essay* 2.23.2; Locke 1823: 4:21-2), or 'the thing in which properties inhere' (cf. Descartes, CSM 2:156). In 'Of the Antient Philosophy' Hume did not consider the kind of the idea the philosopher would specify as the object of his belief. As we shall see in the next section, he raised this issue in 'Of the Immateriality of the Soul'.

Ideas of Substance?

The criticisms of the doctrine of substance Hume raised in 'Of the Antient Philosophy' are generic in so far as they are applicable to virtually any version of the doctrine of substance. Further, his arguments there depend for their plausibility on various principles Hume considered well established, principles such as the copy theory of ideas. At best, they raise doubts regarding substance theories, and in so far as his explanations of the belief in substance are adequate, Hume has done little more than show that, whether or not there are substances, his theory of mind can account for that problematic belief.

The situation is different in 'Of the Immateriality of the Soul'. There Hume provides no explanations of one's belief in immaterial substance, and, I shall argue, his criticisms are directed against a specific and well-articulated theory of substance, namely, the Cartesian theory. My discussion of Hume's attack will consist of two parts. In this section I examine Hume's three initial arguments that one neither has nor can have an idea of substance. I show that the third argument seems to be an effective argument *ad hominem* against the Cartesian definition of 'substance', and that such arguments *ad hominem* are within the classical tradition of scepticism. In the next section I examine Hume's charge that all proponents of the doctrine of immaterial substance are implicit Spinozists. I argue that Hume's criticisms raise doubts regarding the adequacy of the Cartesian theory of substance which are sufficient_ to pave the way for a bundle theory of mind.

Hume begins 'Of the Immateriality of the Soul' by commenting that 'the intellectual world, tho' involv'd in infinite obscurities, is not perplex'd with any such contradictions, as those we have discover'd in the natural', although there are strict limits to what can be known regarding it (*T* 232). Philosophers have attempted to reduce one's ignorance by introducing the doctrine of substance, but, according to Hume, only 'at the hazard of running us into contradictions, from which the subject is of itself exempted' (*T* 232). So Hume asked again what the substance theorists '*mean by substance and inhesion?*' (*T* 232), whether it is possible to have an idea of substance and whether any putative idea is adequate.

Hume's first two arguments rest upon his most basic philosophical principles. He first asks whether it is *possible* to have an idea of substance, and his negative answer rests upon the contentions that ideas are derived from impressions and that representation and the division of the world into kinds is based upon resemblance (cf. *T* 15, 19-20). Hume wrote:

> As every idea is deriv'd from a precedent impression, had we any idea of the substance of our minds, we must also have an impression of it; which is very difficult, if not impossible, to be conceive'd. For how can an impression represent a substance, otherwise than by resembling it? And how can an impression resemble a substance, since, according to this philosophy, it is not a substance, and has none of the peculiar qualities or characteristics of a substance? (*T* 233)

There are several things to notice. First, Hume is concerned with a positive idea of substance. If one grants Hume's principles that all positive ideas are derived from impressions and that ideas can represent only by resemblance, the argument might have some force, but few if any substance theorists would grant that it is a serious objection. Even Descartes held that one has no immediate knowledge of substance as such (Descartes, CSM 2:124 and 156), and this seems to have been the standard view of substance theorists (Locke, *Essay*, 2.23.1-3; Berkeley, *PHK*, I, 27; cf. Reid 1969a: 7-9). Thus, even if one grants that Hume's argument establishes that it is impossible to have a *positive* idea of substance, few would have disputed the point.

Hume's second argument is intended to show that, as a matter of fact, one has no (positive) idea of substance (*T* 233). Hume wrote:

> But leaving the question *of what may or may not be*, for that other *what actually is*, I desire those philosophers, who pretend that we have an idea of that substance of our minds, to point out the impression that produces it, and tell distinctly after what manner that impression operates, and from what object it is deriv'd. Is it an impression of sensation or of reflection? Does it attend us at all times, or does it only return at intervals? If at intervals, at what times principally does it return, and by what causes is it produc'd? (*T* 233)

Hume's argument is little more than a rehearsal of the first argument in 'Of Modes and Substances'. If there is an impression of substance, it must be either an impression of sensation or reflection. Since virtually all substance theorists granted that there was no such impression, it follows that there can be no idea of substance.[9]

The third argument is more interesting, and it poses a more serious challenge to the Cartesian doctrine of substance. Hume argues that the Cartesian definition of substance as 'a thing which exists in such a way as to depend on no other thing for its existence' (Descartes, *Principles* I, 51, cf. CSM 2:210; cf. Spinoza 1985: 408; Arnauld 1964: 39) is too broad. In Hume's words:

If instead of answering these questions, any one shou'd evade the difficulty, by saying, that the definition of substance is *something which may exist by itself;* and that this definition ought to satisfy us: Shou'd this be said, I shou'd observe, that this definition agrees to every thing, that can possibly be conceiv'd; and never will serve to distinguish substance from accident, or the soul from its perceptions. For thus I reason. Whatever is clearly conceiv'd, after any manner, may exist after the same manner. This is one principle, which has been already acknowledg'd. Again, every thing, which is different, is distinguishable, and every thing which is distinguishable, is separable by the imagination. This is another principle. My conclusion from both is, that since all our perceptions are different from each other, and from every thing else in the universe, they are also distinct and separable, and may be consider'd as separately existent, and may exist separately, and have no need of any thing else to support their existence. They are, therefore, substances, as far as this definition explains a substance. (*T* 233)

Hume argues that the Cartesian definition of substance is too broad, and therefore, the substance/accidents distinction is unintelligible. Following two of his most basic tenets, namely, the distinguishability-separability-different principle (*T* 10) and the conceivability criterion of possibility (*T* 32), Hume argues that all perceptions are independent existents. But such a view is contrary to Cartesian principles (cf. *T* 234), and it implies that the Cartesian cannot distinguish perceptions from a substantial mind. Since the definition of substance is a central tenet of Descartes's doctrine, Hume's argument constitutes a *de facto* rejection of that doctrine.[10]

This argument is far stronger than either of Hume's earlier arguments. It is an *ad hominem* against the Cartesian doctrine of substance, in so far as it is based upon principles that were advanced by the Cartesians. Hume's conceiving criterion of possibility is a Cartesian principle. It is the basis upon which the Cartesians distinguished among substances (cf. Descartes, *Principles* I, 60; Descartes 1970: 90-1; Descartes, CSM 2:50; Descartes 1976: 28; Arnauld 1964: 323). Thus, given the factual claim that one can conceive of a perception in isolation, Hume has grounds for claiming that the Cartesian theory of substance fails in so far as it cannot consistently draw a distinction between modes and substances.

There are two further points to note regarding my *ad hominem* interpretation of Hume's argument. First, my account does not, as such, assign an independent role to Hume's distinguishability and separability principle. There are two reasons for this. (1) Descartes himself conflates the conceivability criterion of possibility and the separability principle in his discussions of real connections (Descartes, *Principles* I, 60; Descartes, CSM 2:50). (2) It is the conceivability criterion of possibility that carries the weight of the argument. At best, the separability principle only gives one independent reasons to believe that it is possible to conceive of individual perceptions in isolation from anything else.[11] Second, no Cartesian would accept the argument: no Cartesian would grant that, as a matter of fact, it is possible to conceive of a mode (perception) apart from a substance. But given Hume's argument, the burden of proof shifts: the Cartesian must now present a nonquestion-begging argument to show that, in fact, it is impossible to conceive of a perception apart from a mind. Hume's argument merely raises doubts regarding the adequacy of the Cartesian definition.

Nor should one be surprised that Hume's arguments against substance are *ad hominems*. As a sceptic, Hume's objective was to cast doubt on various doctrines: just as it might be pretentious to claim that a theory is true (*T* 272), it also might be pretentious to assert a theory is false. Nonetheless, it was one of the standard moves among the classical sceptics to engage in arguments *ad hominem*, to show that the principles accepted, or at least asserted, by a dogmatist allow one to reach conclusions that are contrary to those asserted by the dogmatist (cf. Annas and Barnes 1985: passim). Hence, Hume's procedure is well within the sceptical tradition, and as we shall see in the next section, it reaches its highest crescendo in his discussion of Spinozism.

Spinozism

Hume's attack on substance is not completed with his critique of the Cartesian definition. Later in the section he argues that 'the doctrine of the immateriality, simplicity, and indivisibility of a thinking substance is a true atheism, and will serve to justify all those sentiments, for which *Spinoza* is so universally infamous' (*T* 240). The discussion of Spinozism has been largely overlooked in the literature, presumably because Hume seems to be engaged in little more than satire and ridicule.[12] Of course, since charges of Spinozism were raised against virtually all the major philosophers of the late seventeenth century (see Colie 1959: 23-46; Yolton 1956: 13 and 17; Stephen 1949: 2:55-73), Hume's charge of Spinozism against the 'theologians' seems, on the face of it, to be nothing but ridicule. For this reason one can understand why most commentators have had little to say about it. I shall argue, however, that Hume demonstrates, at the very least, that the Cartesian theory of substance cannot be seriously maintained by anyone committed to an empiricist theory of meaning. In so far as the Cartesian doctrine of substance can be made intelligible, it yields conclusions that no Cartesian would find acceptable: Hume is raising more *ad hominem* arguments comparable to those he had raised earlier in the section.

I begin by defining what I shall call 'a complete theory of substance'. Next I examine the three arguments Hume drew from Pierre Bayle's *Historical and Critical Dictionary*.[13] Then I shall discuss the significance of Hume's criticisms of the Cartesian theory of substance.

What I call 'a complete theory of substance' must address at least two issues, and, if it holds essential differences between kinds of substances, three issues. First, it must specify the nature of substance *qua* substance. Only if this is done is there any basis for distinguishing a substance from its modes and attributes. Second, it must specify the relation that obtains between a substance and its modes or attributes. Further, if the theory maintains that there is a further distinction between the modes and attributes of a substance, it must specify the grounds for that distinction. Finally, if the theory holds that there are essential differences between kinds of substances, it must specify the grounds for drawing that distinction.

Descartes proposed such a complete theory of substance. He maintained (1) that a substance is a thing that can exist independently, that is, 'a thing which exists in such a way as to depend on no other thing for its existence.'[14] Distinctions among substances are *real distinctions*, that is, distinctions among distinct existents, and Descartes employed the criterion that if one can distinctly conceive of two things as distinct, then they actually are distinct substances (Descartes, *Principles*, I, 60; Descartes, CSM 2:50 and 54; cf. Descartes 1970: 90-1). He maintained (2) that the only distinction between a substance and its attributes is a *distinction of reason*, and consequently, it is impossible to have a clear and distinct idea of substance apart from a clear and distinct idea of its attributes (Descartes, *Principles*, I, 60). Since the only distinction between a substance and its attributes is a distinction of reason, a substance and its attributes constitute a single entity: the relation between a substance and its attributes is a relation of identity.[15] Descartes drew a further distinction between the modes and attributes of a substance on the grounds of the greater generality of an attribute with respect to the mode that falls under it. The relation is that of a determinable (attribute) to a determinate (mode) (Descartes,

Principles I, 56; cf. Descartes 1970: 186-7). Finally, Descartes maintained (3) that material substance is distinguished from mental (immaterial) substance on the basis of the principal attribute that is essential to each kind of substance. Extension is the principal attribute of material substance; thought or intelligence is the principal attribute of immaterial substance (Descartes, *Principles* I, 53; cf. Descartes, CSM, 2:54, cf. 2:59). Since he maintained that the attributes of thought and extension are simple attributes (Descartes, CSM 1:45), a substance is simple in virtue of its principal attribute.

Given this sketch of a complete theory of substance, we now profitably can turn to Hume's discussion of Spinozism in 'Of the Immateriality of the Soul'.

If Hume's three Baylean arguments constitute a serious criticism of the Cartesian theory of substance, they should focus on the three elements of Descartes's complete theory of substance. We shall see that they do. Given what in Chapter 1 I called Hume's principle of theoretical objects, namely, the principle that all properties one ascribes to theoretical objects must be properties with which one can be immediately acquainted in perception, his arguments show that if the relation between a substance and its attributes is the relation of identity, three consequences follow: (1) extended substances cannot be simple, (2) there is no basis for distinguishing between a substance and its perceivable attributes, and (3) inconsistencies follow from the Cartesian theory of substance, and therefore, that theory cannot describe an existent. So let us turn to Hume's first argument.

Hume wrote:

First, It has been said against *Spinoza*, according to the scholastic way of talking, rather than thinking, that a mode, not being any distinct or separate existence, must be the very same with its substance, and consequently the extension of the universe, must be in a manner identify'd with that simple, uncompounded essence, in which the universe is supposed to inhere. But this, it may be pretended, is utterly impossible and inconceivable unless the indivisible substance expand itself, so as to correspond to the extension, or the extension contract itself, so as to answer to the indivisible substance. This argument seems just, as far as we can understand it; and 'tis plain nothing is requir'd, but a change in the terms to apply the same argument to our extended perceptions, and the simple essence of the soul; the ideas of objects and perceptions being in every respect the same, only attended with the supposition of a difference, that is unknown and incomprehensible. (*T* 243-4)

Hume's first argument rests upon the contention that there is merely a distinction of reason between a substance and its modes or, more properly, its attributes, and therefore, that the relation that obtains between a substance and its attributes is a relation of numerical identity. Given this and his principle of theoretical objects, Hume proceeds to argue that no substance can be both simple and extended. In Book I, Part ii of the *Treatise*, Hume had examined the idea of extension, arguing that the *idea* of extension is inherently complex and that any extension consists of a finite number of indivisible mathematical points (minimum visibles or tangibles) (*T* 32; cf. *T* 38-9). Since extension as a quality of impressions is complex, Hume's principle of theoretical objects requires that extension as a quality of substance also must be complex. But this is contrary to the Cartesian contention that extension is a *simple* attribute, and since the simplicity of a substance rests upon the simplicity of its principal attribute, Hume's criticism inveighs against the simplicity of substance. His colorful way of stating this conclusion is by claiming that either 'the indivisible substance [must] expand itself, so as to correspond to the extension [in which case it is no longer simple], or the extension contract itself, so as to answer to the indivisible substance [in which case it is no longer extended, since extension is necessarily divisible]' (*T* 243). Thus, Hume concluded that an extended substance is not simple.

Hume developed his criticism further by turning explicitly to immaterial substance. Remember, Descartes held that an immaterial (mental) substance is a thing that thinks but is *not* extended (Descartes, *Principles* I, 53; Descartes, CSM 1:54). Hume, on the other hand, argued that some perceptions, namely, all (complex) perceptions of sight and touch, are extended (*T* 34; cf. *T* 240). Assuming that perceptions are modes of an immaterial substance and that a substance is qualitatively identical with the perceptions that are its modes, it follows that an immaterial substance with a mode that is a visual or tactual perception is extended and, therefore, not simple. Furthermore, if the substance is qualitatively identical with an extended mode--and therefore extended--while by hypothesis an immaterial substance is *unextended*, then the Cartesian theory of immaterial substance is inconsistent, and nothing described by that theory can exist.

Hume's second argument reads:

> Secondly, It has been said, that we have no idea of substance, which is not applicable to matter; nor any idea of a distinct substance, which is not applicable to every distinct portion of matter. Matter, therefore, is not a mode but a substance, and each part of matter is not a distinct mode, but a distinct substance. I have

already prov'd, that we have no perfect idea of substance; but that taking it for *something, that can exist by itself*, 'tis evident every perception is a substance, and every distinct part of a perception is a distinct substance: and consequently the one hypothesis labours under the same difficulties in this respect with the other. (*T* 244)

There are several things to notice in this argument. First, Hume again is focusing primarily on material substance and only extends his argument to include immaterial substance. His claim 'that we have no distinct idea of substance, which is not applicable to matter' again assumes that materiality, as the principal attribute of substance, is numerically identical with the substance of which it is an attribute. Consequently, due to the identity of substance and its attribute, matter may be taken to be the substance itself, and anything one can claim regarding matter is true of material substance. Since one can conceive of any bit of matter existing independently of any other bit of matter, each bit of matter is a distinct substance. Notice that this is consistent with Descartes's claim regarding one's knowledge of distinct substances on the basis of conceivability. As Descartes wrote:

For when we come to know God, we are certain that he can bring about anything of which we have a distinct understanding. For example, even though we may not yet know for certain that any extended or corporeal substance exists in reality, the mere fact that we have an idea of such a substance enables us to be certain that it is capable of existing. *And we can also be certain that, if it exists, each and every part of it, as delimited by us in our thought, is really distinct from the other parts of the same substance* (Descartes, *Principles*, I, 60, emphasis added)

Notice that it is the conceivability of a distinct thing that provides the grounds for claiming that it is a substance, and consequently, the conceivability of distinct bits of matter is sufficient to establish that each *bit* of matter is a distinct substance.[16]

Second, if there is merely a distinction of reason between a substance and its attributes--if, in Hume's parlance, they are distinguishable but not separable (*T* 25)--then there must be some grounds for drawing that distinction. Regarding other distinctions of reason-- the distinction between color and shape, for example--Hume contended that one could draw such distinctions on the basis of the resemblance of one aspect of an object to aspects of other objects (*T* 25), and it might be that such grounds could be extended to the case of substances and attributes. Attributes of substances of a particular kind resemble one another. Substances also 'resemble' one another in so far as they are capable of existing independently. But, as we have seen, Hume argued on basically Cartesian grounds that the modes of immaterial substances (perceptions) are capable of independent existence, and consequently there are no grounds for distinguishing between a substance and its modes or attributes. Hume's point is that if the independence criterion of substance is employed, the distinction between an immaterial substance and its modes collapses; if the independence criterion is rejected, there are no grounds for drawing a distinction between a substance and its modes or attributes. In either case, there cannot even be a distinction of reason between a substance and its modes or attributes.

Hume's third argument reads as follows:

> Thirdly, It has been objected to the system of one simple substance in the universe, that this substance being the support of *substratum* of every thing, must at the very same instant be modify'd into forms, which are contrary and incompatible. The round and square figures are incompatible in the same substance at the same time. How then is it possible that the same substance can at once be modify'd into that square table, and into this round one? I ask the same question concerning the impressions of these tables; and find that the answer is no more satisfactory in the one case than in the other. (*T* 244)

Again, the problem to which Hume points rests upon the dual contentions that a substance is simple and that the relation of identity obtains between a substance and its modes. If a mode and its substance are identical, and if one allows that one can have perceptions of a round table and a square table at the same time, it follows that the substance that has these modes is both round and square. But if a substance is simple, and if roundness and squareness are incompatible properties, a substance cannot be both round and square at the same time. Since, Hume contended, the Cartesian theory of substance requires that when one perceives both a round table and a square table the immaterial substance must be simultaneously round and square, the Cartesian theory of substance must be rejected. Such is Hume's argument.

Although Hume's conclusion follows if it is assumed that the essential properties of a substance are identical with the qualities of the modes of that substance, it is clear that Descartes would reject this identification at the level of modes rather than attributes. Roundness and squareness are both modes falling under the attribute of extension. Consequently, even if one simultaneously perceived a round table and a square table, one could conclude nothing more than that, since roundness and squareness are modes of extension, the attribute of extension is applicable to the mind, and therefore the mind is extended. But if this were allowed, it would constitute a decisive criticism of Descartes's theory of immaterial substance, since Descartes maintained that the mind is *immaterial* and *essentially unextended,* while Hume's principle of theoretical objects would seem to demand that the mind is (at least sometimes) extended. Furthermore, it provides the basis for a still stronger criticism, for Hume maintained that while some perceptions are extended, namely, those of sight and touch, all other kinds of perceptions are unextended (*T* 235-6).[17] Consequently, to maintain that the qualities of a substance are identical with its attributes would entail that if one simultaneously perceived the shape and aroma of an apple, then the mind is both extended and unextended. Such a claim is incompatible with the Cartesian contention that a substance is simple in virtue of having only one principal attribute.[18]

I have argued that Hume's discussions of Spinozism provide a serious criticism of the Cartesian theory of substance. His arguments pose the following dilemma. In claiming that a substance is a simple, independent entity that is identical with its attributes, either one is using the term for the attributes in the same sense as one uses them in applying them to impressions or one is not. If one is using the terms in the same sense as when one applies them to impressions, it follows that a substance can be neither extended nor both simple and unextended. If one uses these terms in a sense that is not applicable to impressions, then the nature of substance is unknowable and the doctrine of substance can fulfill no theoretical purposes. Hence, the Cartesian theory of substance must be rejected.

If my interpretation is correct, what are the consequences? Can Hume claim that there are neither material nor immaterial substances? No. At most he can claim that the Cartesian theory of substance, and any substance theory that is similar to it in the relevant details, is incoherent: while such a theory cannot describe an existent, that does not entail that there is nothing denoted by the terms 'substance' and 'substratum'. It is for this reason Hume could write in 1745:

> The Author has not anywhere that I remember denied the Immateriality of the Soul in the common Sense of the Word. He only says, That the Question did not admit of any distinct Meaning; because we had no distinct Idea of Substance. (*LGFE* 29-30)

By 'the Immateriality of the Soul in the common Sense of the Word' Hume almost certainly means the doctrine of immaterial substance. While Hume did not deny that there are immaterial substances, his criticisms are sufficient to require any defender of that doctrine more carefully to define what it is for a substance to be simple, how the various distinctions of reason germane to a substance theory are to be defended, what versions of the conceivability criterion of possibility, and what notions of divisibility, possibility, and identity are acceptable. By taking seriously the 'scholastic way of talking', that is, the suggestion that a mode is identical with its substance (*T* 243), the mode/attribute/substance distinctions break down. With this, the basis for drawing distinctions among substances is lost: there can be at most one substance. And if substance is simple, it can have no characteristics. These consequences are contrary to both common sense and theology and allow Hume to characterize the doctrine as 'atheistic' (cf. *D* 159). Since Hume's critique raises the possibility that the relevant clarifications and distinctions cannot be made, it calls the doctrine of substance into doubt and paves the way for a nonsubstantial (bundle) theory of mind. It shows that if a bundle theory of mind is intelligible and can explain the same beliefs that are allegedly explained by a substance theory, the bundle theory is preferable.

Conclusions

We have seen that Hume raised various kinds of objections to the doctrine of substance. In 'Of Modes and Substances', as well as in 'Of the Immateriality of the Soul', Hume argued that one, as a matter of fact, has no positive idea of substance *qua* substratum. In 'Of the Antient Philosophy' he explained why it is possible to believe in the existence of material substance, that is an imperceptible being that is simple and identical through time, on the basis of his principles of the association of ideas. In 'Of the Immateriality of the Soul', Hume first objected to the Cartesian definition of substance on the ground that it is too broad: on basically Cartesian principles, Hume shows that even a perception must be deemed a substance, a position that is absurd on Cartesian principles. This is an *ad hominem* argument in the tradition of the ancient sceptics: it takes the principles of a particular philosopher and shows that they entail claims that are inconsistent with the positive dogmas of that philosopher. His *ad hominem* procedure was basically the same in his argument that proponents of the doctrine of immaterial substance are implicit Spinozists.

Notes

[1]Cf. Reid 1970: 14; Reid 1969a: 27; Copleston 1959: 74-5. Not all commentators, however, grant that Hume rejected the doctrine of substance. See Anderson 1966: 10, 90, and 170-1; Mouton 1974: 257; Robison 1976: 39.

[2]Cf. Descartes 1976: 17; Locke, *Essay* 2.23.1. There were alternative accounts of substance, and in Chapter 5 we shall briefly examine Shaftesbury's holistic alternative.

[3]Smith 1905: 149-73 and 335-47; Smith 1941: 443-94; cf. Hearn 1969: 3-7. It is beyond the scope of this work to ask whether Hume considered the belief in the existence of God to be a 'natural belief'. On that issue see Tweyman 1986.

[4]According to Bricke, the argument at *T* 15-16 fails on two counts. First, 'it rests on the principle that perceptions must have the pertinent properties of their objects, but the principle is absurd'. Second, it begs the question regarding the reification of perceptions (Bricke 1980: 63). If one pays sufficient attention to Hume's methodological constraints, I believe both of these objections can be answered. Hume could reply to the first on the basis of the principle of theoretical objects (see page 8 above): in so far as 'external' objects, substances, and so forth are merely constructs ('realities'), any property one attributes to the object must be fundamentally a property of a perception. But there are properties and there are properties. Bricke illustrates the alleged absurdity as follows: 'It is absurd to say that my perception of something that is red, sticky, cubical, and cold, and that weighs forty pounds, is itself red, sticky, cubical, cold, and forty pounds in weight' (Bricke 1980: 63). Redness is nonproblematic: it is not absurd to claim that both a perception and the object it presumably represents are red, even if the best scientific evidence suggests that there is a specific difference (nonresemblance) between the redness of a perception and the property in the corresponding object. Much the same might be said regarding coldness. Being sticky or cubical are different, for they involve correlations between perceptions of sight and touch. Both might be known primarily on the basis of touch, and only with a certain amount of experience might one correlate the relevant perceptions of sight. Indeed, stickiness is even more peculiar, since, for example, honey might 'look' sticky only if one has had certain tactile experiences with honey, that is, one might need to recognize that something is honey before it 'looks' sticky. Finally, it is questionable whether weighing forty pounds can be deemed a property at all. If it can be, it must involve a correlation between certain tactile perceptions (kinesthetic sensations) and visual perceptions of things on scales. Bricke blurs these points by talking of a singular perception: the 'perception' must be a construct made up of perceptions of the several senses.

Regarding the second point, there is a clear sense in which Hume 'reifies' perceptions: they are the fundamental elements of his theory. And this means that there is a fundamental difference between Humean perceptions and their analogues on a substance theory. But if Hume's objective was to defend a nonsubstance theory of mind, he can no more be faulted for his fundamental theoretical assumptions than Lavoisier can be faulted for beginning with assumptions that are incompatible with explaining burning on the basis of the phlogiston theory. The issue is whether the theory one proposes can provide an adequate, though simpler, explanation of a range of phenomena than an alternative theory under consideration, in this case, the substratum theory.

But it is, perhaps, unnecessary to worry about Bricke's objections to the argument, since many of the proponents of a substance theory were quite willing to grant that one has no immediate perception of substance. Hume's argument is well within the Lockean heritage (Locke, *Essay* 2.23.1-3), and even Descartes held that one has no immediate knowledge of substance (CSM 2:124).

[5]Hume is concerned here with 'positive ideas', and until I explicitly note a change to a concern with relative ideas, I shall use the word 'idea' as a shorthand for 'positive idea'.

[6]Various commentators have questioned the adequacy of Hume's definition of 'identity', especially in light of his self-acknowledged problems with personal identity (cf. Neujahr 1978: 18-28; Fang 1984: 59-68). While these are interesting problems, I argue in Chapter 7 that Hume's primary problem with the belief in personal identity stems from the belief that the mind is simple, not the belief that the mind is identical over time. For this reason I am unconvinced that Hume recognized any problems there might be with his definition of identity.

[7]Recall that this assumption is also operative in the Lockean-Humean division of objects into kinds (*T* 16).

[8]Hume's discussion of the belief in occult qualities (*T* 222-4) adds nothing new to his discussion, and we may safely ignore it.

[9]Hume's cousin Lord Kames eventually argued that there is an impression of immaterial substance or self, but it is not constantly present. See Kames 1751: 231; cf. *Letters* 1:94.

[10]Nor can one plausibly suggest, as Anderson and Mouton do (Anderson 1966: 10, 90, and 170-1; Mouton 1974: 257), that Hume considered perceptions substantial, for the remark at *T* 234 that 'A substance is entirely different from a perception' clearly indicates that Hume was following out the presumptions of the Cartesian theory of substance.

[11]Bricke has argued at length that Hume's use of the separability principle in the argument fails (Bricke 1980: 69-71). If the argument is primarily an *ad hominem* against the Cartesian theory of substance, whether or not the separability principle is itself plausible is of little consequence.

[12]Although Hume's discussion of Spinozism is mentioned in many studies, generally it is treated as little more than a historical curiosity. (See Laing 1932: 68, 156, and 174; Laird 1932: 158, 163-5, and 282; Smith 1941: 322, 325, and 506-16; Price 1940: 104-5; Popkin 1979: 66-9.) Yolton is one of the few who has taken the discussion seriously (Yolton 1983: 49-63), although as I argue in Chapter 6, he does not carefully distinguish between Hume's positive claims and his criticism of the doctrine of immaterial substance.

[13]In one of his few reference footnotes, Hume acknowledged that his three specific arguments were drawn from the article 'Spinoza' in Bayle's *Historical and Critical Dictionary* (*T* 243n). They were drawn primarily from note N of the article. (See Bayle 1964: 300-14. The relevant sections also are quoted in Smith 1941: 506-16.) As Laird has acknowledged, it is quite probable that Hume's familiarity with Spinoza was limited to Bayle's article (Laird 1932: 164).

[14]Descartes, *Principles*, I, 51. Descartes's theory of substance was, to a greater or lesser degree, anticipated by many of the medievals. For example, Thomas Blundevile wrote, 'Substance is a thing consisting of it selfe, and needeth no help to sustain the being thereof' (Blundevile 1599: 17). Hence, to the extent that Descartes's theory of substance was anticipated, Hume's criticisms of the Cartesian theory of substance constitute a general criticism of the doctrine of substance.

[15]This identity is not identity of form. It is at least similar to the type of identity that obtains between the Morning Star, the Evening Star and the planet Venus: there is exactly one thing that can be described on the basis of three sets of properties. Nonetheless, since both the Evening Star and the planet Venus would cease to exist if the Morning Star ceased to exist, this is similar to Descartes's suggestion that an immaterial substance would cease to exist if it ceased to think (cf. Descartes, CSM 2:18). On Hume's distinctions of reason, see *T* 25.

[16]If Bayle's reading of Spinoza were correct, this consequence might raise problems for Spinoza's metaphysical theory. It is consistent with some of Descartes's remarks to suggest that each bit of matter is a distinct substance (CSM 2:155-7; but cf. CSM 2:10).

[17]I shall discuss this claim in Chapter 6.

[18]In the person of Cleanthes, Hume raises similar criticisms in the *Dialogues concerning Natural Religion*. See *D* 159.

5

Necessary Connection

If a primary objective of the first book of the *Treatise* was to state and defend a bundle theory of mind, why does Hume devote the third part of that book to a discussion of induction and necessary connection? Two reasons might be cited. First, substance theorists generally held that (ultimately) only substances can be causes. If there are no substances, it was incumbent upon Hume to explain the circumstances under which the word 'cause' might continue to be used. Second, although the Cartesian theory of substance was the most common and well-articulated theory of substance current in Hume's time, it was not the only theory. One alternative theory of substance was proposed by Shaftesbury, a theory according to which a substantial mind is a collection of necessarily connected perceptions.[1] If Hume was to show that his theory of mind was theoretically more plausible than the theory of Shaftesburian substance, it was incumbent upon him to attack the notion of a necessary connection among existents.

In this chapter I begin by discussing the Shaftesburian theory of substance. Next, I examine Hume's critique of the notion of necessary connection. Finally, I discuss Hume's explanation of the belief in necessary connection between objects. As we shall see, the discussion of necessary connection is another of Hume's several studies in doxastic pathology.

Shaftesburian Substance

In the Appendix to the *Treatise*, Hume laments the inadequacy of his theory of mind.[2] After commenting that the fundamental problem with his theory of mind was that it rests on two inconsistent principles (*T* 636), Hume comments, 'Did our perceptions either inhere in something simple and individual, or did the mind perceive some real connexion among them, there wou'd be no difficulty in the case' (*T* 636). The alternative to the substratum theory to which Hume alludes is Shaftesbury's account of individuals (cf. *T* 254n), for Shaftesbury held that it is the necessary connections among the components of a thing that make it into an individual. I shall call this the Shaftesburian theory of substance.[3] So let us briefly turn to Shaftesbury's discussions of individuals.

Shaftesbury was a holist. Throughout his works, he alludes to the need to have knowledge of nature as a whole in order to properly understand the parts of it. In his *Inquiry concerning Virtue or Merit*, for example, one finds this:

> WHEN we reflect on any ordinary frame or constitution either of Art or Nature, and consider how hard it is to give the least account of a particular part without a competent knowledge of the whole, we need not wonder to find ourselves at a loss in many things regarding the constitution and frame of Nature herself. For to what end in Nature many things, even whole species of creatures, refer, or to what purpose they serve, will be hard for any one justly to determine; but to what end the many proportions and various shapes of parts in many creatures actually serve, we are able, by the help of study and observation, to demonstrate with great exactness. (Shaftesbury 1964: 1:243)

This passage shows us two things. First, it shows Shaftesbury was an epistemic holist: he held that knowledge of a part depends upon knowledge of the whole. Second, it shows that Shaftesbury was a proponent of teleological explanation.

Maintaining that the system of nature is a unified whole, Shaftesbury gave an example of 'the many proportions and various shapes of parts in many creatures [that] actually serve' to provide us with knowledge of the purposes of the various kinds of individuals, to divide the world into species, that is, subsystems of entities, and to explain how these species may be understood in terms of Nature as a whole. He wrote:

> If therefore in the structure of this or any other animal, there be anything which points beyond himself, and by which he is plainly discovered to have relation to some other being or nature besides his own, then will this animal undoubtedly be esteemed a part of some other system. For instance, if an animal has the proportions of a male, it shows he has relation to a female. And the respective proportions both of the male and female will allow, doubtless, to have a joint relation to another existence and order of things

beyond themselves. So that the creatures are both of them to be considered as parts of another system, which is that of a particular race or species of living creatures, who have one common nature, or are provided for by some order or constitution of things subsisting together, and co-operating towards their conservation and support.

In the same manner, if a whole species of animals contribute to the existence or well-being of some other, then is that whole species, in general, a part only of some other system.

For instance, to the existence of the spider that of the fly is absolutely necessary. The heedless flight, weak frame, and tender body of the latter insect, fits and determines him as much a prey as the rough make, watchfulness, and cunning of the former fits him for rapine and the ensnaring part. The web and wing are suited to each other. And in the structure of each of these animals there is as apparent and perfect a relation to the other as in our own bodies there is a relation of limbs and organs; or as in the branches or leaves of a tree we see a relation of each to the other, and all, in common, to one root and trunk. (Shaftesbury 1964: 1:245)

These passages illustrate Shaftesbury's commitment to the systematic interrelationship of the several distinct entities and kinds of entities to one another. It is in part on the basis of the 'relation' of one individual to another that the world is divided into kinds. Further, even across species one can notice that the existence of one species is 'absolutely necessary' for the existence of another, and, as he illustrates in terms of the spider and the fly, one can discern the purposive relation between the structure of the predator and its prey: the structure of the fly is as it must be to serve as the prey of the spider. The world is a single system itself composed of 'necessarily' (purposively) related systems.

While Shaftesbury's objective throughout many of his works is to show the plausibility of the argument from design (cf. Shaftesbury 1964: 2:63-6), Hume's concern was with the more general contention that there are 'real relations' or necessary connections among the parts of an individual. Although Shaftesbury alludes to this in his remarks on the the relations among parts of a body and the parts of a tree, the theme comes to the fore in his *Moralists, A Philosophical Rhapsody*.

The Moralists is presented as Philocles' description of a conversation he had had primarily with Theocles. Theocles is presented as a defender of the sentiments expressed in Shaftesbury's *Inquiry concerning Virtue or Merit* (Shaftesbury 1964: 2:50-60), while Philocles is assigned the part of the sceptic. Theocles alludes to the oneness of the universe and suggests that simple unity can be observed in everything. He says to Philocles:

> I know you look upon the trees of this vast wood to be different from one another; and this oak, the noblest of the company, as it is by itself a different thing from all its fellows in the wood, so with its own wood of numerous spreading branches (which seem so many different trees) 'tis still, I suppose, one and the self-same tree. Now should you, as a mere caviller, and not as a fair sceptic, tell me that if a figure of wax, or any other matter, were cast in the exact shape and colours of this tree, and tempered, if possible, to the same kind of substance, it might therefore possibly be a real tree of the same kind or species, I would have done with you, and reason no longer. But if you questioned me fairly, and desired I should satisfy you what I thought it was which made this oneness or sameness in the tree or any other plant, or by what it differed from the waxen figure, or from any other such figure accidentally made, either in the clouds, or on the sand by the sea shore, I should tell you that neither the wax, nor sand, nor cloud thus pieced together by our hand or fancy had any real relation within themselves, or had any nature by which they correspond any more in that near situation of parts than if scattered ever so far asunder. But this I should affirm, "that wherever there was such a sympathizing of parts as we saw here in our real tree, wherever there was such a plain concurrence in one common end, and to the support, nourishment, and propagation of so fair a form, we could not be mistaken in saying there was a peculiar nature belonging to this form, and common to it with others of the same kind." By virtue of this, our tree is a real tree, lives, flourishes, and is still one and the same even when by vegetation and change of substance not one particle in it remain the same. (Shaftesbury 1964: 2:99-100)[4]

There are several things to notice here. First, Shaftesbury refers to a 'real relation' among the parts of the tree. Recalling the earlier discussion in the *Inquiry concerning Virtue or Merit*, Shaftesbury's point is that the parts of a particular tree are essentially parts of that tree; each part is necessarily connected with every other part of the tree. They are parts in the same sense that the subject and predicate of a certain simple proposition are parts of that proposition. In a simple proposition each term is logically incomplete: each term is essentially a part of a proposition. It is the whole to which simplicity can be attributed (cf. Shaftesbury 1964: 2:106), and this simplicity rests upon these 'real relations' or necessary connections.[5] And, of course, each particular system, such as a particular tree, is essentially related to every other system in Nature, thus making Nature itself essentially one thing (Shaftesbury 1964: 2:102 and 104-5). Second, Shaftesbury refers to 'a sympathizing of parts . . . in one common end'. By 'sympathizing of parts', Shaftesbury is concerned with the real or essential connections among the parts of a particular object, connections that tend toward the self-perpetuation of that object.[6]

Shaftesbury's account of the nature of a person seems to be exactly similar to that of a tree, namely, the components of a person are necessarily connected to one another, and it is in virtue of these necessary connections that a person is one thing and remains the same through time (cf. Shaftesbury 1964: 2:100-2). Given this, it was incumbent on Hume to clear the philosophical ground in preparation for his bundle theory of mind. To do this, he attempted to cast doubt on the claim that there are necessary connections among objects in general and perceptions in particular. It is to these arguments that we now turn.

Necessary Connection and Inductive Inference

The discussions of causation and necessary connection are among the most familiar in the Hume corpus. In examining these discussions, I focus on the arguments against necessary connection and against the absolute certainty of inductive reasoning. These will be sufficient to show that, as in the case of his argument against the Cartesian definition of substance (*T* 233), Hume held that all perceptions are metaphysically independent beings, and in this sense they are not necessarily connected with any others.[7]

In *Treatise* I.iii.2 Hume discusses the elements of the idea of a causal relation. After indicating that the relations of contiguity in space and time and temporal priority of cause to effect are 'essential to that of causation; or at least may suppose [them] such, according to the general opinion' (*T* 75), Hume notes that in addition to these 'There is a NECESSARY CONNEXION to be taken into consideration; and that relation is of much greater importance, than any of the other two above-mention'd' (*T* 77). But discovering the nature of this necessary connection is no mean task. As Hume wrote:

> Here again I turn the object on all sides, in order to discover the nature of this necessary connexion, and find the impression, or impressions, from which its idea may be deriv'd. When I cast my eye on the *known qualities* of objects, I immediately discover that

the relation of cause and effect depends not the least on *them*. When I consider their *relations*, I can find none but those of contiguity and succession; which I have already regarded as imperfect and unsatisfactory. Shall the despair of success make me assert, that I am here. possest of an idea, which is not preceded by any similar impression? This wou'd be too strong a proof of levity and inconstancy; since the contrary principle has been already so firmly establish'd, as to admit of no farther doubt; at least, till we have more fully examin'd the present difficulty. (*T* 77)

Necessary connections are neither observable monadic properties nor observable relations. The fact that one has an idea of a necessary connection cannot be based upon an impression of sensation. This seems to raise the possibility that there is an idea that is not derived from an impression (cf. *T* 164-5). Here Hume leaves open the possibility that there are necessary connections among objects, but raises doubts regarding the possibility of knowing that there are such.

In *Treatise* I.iii.3, Hume examines the evidence for the causal maxim, 'that *whatever begins to exist, must have a cause of existence*' (*T* 78) and argues that there can be no necessary connections among objects. Hume begins by arguing that the maxim cannot be known on the basis of intuition (it is not a necessary truth), since it cannot be based solely upon a comparison of ideas (*T* 79; cf. *T* 70). Next he develops an argument that is independent of his earlier discussion of knowledge. He wrote:

We can never demonstrate the necessity of a cause to every new existence, or new modification of existence, without shewing at the same time the impossibility there is, that any thing can ever begin to exist without some productive principle; and where the latter proposition cannot be prov'd, we must despair of ever being able to prove the former. Now that the latter proposition is utterly incapable of a demonstrative proof, we may satisfy ourselves by considering, that as all distinct ideas are separable from each other, and as the ideas of cause and effect are evidently distinct, 'twill be easy for us to conceive any object to be non-existent this moment, and existent the next, without conjoining to it the distinct idea of a cause or productive principle. The separation, therefore, of the idea of a cause from the beginning of existence, is plainly possible for the imagination; and consequently actual separation of these objects is so far possible, that it implies no contradiction nor absurdity; and is therefore incapable of being refuted by any reasoning from mere ideas; without which 'tis impossible to demonstrate the necessity of a cause. (*T* 79-80; cf. *T* 161-2)

Hume's argument is directed against the pretension that the causal maxim is a necessary truth, and he focuses on the formulation, 'It is not possible that there is a thing that is not caused by some other thing.' His argument is based upon two of his most fundamental philosophical principles, namely, his separability principle (*T* 10, 18), and the conceivability criterion of possibility (*T* 32). Where by 'any object' one means any arbitrarily chosen object, the basic argument can be stated as follows:

(1) I can distinguish and separate my ideas of any given object *qua* effect from my idea of the object which is its putative cause.

(2) Whatever objects are distinguishable are separable, and whatever objects are separable are different.

(3) Therefore, my idea of any object *qua* cause is different from my idea of any object conjoined with it *qua* effect.

(4) '[W]hatever the mind clearly conceives includes the idea of possible existence' (*T* 32).

(5) Therefore, it is possible for an object *qua* effect to exist independently from any object conjoined with it *qua* cause.

(6) If objects are necessarily connected, then it is impossible for any object *qua* effect to exist independently from whatever kind of object is constantly conjoined with it *qua* cause.

(7) Therefore, no objects are necessarily connected.

Since the relation between a substance and an accident is normally taken to be a necessary connection (cf. Locke 1823: 4:21), this is precisely the kind of argument one would expect Hume to advance against the general claim that there are necessary connections among perceptions or objects, for it parallels his arguments that perceptions do not depend for their existence on minds (cf. *T* 207, 233).[8]

Hume's argument against necessary connections is a metaphysical argument. If sound, this argument alone is sufficient to show that perceptions are independent entities, a point that is crucial for the theoretical primacy of Humean perceptions. In *Treatise* I.iii.6 he turns to the epistemological issue of induction and the belief in the uniformity of nature. The relation between these issues should be clear. *If* necessary connections obtain among objects, this would provide the metaphysical ground for the principle of the uniformity of nature and inductive arguments regarding future events would have complete certainty. If, as Hume argued, there are no necessary connections among objects, then the metaphysical basis for the principle of the uniformity of nature is undercut, but since the belief in uniformity persists,[9] one must ask whether there is any other basis for the belief. After noting that it is only the constant conjunction of past experiences that can provide the basis for an inference from the past to the future (*T* 87-8), he asks whether reason supports the principle '*that instances, of which we have had no experience, must resemble those, of which we have had experience, and that the course of nature continues always uniformly the same*' (*T* 89). The uniformity principle cannot be based upon reason, since

> We can at least conceive a change in the course of nature; which sufficiently proves, that such a change is not absolutely impossible. To form a clear idea of any thing, is an undeniable argument for its possibility, and is alone a refutation of any pretended demonstration against it. (*T* 89; cf. *EHU* 35)

Since what is conceivable is possible (*T* 32), and since one can conceive of a change in the course of nature, that is, one can at least conceive of one instance in which a presumptive cause was not followed by its usual effect, the principle of the uniformity of nature cannot be known by reason. Given that there are no necessary connections among objects, this is as one would expect.

Nor can the principle of the uniformity of nature be justified on the basis of experience. Hume's primary argument is as follows:

> The idea of cause and effect is deriv'd from *experience*, which informs us, that such particular objects, in all past instances, have been constantly conjoin'd with each other: And as an object similar to one of these is suppos'd to be immediately present in its impression, we thence presume on the existence of one similar to its usual attendant. According to this account of things, which is, I think, in every point unquestionable, probability is founded on the presumption of a resemblance betwixt those objects, of which we have had experience, and those, of which we have had none; and therefore 'tis impossible this presumption can arise from probability. The same principle cannot be both the cause and the effect of another; and this is, perhaps, the only proposition concerning that relation which is either intuitively or demonstratively certain. (*T* 89-90; cf. *EHU* 35-6; Sextus Empiricus 1985: 105)

Experience cannot justify one's belief in the principle of the uniformity of nature, since, at best, experience shows us only that two kinds of objects constantly have been conjoined in the past. But if one needs the uniformity principle to make inferences regarding the future, this cannot be obtained from experience, since it is presupposed by any probabilistic reasoning. As Hume puts it here, 'The same principle cannot be both the cause and effect of another'; as he puts it in the first *Enquiry*, 'To endeavour, therefore the proof of this last supposition by probable argument, or arguments regarding existence, must be evidently going in a circle, and taking that for granted, which is the very point in question' (*EHU* 35-6).[10]

Thus, as in the case of the belief in necessary connections among objects, one never can prove that the principle of the uniformity of nature is true. It is not a necessary truth, since exceptions to it are conceivable. It cannot be proven by means of an argument from experience, since the principle is presupposed by such an argument. Thus, 'We suppose, but are never able to prove, that there must be a resemblance betwixt those objects, of which we have had experience, and those which lie beyond the reach of our discovery' (*T* 91-2). One continues to believe that the principle is true, even though one typically neither thinks about past instances of constant conjunctions between objects nor the uniformity principle in drawing causal inferences (cf. *T* 93). What will explain this tendency to draw epistemically unwarranted inferences? Hume explains this tendency on the basis of the association of ideas (*T* 92), and it is to his explanations that we now turn.

Explanations

The bulk of *Treatise* Book I, Part iii is devoted to the discussion of belief. We examined the discussion of belief as the force and vivacity of an idea following an impression (*T* 96) in Chapter 3, and we briefly discussed the role of the principles of the association of ideas in belief in Chapter 2. In this section we will look first at the explanations Hume provides of the belief in the principle of the uniformity of nature in *Treatise* I.iii.8, and then at his explanation of the belief that there are necessary connections among causally related ideas in *Treatise* I.iii.14. In both of these cases we shall see that the explanation proceeds in accordance with the principles of the association of ideas.

In *Treatise* I.iii.8, Hume provides a general discussion of the causes of belief, i.e., the increase in the force and vivacity of an idea associated with an impression, arguing that belief can be explained on the basis of the principles of the association of ideas. He begins with resemblance, providing various examples to show that resemblance can cause an increase in the force and vivacity of an idea associated with a present impression (*T* 99-100).[11] He then turns to contiguity (*T* 100) and causation. His initial discussion of causation focuses on the increase in force and vivacity on the presumption that there was a causal relation between an object seen and something about which one is concerned, as in the case of religious relics (*T* 101). He then turns to a more general explanation of the causes of one's belief in the uniformity of nature. It is with the latter discussion that we shall be concerned.

Hume claims that all causal reasoning is based on a psychological custom or habit, rather than any type of reasoning. Hume begins by summarizing the conclusions he had reached regarding the causes of belief, namely, 'There enters nothing into this operation of the mind [belief] but a present impression, a lively idea, and a relation or association in the fancy' (*T* 101). He then goes on to consider an example. He wrote:

> In order to put this whole affair in a fuller light, let us consider it as a question in natural philosophy, which we must determine by experience and observation. I suppose there is an object presented, from which I draw a certain conclusion, and form to myself ideas, which I am said to believe or assent to. Here 'tis evident, that however that object, which is present to my senses, and that other, whose existence I infer by reasoning, may be thought to influence each other by their particular powers or qualities; yet as the phenomenon of belief, which we at present examine, is merely internal, these powers and qualities, being entirely unknown, can have no hand in producing it. 'Tis the present impression, which is to be consider'd as the true and real cause of the idea, and the belief which attends it. We must therefore endeavour to discover by experiments the particular qualities, by which 'tis enabled to produce so extraordinary an effect. (*T* 101-2)

Hume's concern is with the cause of causal beliefs. Consequently, he focuses on the cause of an idea by an impression. The presumption that there are unperceived powers or necessary connections among the objects represented by the impression and the idea plays no role in the consideration. He is concerned with the 'inference' from cause to effect, that is, the way in which one perception causes another perception in making such an inference. Hence, it is reasonable for him to claim that only an impression can be the cause of the idea which is the object of belief.

He proceeds by providing two 'experiments' or observations to determine the conditions under which an impression of some object *a* can cause an idea of an object *b* which is deemed the effect of *a*. He wrote:

> First then I observe, that the present impression has not this effect by its own proper power and efficacy, and when consider'd alone, as a single perception, limited to the present moment. I

find, that an impression, from which, on its first appearance, I can draw no conclusion, may afterwards become the foundation of belief, when I have had experience of its usual consequences. We must in every case have observ'd the same impression in past instances, and have found it to be constantly conjoin'd with some other impression. This is confirm'd by such a multitude of experiments, that it admits not of the smallest doubt. (*T* 102; cf. *EHU* 42)

Hume takes it to be a fact that no causal inference will be drawn from a solitary impression taken in isolation from all experience. This presumption seems justified by his earlier argument that there are no necessary connections among any objects, including perceptions. Hence, a solitary impression cannot be the cause of a belief. Yet, once one has had a certain amount of experience, notably experience of the constant conjunction between objects of kind *a* and objects of kind *b* (cf. *T* 87), an impression of an object of kind *a* can be the foundation for the belief in the existence of an object of kind *b*. How can this be?

Hume answers that question in his second observation. In his words:

From a second observation I conclude, that the belief which attends the present impression and is produc'd by a number of past impressions and conjunctions; that this belief, I say, arises immediately, without any new operation of the reason or imagination. Of this I can be certain, because I never am conscious of any such operation, and find nothing in the subject, on which it can be founded. Now as we call every thing CUSTOM, which proceeds from a past repetition, without any new reasoning or conclusion, we may establish it as a certain truth, that all the belief, which follows upon any present impression, is deriv'd solely from that origin. When we are accustom'd to see two impressions conjoin'd together, the appearance or idea of the one immediately carries us to the idea of the other. (*T* 102-3; cf. *EHU* 43)

The belief that arises from an impression is *not* the result of any kind of argument or reasoning. The belief occurs immediately upon perceiving the impression (cf *T* 103-4). Hume calls this phenomenon a case of custom or habit (cf. *EHU* 43). Having perceived a constant conjunction between two types of objects in the past, the mind develops a 'habit' of expectation, and this 'habit' explains the transition from the impression to the belief.[12]

If Hume takes this to be an explanation of the phenomenon, he is confused. His allusion to custom or habit cannot be taken to imply that a mind is composed of something more than perceptions and relations among them (cf. *T* 207, 252). This 'custom' or 'habit' can be nothing more than the fact that, after a certain amount of experience, one actually moves directly from a certain kind of impression to the idea with which it is constantly conjoined. This, of course, is the phenomenon that was to be explained.

Up to this point Hume has not explicitly addressed the belief in the principle of the uniformity of nature, although the discussions we have examined show how that belief is to be explained. His discussions focus on a particular arbitrarily chosen object. In any case of causal relations, one's tendency to believe that an object of kind *b* will follow an object of kind *a* is based upon a constant conjunction between observed instances of objects of kinds *a* and *b*. The belief in the principle of the uniformity of nature is a generalized statement of one's belief that if experience indicates that objects of kind *a* have been constantly conjoined with objects of kind *b*, then given any *arbitrarily chosen* object of kind *a*, it will be followed by an object of kind *b*. Hume says as much when considering those 'rare and unusual' cases in which the inference from cause to effect is *mediate* (based upon reasoning), rather than immediate. He wrote:

> 'Tis certain, that not only in philosophy, but even in common life, we may attain the knowledge of a particular cause merely by one experiment, provided it be made with judgment, and after a careful removal of all foreign and superfluous circumstances. Now as after one experiment of this kind, the mind, upon the appearance either of the cause or the effect, can draw an inference concerning the existence of its correlative; and as a habit can never be acquir'd merely by one instance; it may be thought, that belief cannot in this case be esteem'd the effect of custom. But this difficulty will vanish, if we consider, that tho' we are here suppos'd to have had only one experiment of a particular effect, yet we have many millions to convince us of this principle; *that like objects, plac'd in like circumstances, will always produce like effects;* and as this principle has establish'd itself by a sufficient custom, it bestows an evidence and firmness on any opinion, to which it can be apply'd. The connexion of the ideas is not habitual after one experiment; but this connexion is comprehended under another principle, that is habitual; which brings us back to our hypothesis. In all cases we transfer our experience to instances, of which we have no experience, either *expressly* or *tacitly*, either *directly* or *indirectly*. (*T* 104-5)

Hume claims one often draws a causal inference mediately on the basis of a single case, since the general principle that similar objects placed in similar circumstances always produce similar effects is believed on the basis of experience. This principle is nothing more than another formulation of the uniformity principle. Hence, the belief that the uniformity principle is true is explained on the basis of the same psychological mechanisms that allow one to explain particular causal beliefs, namely, the principles of the association of ideas.

Having explained the belief in the principle of the uniformity of nature, Hume proceeds to explain the beliefs in the several kinds of probability along similar lines (*T* 124-55). To complete his explanations of belief, he returns to the idea of necessary connection. Recall that Hume had argued that the belief that there are necessary connections among objects is false. Yet, like the belief in the uniformity principle, the belief that there are necessary connections among objects persists. Further, he never denied that one has an idea of a necessary connection. In *Treatise* I.iii.14, he examines both the nature of the idea of a necessary connection and explains one's tendency to believe that such connections obtain among objects.

In 'Of the Idea of Necessary Connexion' Hume begins by reviewing both some of the most general claims of his philosophy and the conclusions he had reached regarding causation and necessary connection. He stresses that 'we have no idea, that is not deriv'd from an impression' (*T* 155), and that 'I immediately perceive that [causally related objects] are *contiguous* in time and place, and that the object we call cause *precedes* the other we call effect. In no one instance can I go any farther, nor is it possible for me to discover any third relation betwixt these objects' (*T* 155). But when one repeatedly observes the two (kinds) of objects that stand in the relations of contiguity and precedence, one finds

> that the repetition is not in every particular the same, but produces a new impression, and by that means the idea, which I at present examine. For after a frequent repetition, I find, that upon the appearance of one of the objects, the mind is *determin'd* by custom to consider its usual attendant, and to consider it in a stronger light upon account of its relation to the first object. 'Tis this impression, then, or *determination*, which affords me the idea of necessity. (*T* 155-6)

Hume reviews the several philosophical accounts of the origin of one's idea of power or necessary connection among objects, finding each wanting (*T* 157-62). He concludes that in using words such as 'power' or 'necessary connection' 'we have really no distinct meaning, and make use only of common words, without any clear and determinate ideas' (*T* 162). But Hume continues:

But as 'tis more probable, that these expressions do here lose their true meaning by being *wrong apply'd*, than that they never have any meaning; 'twill be proper to bestow another consideration on this subject, to see if possibly we can discover the nature and origin of those ideas, we annex to them. (*T* 162)

In looking for a source of one's ideas of power or necessary connection, Hume notes that the 'multiplicity of resembling instances . . . constitutes the very essence of power or connexion, and is the source, from which the idea of it arises' (*T* 163). Since 'the several resembling instances, which give rise to the idea of power, have no influence on each other, and can never produce any quality *in the object*, which can be the model of that idea', Hume concludes:

> the *observation* of this resemblance produces a new impression *in the mind*, which is its real model. For after we have observ'd the resemblance in a sufficient number of instances, we immediately feel a determination of the mind to pass from one object to its usual attendant, and to conceive it in a stronger light upon account of that relation. This determination is the only effect of the resemblance; and therefore must be the same with power or efficacy, whose idea is deriv'd from the resemblance. The several instances of resembling conjunctions lead us into the notion of power and necessity. These instances are in themselves totally distinct from each other, and have no union but in the mind, which observes them, and collects their ideas. Necessity, then, is the effect of this observation, and is nothing but an internal impression of the mind, or a determination to carry our thoughts from one object to another. (*T* 164-5)

The idea of power or necessary connection is derived from an impression, but it is not an impression of sensation. It is an 'internal impression' or impression of reflection. Hume explains the origin of this idea on the basis of resemblance. After the observation of resembling instances of the conjunction between objects, the mind forms an idea of an object of the second kind upon the observation of an idea of the first kind. When that happens, the mind is determined; there is an internal impression, an impression that is distinct from the perceptions that might be united by a causal relation. This internal impression is the source of one's idea of necessary connection.

Hume's conclusion is surprising. It is also one that does not engender belief. Even if one accepts his argument that necessary connections are nothing but determinations of the mind, one continues to believe that necessary connections obtain among causally related objects. Hence, it was incumbent upon Hume to explain why one believes that necessary connections obtain among objects, even if they are merely impressions of reflection. His explanation is as follows:

> 'Tis a common observation, that the mind has a great propensity to spread itself on external objects, and to conjoin with them any internal impressions, which they occasion, and which always make their appearance at the same time that these objects discover themselves to the senses. Thus as certain sounds and smells are always found to attend certain visible objects, we naturally imagine a conjunction, even in place, betwixt the object and qualities, tho' the qualities be of such a nature as to admit of no such conjunction, and really exist no where. But of this more hereafter. Mean while 'tis sufficient to observe, that the same propensity is the reason, why we suppose necessity and power to lie in the objects we consider, not in our mind that considers them; notwithstanding it is not possible for us to form the most distant idea of that quality, when it is not taken for the determination of the mind, to pass from the idea of an object to that of its usual attendant. (*T* 167)

When several qualities are present to the mind at the same time, there is a tendency for the mind to 'project' those qualities that do not exist in space--that 'exist only in the mind'--into a spatially located object. This general theme was fairly common among the proponents of the primary/secondary qualities distinction, since they held that although such secondary qualities 'exist only in the mind', that is, there is nothing in a material object that resembles one's idea of a secondary quality, one perceives those qualities as if they are components of objects.[13] Hume later argued that all ideas of reflection and all sensible qualities save those of sight and touch '*exist, and yet be no where*' (*T* 235), although one has a tendency to 'project' such qualities into extended objects. Of this tendency he wrote:

> These relations, then, of *causation*, and *contiguity in time of their appearance*, betwixt the extended object and quality, which exists without any particular place, must have such an effect on the mind, that upon the appearance of one it will immediately turn its thought to the conception of the other. Nor is this all. We not only turn our thought from one to the other upon account of their relation, but likewise endeavour to give them a new relation, *viz.* that of a *conjunction in place*, that we may render the transition more easy and natural. (*T* 237)

It is precisely this tendency to 'project' qualities into objects, a tendency itself explained on the basis of the principles of the association of ideas, that Hume explains one's belief that necessary connections obtain among objects: by projecting the connection on to the objects, there appears to be greater regularity in the world.

Conclusions

In this chapter we have examined Hume's arguments against necessary connections among objects in general, and perceptions in particular. We began by observing that Shaftesbury seemed to hold that it is necessary connections among objects that unite them into a single whole. Hume's arguments that no necessary connections can obtain among objects parallel his arguments against substance. Similarly, he argued that there is no evidential basis for the belief in the principle of the uniformity of nature. These arguments entail that perception, the fundamental entities of Hume's theory of mind, are independent entities. But as in the case of his arguments against substance, he claimed that the belief in uniformity and necessary connection persists, and he explains those beliefs on the basis of the principles of the association of ideas.

In turning next to his discussion of the belief in external objects, we shall see that his studies in doxastic pathology continue. Ultimately, his account of the mind as a bundle of distinct and independent perceptions will be deemed plausible only in so far as his theory will allow him to explain such unwarranted 'natural' beliefs as the belief in the external world and the substantiality of the mind (personal identity).

Notes

[1]Similarities between Shaftesbury's theory and Spinoza's have not gone without notice. See Robertson's notes to Shaftesbury 1964.

[2]I shall consider this in detail in Chapter 7.

[3]For our present purposes it is irrelevant to ask whether Shaftesbury drew a distinction between substances and individuals (cf. Shaftesbury 1964: 2:275-6). As we shall see, there is an account of what it is for an individual to be simple and perfectly identical through time--what Hume considers the characteristics of substance as such--that is found in Shaftesbury's works.

[4]It is almost certainly this passage to which Hume refers at *T* 254n.

[5]Hume took the difference between 'real relations' and 'real' or 'necessary connections' to be merely verbal. Cf. *T* 458.

[6]As we shall see in Chapter 7, Hume gives an alternative explanation of the notion of a 'sympathy of parts to a common end' (cf. *T* 257).

[7]It is worthy of notice that Hume was not the first to raise sceptical doubts regarding causal relations. In *The Outlines of Pyrrhonism*, Book 3, Chapter 5, Sextus Empiricus also raises doubts regarding the causal relation, although his arguments differ significantly from Hume's and show little more than that the evidence for the existence of causal relations is balanced by the evidence against the existence of such relations. See Sextus Empiricus 1985: 113-16. See also Nicholas of Autrecourt 1986: 710-11.

[8]Not all commentators take seriously Hume's criticisms of necessary connection. Citing Hume's remark that 'we have no idea of power or agency separate from the mind, and belonging to causes' (*T* 223), John Wright notes, 'He is saying that we have no idea of the necessity, power or agency of causes, *not* that there is no necessity, power, or agency in the objects themselves. For Hume tells us he is quite "ready to allow, that there may be several qualities both in material and immaterial objects, with which we are utterly unacquainted" and which correspond "to the terms of power and efficacy".' (Wright 1983: 132; the passage cited is from *T* 168; cf. Broughton 1987: 217-244.) Even if one takes the passage on *T* 168 to allow that one has an idea of power *in some sense*, Wright's interpretation of it constitutes a complete rejection of the argument against necessary connections at *T* 79-80. That argument shows that in so far as it is possible for any arbitrarily chosen object to exist independently of all others, there are no necessary connections. Notice that at *T* 168 Hume remarks that 'if we please to call these [unknown qualities] *power* or *efficacy*, 'twill be of little consequence to the world.' The passage does not commit Hume to the existence of necessary connections or powers in any strong sense. Indeed, in the first *Enquiry* Hume allows that there are powers, and even ideas of powers as unknown qualities, but he claims this only after providing his 'definitions' of cause and effect, and such an idea of power is nothing more than a relative idea of 'the *unknown* circumstance of an object, by which the degree of quantity of its effect is fixed and determined' (*EHU* 77n). Such a 'power' does not entail the impossibility of an effect following from something other than that from which it does follow, a point required by the discussion at *T* 79-80. Hence, even though Hume suggested that the terms 'power' and 'necessary connexion' seem to be synonymous (*T* 157; *EHU* 62), his remark that 'This multiplicity of resembling instances, therefore, constitutes the very essence of power or necessary connexion, and is the source from which the idea of it arises' (*T* 163) seems to imply the power *qua* unknown quality is nothing more than a certain property of an object that is constantly conjoined with an observable effect of a certain degree: it provides no grounds for suggesting that Hume reintroduced necessary connections in the sense rejected at *T* 79-80.

[9]As does the belief in necessary connections among objects, an issue Hume addresses in *Treatise* I.iii.14.

[10]Hume develops a second argument in reply to an objection at *T* 90-1, but that argument adds virtually nothing further to his case.

[11]Cf. Montaigne 1976: 381.

[12]Hume includes a third observation at *T* 103, an observation that it is *only* the transition from an impression to an idea that engenders belief, but that is not of concern in this context. See also *T* 105-6.

[13]In his careful moments, Locke distinguished between the sensation in the mind and the secondary quality as the power in the object to cause that quality (*Essay* 2.8.13-14), but talk of secondary qualities as 'existing only in the mind' was fairly common. Cf. Berkeley, *PHK* I, 10.

6
Bodies and Bundles

If Hume's theory of mind is adequate, it must explain why one holds certain beliefs that are unwarranted or false. We already have seen that he provides explanations of one's belief in material substance and necessary connections. In this chapter I examine his discussion of beliefs in the external world. First, I examine the interrelationships between the vulgar and the philosophical beliefs in the existence of external objects. Next I ask whether Hume countenanced material objects as entities categorially distinct from perceptions. I argue that he did, showing (1) that Hume considered positing material objects provides the best causal explanation of impressions, (2) that the evidence for a phenomenalistic interpretation of the *Treatise* is, at best, suspect, and (3) even if one were to deem Hume a phenomenalist, one cannot plausibly claim that Hume was a neutral monist, since Hume introduced distinctions that are incompatible with the contention that both minds and bodies are composed of perceptions. Finally, I argue that Hume championed a sophisticated form of dualism, that he drew categorial distinctions among perceptions and distinguished the mental realm from the physical realm on the basis of considerations of the spatial relations among the entities in each realm.

Constancy and Coherence

In so far as Hume provides an account of the perceptual foundations for the belief in the existence of material objects, 'Of Scepticism with Regard to the Senses' is that account. Yet the 'account' is hardly a typical epistemological discussion. His epistemic conclusion is that there is no theory of sense perception that is adequate to provide one with knowledge of the external world, and one can be no better counseled than to be a Pyrrhonian sceptic (*T* 217-18). But the explicit topic of the section has little to do with the truth of one's belief in the external world, a point 'which we must take for granted in all our reasonings' (*T* 187). The question on which Hume focuses is '*What causes induce us to believe in the existence of body?*' (*T* 187). The discussion is a study in doxastic pathology: the belief in the existence of an external world is another problematic belief that must be explained if Hume's theory of mind is to be plausible.

To gain a proper understanding of the position Hume developed in 'Of Scepticism with Regard to the Senses' and thereby demonstrate the consistency of the views expressed there with the thesis that bodies exist, it will be useful to explain Hume's implicit distinction between *ordinary thinking*, *critical thinking*, and *philosophical invention*, and to specify the ways in which the three modes of thought are employed.[1] In the *ordinary* mode of thought, the dominant associative principles of inference and belief operate without interference. For this reason, only the ordinary mode of thought is capable of originating belief. This is the only mode of thought employed by the common person, that is, 'all the unthinking and unphilosophical part of mankind (that is, all of us, at one time or another)' (*T* 205). Since only the ordinary mode of thought can produce belief, it is doxastically fundamental and a necessary condition for critical thinking.

While the common person is restricted to the ordinary mode of thinking, some individuals, namely, philosophers, are capable of a quite different mode of thought. The task of *critical thinking* is to assess evidence and to discover inconsistencies and absurd consequences. Like mathematical reasoning it is a process of reasoning; unlike mathematical reasoning, it is never constructive. The initial subject matter of critical thinking is ordinary belief; the tendency is negative and refutational; the result is puzzlement. But such a result is psychologically unacceptable. The critic finds his or her beliefs unfounded but cannot abandon them. This intellectual crisis brings forth *philosophical invention*, a mode of thinking which revises ordinary beliefs so as to make them consistent with the evidence uncovered in critical thinking. Like ordinary thinking, philosophical invention is a function of the imagination; unlike such thinking, it cannot originate belief. It yields philosophical positions whose persuasive force is provided by an ordinary belief. Inventions are parasitic. They are also subject to further critical thinking, and in Hume's view are generally found wanting.

Subjecting a philosophical position to further critical analysis generally yields a complete, though fleeting, suspension of belief. The critical state of mind is neither stable nor persisting, and the suspension of belief it yields is limited to the moments in one's 'closet'. Normally, the best one can do is vacillate between ordinary belief and philosophical invention, with ordinary belief remaining the dominant mode of thought. Thus, when critical thought is inoperative, one believes with the 'rabble without doors'; when it yields philosophical invention, one accepts a philosophical theory. Only when critical thought focuses on a philosophical theory can one obtain those rare Pyrrhonistic interludes in one's closet.

In 'Of Scepticism with Regard to the Senses' Hume utilized this three-fold distinction, though he did not spell it out in its general form. He focuses primarily on an explanation of the ordinary and philosophical beliefs in the external world, devoting only limited space at the end of each discussion to a critical evaluation of the belief. He begins by specifying the essential elements of a belief in the existence of body. To believe in an external world is to believe that some objects are distinct from their perceivers and continue to exist unperceived (*T* 188). Distinctness is analyzed further. Bodies are *external to* consciousness and *independent* of it in their existence and operation (*T* 188). Of these three elements of one's belief in the existence of external objects, Hume focused his attention on the continued and independent existence of bodies. His reason for this rests upon the tendency to place greater store in the independence of an object than in its external position. As he wrote:

> Mean while we may observe that when we talk of real distinct existences, we have commonly more in our eye their independency than external situation in place, and think an object has sufficient reality, when its Being is uninterrupted, and independent of the incessant revolutions, which we are conscious of in ourselves. (*T* 191)

Notice that this characterization of the independence of objects corresponds to the criteria for perfect numerical identity, namely, invariability and uninterruptedness (*T* 201).

Equipped with this analysis of one's belief in the existence of external objects, Hume proceeds to develop his causal explanation of that belief. He asks, first, whether the belief is produced by the senses, the reason or the imagination. He argues at some length that the senses can neither cause the belief in the continued existence of an object that no longer appears to the senses (*T* 188-9) nor the belief in an existence distinct from or external to perceptions, since perceptions are the sole objects of the senses and do not 'point beyond' themselves (*T* 189, 190-2).[2] Hence, the senses alone cannot provide the basis for the belief in the existence of external objects. Nor can 'REASON, or weighing our opinions by any philosophical principles' (*T* 193) be the basis for the belief, since a belief in the existence of external objects is held by persons incapable of understanding philosophical arguments (*T* 193). Hence, the belief must be caused by the imagination.

Hume continues by noting that 'Since all impressions are internal and perishing existences, and appear as such, the notion of their distinct and continu'd existence must arise from a concurrence of some of their qualities with the qualities of the imagination; and since this notion does not extend to all of them, it must arise from certain qualities peculiar to some impressions' (*T* 194). Contrary to Descartes and Locke (Descartes, CSM 2:52; Locke, *Essay* 4.11.5), Hume dismisses the involuntariness of perceptions as a mark of their externality, since pain, which philosopher and commoner alike deem nothing more than a perception in the mind (*T* 192), is as involuntary as any putative perception of an external object (*T* 192). And for the same reason, passivity cannot be the characteristic of the imagination Hume seeks. The characteristics Hume seeks are constancy and coherence. Anything one will deem an external object generally tends to remain the same through time, and in so far as it changes, the changes are coherent: they follow certain 'natural laws' and can be predicted on the basis of past experience (*T* 194-5).[3]

Hume proceeds to offer a general explanation of the belief in external objects on the basis of the correlation between constancy and coherence as putative characteristics of external objects and the relations of resemblance and causation that obtain among perceptions. As we shall see, his discussion shows both that he presumed that one ordinarily--if unconsciously--uses something very much like the method of evidential evaluation I sketched in Chapter 1.[4] Further, the discovery of inconsistent beliefs results in philosophical invention: the positing of 'something, of which we are insensible' (*T* 198) that unites appearances.

Beginning with coherence, Hume notes that the fleeting perceptions in the mind possess a certain coherence, although "tis of somewhat a different nature, from that which we discover in bodies' in so far as passions are mutually interdependent but are *not* presumed operative when unperceived (*T* 195). He then provides the example of a porter bringing him a letter. He hears a sound like the sound of a door opening, before seeing the porter.

This gives occasion to many new reflexions and reasonings. First, I never have observ'd, that this noise cou'd proceed from any thing but the motion of a door; and therefore conclude, that the present phenomenon is a contradiction to all past experience, unless the door, which I remember on t'other side the chamber, be still in being. Again, I have always found, that a human body was possest of a quality, which I call gravity, and which hinders it from mounting in the air, as this porter must have done to arrive at my chamber, unless the stairs I remember be not annihilated by my absence. (*T* 196)

Notice that Hume is here reasoning from effect to cause. The best explanation--the only explanation consistent with past experience--of his hearing the sound of a door opening is that it is correlated with an opening door. Similarly, the best explanation of the appearance of the porter in the second-story room of his house, is that the porter climbed the stairs, and, therefore, that the stairs exist. And the same kind of reasoning will explain how the letter from a distant friend came to be carried in by the porter (*T* 196). It is only the supposition of an unperceived cause of one's impressions that will, consistent with past experience, explain the phenomenon. On this point Hume was explicit. Referring to the sound of a door and its unperceived cause, Hume wrote:

I am accustom'd to hear such a sound, and see such an object in motion at the same time. I have not receiv'd in this particular instance both these perceptions. These observations are contrary, unless I suppose that the door remains, and that it was open'd without my perceiving it: And this supposition, which was at first entirely arbitrary and hypothetical, acquires a force and evidence by its being the only one, upon which I can reconcile these contradictions. There is scarce a moment in my life, wherein there is not a similar instance presented to me, and I have not occasion to suppose the continu'd existence of objects, in order to connect their past and present appearances, and give them such a union with each other, as I have found by experience to be suitable to their peculiar natures and circumstances. Here then I am naturally led to regard the world, as something real and durable, and as preserving its existence, even when it is no longer present to my perception. (*T* 196-7)

Since Hume is here giving a general account of the reasoning that is involved in positing the existence of external objects, the concern with the use of the best explanation to overcome apparent inconsistencies shows that Hume assumed even the vulgar unwittingly comply with some of the strictures of his philosophical method.

Throughout his discussion of coherence Hume notes the similarity between the notion of coherence and causal reasoning (*T* 195). We have noted that in his discussion of the porter, it is the explanatory character of the *supposition* that there are external objects that is operative--although some will argue that it would be sufficient for Hume to claim that there are unperceived perceptions (unsensed sensa), an assumption that is consistent with Hume's account of perceptions (cf. *T* 207, 233; Price 1940: 32ff). Hume suggests one posits external objects to reconcile the apparent inconsistency between the interrupted appearance of objects and their coherence. Although in positing the existence of an external object one goes beyond the degree of regularity observable among perceptions to a realm of entities that are categorially distinct from perceptions, and in this regard the appeal to constancy is 'at the bottom considerably different from' causal reasoning (*T* 197), this is explainable in part on the basis of the principle that 'as the mind is once in the train of observing an uniformity among objects, it naturally continues, till it renders the uniformity as compleat as possible' (*T* 198).

But this principle is 'too weak to support so vast an edifice, as is that of the continu'd existence of all external bodies; and we must join the *constancy* of their appearance to the *coherence*, in order to give a satisfactory account of that opinion' (*T* 198-9). Just as coherence corresponds to the relation of causation, the relation of constancy corresponds to the relation of resemblance (*T* 199). Those interrupted perceptions one takes to be perceptions of a particular object resemble one another. It is on the basis of these relations of resemblance and causation among perceptions that Hume explains the several versions of the belief in external objects, beginning with the common person's belief.

From the Vulgar to the Philosophical

After explaining the principle of identity in terms of 'the *invariableness* and *uninterruptedness* of any object, thro' a suppos'd variation of time, by which the mind can trace it in different periods of its existence, without any break of the view, and without being oblig'd to form the idea of multiplicity of number' (*T* 201; cf. Locke, *Essay* 2.27.1), Hume focuses his attention on the ordinary mode of thought: the common person's belief in the existence of external objects. He began by making an important point about what commonly is believed to be external: it is the impression of sensation itself. The common person does not differentiate the objects with which he or she is immediately acquainted (impressions) from external objects, and for the sake of the discussion of the common belief Hume also used the terms 'object' and 'perception' interchangeably, while maintaining that such a conflation strictly is mistaken (*T* 193, 202, 205). The source of this error lies in the tendency of the mind to equate or identify objects of experience or thought that closely resemble one another, that is, the tendency to conflate perfect numerical identity and specific identity (cf. *T* 257-8). Since resembling impressions affect the mind in nearly the same way as identical ones, the tendency to confuse them is quite natural: it involves resemblances among both the acts of the mind and the objects of those acts (*T* 204n-205n). This identification of resembling objects of experience becomes problematic, however, when there is a gap between one's experience of an object and a later experience of an object identified as the first. Such an interruption yields the idea of distinct though resembling existences, an idea which is contrary to the assumption of identity. Nonetheless, since in the ordinary mode of thought the appearance of an object is not distinguished from one's perceiving it, everyone ordinarily believes that the object perceived at t_3 is identical with the object perceived at t_1, even though it was not perceived at t_2. So long as Hume can demonstrate that the appearance/existence distinction can be maintained consistently with the impression-object equation, the ordinary mode of belief can be proven consistent.

Given the impression-object equation, the distinction between appearance and existence can be proven consistent only if it is possible for the immediate objects of sensory experience to exist unperceived. This raises two questions:

> *First*, How we can satisfy ourselves in supposing a perception to be absent from the mind without being annihilated. *Secondly*, After what manner we conceive an object to become present to the mind, without some new creation of a perception or image; and what we mean by this *seeing*, and *feeling*, and *perceiving*.

Hume responded to the first question as follows:

> As to the first question; we may observe, that what we call a *mind*, is nothing but a heap or collection of different perceptions, united together by certain relations, and suppos'd, tho' falsely, to be endow'd with a perfect simplicity and identity. Now as every perception is distinguishable from another, and may be consider'd as separately existent; it evidently follows, that there is no absurdity in separating any particular perception from the mind; that is, in breaking off all its relations, with that connected mass of perceptions, which constitute a thinking thing. (*T* 207)

Perceptions, be they impressions or ideas, are distinct and independent existents. As such, they are capable of existing apart from those other perceptions that, with it, constitute consciousness, that is, perceptions are capable of existing unperceived. But if it is possible for objects of experience and thought (perceptions) to exist unperceived, no contradiction is implied if one attributes identity to one's perceptions in spite of an interruption in their appearance to the mind.

Turning to the second question, Hume wrote:

> The same reasoning affords us an answer to the second question. If the name of *perception* renders not this separation from a mind absurd and contradictory, the name of *object*, standing for the very same thing, can never render their conjunction impossible. External objects are seen, and felt, and become present to the mind; that is, they acquire such a relation to a connected heap of perceptions, as to influence them very considerably in augmenting their number by present reflexions and passions, and in storing the memory with ideas. The same continu'd and uninterrupted Being may, therefore, be sometimes present to the mind, and sometimes absent from it, without any real or essential change in the Being itself. An interrupted appearance to the senses implies not necessarily an interruption in the existence. The supposition of the continu'd existence of sensible objects or perceptions involves no contradiction. We may easily indulge our inclination to that supposition. When the exact resemblance of our perceptions makes us ascribe to them an identity, we may remove the seeming interruption by feigning a continu'd being, which may fill those intervals, and preserve a perfect and entire identity to our perceptions. (*T* 207-8)

Just as it is logically possible for an impression to continue to exist when it is not experienced, even though it is called a perception only when experienced, so it can have those relations to other impressions and ideas which make it a perception or element of consciousness, even though we may consistently believe in its externality. For Hume's account of the ordinary belief in external objects, what is important is that the existence of an impression-object is not logically dependent upon being perceived by the mind. Thus, the belief that some immediate objects of experience exist unperceived is consistent, even if unwarranted by the evidence. And given its consistency, the exact resemblance of two or more of one's impressions can with some plausibility be offered as the ground which leads one to *feign* the existence of a continually existent object, and to *discount or ignore* the gaps between one's experiences of that object (*T* 208).

Hume's discussion of the ordinary mode of thought focused on one aspect of the belief in the identity of external objects, namely, the belief that certain objects of experience possess a temporally uninterrupted existence. It is on the basis of the resemblance between temporally separated and interrupted perceptions that the 'imagination is seduc'd into such an opinion' (*T* 209), a seduction that obtains the strength of a belief from the influence of the memory (*T* 209-10). Throughout the discussion the impression-object equation has been in force. But the falsehood of the belief that impressions are identical with external objects and retain their identity through time is 'acknowledg'd by all philosophers' (*T* 209; cf. *T* 193, 210), and can be demonstrated by several simple 'experiments'. As Hume wrote:

'Twill first be proper to observe a few of those experiments, which convince us, that our perceptions are not possest of any independent existence. When we press one eye with a finger, we immediately perceive all the objects to become double, and one half of them to be remov'd from their common and natural position. But as we do not attribute a continu'd existence to both these perceptions, and as they are both of the same nature, we clearly perceive, that all our perceptions are dependent on our organs, and the disposition of our nerves and animal spirits. This opinion is confirm'd by the seeming encrease and diminution of objects, according to their distance; by the apparent alterations in their figure; by the changes in their colour and other qualities from our sickness and distempers; and by an infinite number of other experiments of the same kind; from which we learn, that our sensible objects are not possest of any distinct of independent existence. (*T* 210-11)

Hume provided some of the standard arguments for distinguishing between impressions and objects (cf. Montaigne 1976: 451-2). If one presses one's eye, the number of objects perceived doubles, but no one, including the common person, would grant that both of these objects exist externally to the mind. The apparent size of an object diminishes as the distance between one's own body and the object increases. Bodily disorders alter one's impressions of the qualities of bodies. Each of these experiments indicates that one's sensory impressions are (causally) dependent upon the state of one's body, while it is presumed that bodies external to one's body are not. Thus, external objects and impressions are distinct entities. The former are both logically and causally independent of perceivers, whereas impressions are causally dependent upon perceivers.[5]

The causal dependence of one's sense perceptions on one's body is the first insight of the critical mode of thought. That conclusion leads to the further conclusion that none of those objects is external. From the experience of the interruption of sensed objects in perceiving them, the critical thinker infers that there is an interruption in their existence. That in turn implies that they are discontinuous, nonidentical, and subjective (*T* 211). They are not bodies. But the belief that bodies exist cannot be eradicated merely by concluding that sensory impressions are not bodies (*T* 214; cf. *T* 187). Once developed by the associative mechanisms, that belief retains its force. Yet the critical arguments also have force. This results in an intellectual crisis. It calls for philosophical invention, a mode of thinking that gains all its doxastic influence from the ordinary mode and is in this sense parasitic upon it (*T* 211-13). Since reason demands that impressions are dependent entities, while the imagination demands that objects are continuants, the imagination produces a philosophical theory that gives both elements of the understanding their due. One's pre-critical beliefs are transformed into the doctrine of representative realism. Since the position that distinguishes impressions from their proper external objects is a product of philosophical invention, one will believe one's theory only so long as one attends to the problem of perception and is motivated to invent, reverting back to the ordinary mode of belief upon leaving one's study (*T* 214, 216, 218).

Philosophical invention, spurred by the critical mode of thought, yields a representational theory of perception. An object is conceived as the thing that causes and resembles a certain positive perception, and continued existence is attributed to this object (*T* 215). But critical thinking knows no bounds and may be used to examine such reasoned inventions.[6] When one examines representative realism, one finds that the supposition that perceptions are caused by and resemble external objects cannot be known to be true. Hume first attacks the causal thesis. Noting that the causal relation provides the sole basis for inferring the existence of objects (*T* 212), Hume argues that one can never know that a causal relation obtains between a putative external object and a perception. As he wrote:

> The idea of this relation [causation] is deriv'd from past experience, by which we find, that two beings are constantly conjoin'd together, and are always present at once to the mind. But as no beings are ever present to the mind but perceptions; it follows that we may observe a conjunction or a relation of cause and effect between different perceptions, but can never observe it between perceptions and objects. 'Tis impossible, therefore, that

from the existence or any of the qualities of the former, we can ever form any conclusion concerning the existence of the latter, or ever satisfy our reason in this particular. (*T* 212; cf. Montaigne 1976: 454)

While Hume allowed that 'Any thing may produce any thing' (*T* 173), and while, as we have seen, he allowed that considerations of coherence and causation suggest that the existence of external objects provides the best explanation of one's interrupted experience of objects (cf. *T* 196-7), the nature of one's knowledge of causal relations does not allow one to claim that there is an external cause. Properly speaking, it is only on the basis of perceptions that one forms causal beliefs, and it is only among perceptions that one can claim causal relations obtain. Hence, whatever propensity one might have to extend the domain of causal relations, one never is properly justified in doing so.

Hume's remarks on resemblance are briefer still, being little more than the comment that 'I have already shewn, that the relation of cause and effect can never afford us any just conclusion from the existence of qualities of our perceptions to the existence of external objects: And I shall farther add, that even tho' they cou'd afford such a conclusion, we shou'd never have any reason to infer, that our objects resemble our perceptions' (*T* 216; cf. Sextus Empiricus 1985: 149). Hume's point throughout his discussion of the philosophical position on perception is that, while one has a natural tendency to ascribe continued existence to external objects and while one can explain how this natural tendency leads to the philosophical belief in the 'double existence of perceptions and objects', 'perceptions have no perceivable connexion with such an existence' (*T* 217), and therefore, one can never properly know that the philosophical account is true. Hence, one should suspend all belief in the existence of unperceived continuants. Yet such a suspension of belief is limited to the rare moments of intense reasoning, and any further adherence to it is merely verbal (*T* 214, 218). Though philosophical invention succumbs to ordinary belief when one does not closely attend to a philosophical problem (cf. *T* 216), critical thought more quickly yields to philosophical invention and ordinary belief (*T* 218, 267-70).

Given the distinction between these three modes of thought, there is no inconsistency between Hume's discussion in 'Of Scepticism with Regard to the Senses' and the presuppositions in the remainder of his philosophical writings. He spoke *for himself* as well as all others when he asserted that the belief in the existence of body 'is a point, which we must take for granted in all our reasonings' (*T* 187). Though not all humans can obtain all three, the distinctions between ordinary thinking, critical thinking and philosophical invention have general application. Those who attain all three vacillate among them. Hume also shifted among the three roles. He was an ordinary human (naive realist) when indulging in ordinary thinking, a scientific inquirer (representationalist) when presuming his philosophical invention, and--most rarely--a pure philosopher (sceptic concerning external objects) when subjecting philosophical invention to further critical thought.

Thus, we have seen that in 'Of Scepticism with Regard to the Senses' Hume critically examined the ordinary and philosophical beliefs in the existence of the external world. Both beliefs were deemed epistemically suspect. While the ordinary belief is false, the philosophical belief is unsupported by the evidence. Nonetheless, both beliefs can be explained on the basis of the principles of the association of ideas, and consequently, the explainability of the beliefs tends to support Hume's theory of mind. Further, we have noticed that Hume did not explicitly cast his lot with either the common person or with the philosopher, but suggested that he himself vacillated among the positions on the scale from naive realism to Pyrrhonism. Yet the question remains, given his meta-theoretical principles, which account of the external world did Hume consider most plausible?

I wish to suggest that he favored a version of indirect realism which describes material objects as the things that cause impressions of sensation, while leaving open a detailed characterization of most of their properties.[7] There are several reasons why I believe this is correct. First, as we have seen, in his discussion of coherence, Hume suggests that positing the existence of material objects provides the best explanation of the phenomenon of interrupted appearance of objects (*T* 196-7). Certainly, such an explanation is simpler than one that interposes God as the cause of one's perceptions (cf. *T* 84), for even if Humean material objects are categorially distinct from perceptions, the 'ontological distance' between perceptions and material objects is not as great as that between perceptions and God (cf. *T* 159-60). Second, in Book II of the *Treatise*, Hume seems to take it as a working hypothesis that material objects cause impressions of sensation (*T* 275-6). Third, in the *Natural History of Religion*, Hume describes 'the most probable, at least the most intelligible philosophy' of nature in terms of the corpuscular hypothesis (*NHR* 29). Corpuscles are at least those things describable in terms of the laws of Newtonian mechanics. Nonetheless, Hume the corpuscularian retains his scepticism regarding the properties of corpuscles, for as he shows in 'Of the Modern Philosophy', primary qualities cannot be conceived as entirely distinct from secondary qualities. Since the primary/secondary qualities distinction was an explanatory hypothesis -- the primary qualities explaining the secondary qualities -- the fact that the qualities in the explanans (the primary qualities) cannot be conceived distinctly from those in the explanandum (the secondary qualities) shows that the hypothesis fails. Thus, although there might be material objects, little can be known of their positive nature.[8] But to discover what can be known regarding material objects within the context of Hume's philosophy, it will be beneficial to consider a different but related issue, namely, the grounds Hume provides for a mind/body distinction.

In the remaining sections of this chapter I argue that Hume was committed to a rather sophisticated form of dualism. I begin with a negative argument that the prevalent interpretation of Hume's position, neutral monism, lacks substantive evidence. This discussion will call into doubt the major competitor to a realistic reading of Hume's views on the external world, namely, a phenomenalistic reading. Next I show that Hume drew a systematic distinction among perceptions, a distinction I call the 'material/immaterial distinction'. Finally, I argue that minds and bodies constitute two systems of entities, and that their distinction is based upon the susceptibility of the entities in each system to spatial relations.

Neutral Monism

Throughout the twentieth century numerous scholars have maintained that Hume accepted or anticipated neutral monism.[9] To evaluate this interpretation we should begin with a commonly held definition of neutral monism (M) and evaluate the textual evidence. Unfortunately, there is no settled definition of M. Consider the following theses: N: All fundamental entities are of only one sort and are neither mental (immaterial) nor physical (material); R: Minds and bodies are reducible to momentary immediate objects of consciousness. One could define M solely in terms of N. On this view HM (Hume held M) is equivalent to HN (Hume held N). One could, on the other hand, define M as the conjunction of N and R, in which case HM would be equivalent to HNR.[10] For my purposes the differences between these two ways of defining M are of no consequence. As I shall show, there are three major difficulties confronting anyone attempting to establish HM. First, one cannot establish N on the basis of R, so one cannot establish HN on the basis of HR. Second, the evidence for HR is, at best, inadequate. Finally, there is no independent evidence for HN.

One who defends *M* in terms of *N* might argue for *HN* on the basis of *HR*, that is, one might argue that since Hume reduced both bodies and minds to perceptions (*HR*), he held *N* and thus was a neutral monist (cf. Shaffer 1967: 340). Is this argument sound? Does *HR* entail *HN*? No, since *R* does not entail *N*. One need not grant *HN* even if one grants that for Hume both minds and bodies are 'bundles' of perceptions. Why should we suppose that Hume did not recognize categorial differences within the class of perceptions which are incompatible with the truth of *N*? It is recognized that he divided perceptions into impressions and ideas and encouraged us to consider them as two kinds of perceptions, so why not consider the possibility of a further division of both into material and immaterial perceptions?

Consider the second difficulty. Assume for the sake of the argument either that *R* does entail *N* or that one defines *M* as *R* and *N* and asserts *HNR*. Did Hume hold *R*? I concede that the Hume of the *Treatise* reduced minds to perceptions. What I hope to show is that there is insufficient evidence to prove that Hume provided a phenomenalistic reduction of bodies to perceptions. Let us begin by considering some arguments that Hume did provide such a reduction.

One argument for his phenomenalism, *HR*, might be based upon Hume's assertion that one's idea of body or substance is nothing but a collection of sensible qualities (*T* 16 and 219). Since phenomenalists claim that bodies consist of nothing but sensible qualities (sense data), it allegedly follows that Hume was a phenomenalist (cf. Hammond 1964: 211). But surely this inference is fallacious. Many non-phenomenalists have held the same view. For example, John Locke, who accepted a theory of material substance, made this claim (Locke, *Essay* 2.23.3-4). Presumably Hume's concern with the idea of body as a collection of qualities was, like Locke's, with providing a method for dividing the world into kinds (cf. *T* 16; Locke, *Essay* 2.23.3-4, 3.6.2-5). But a phenomenalist is not primarily concerned with the meanings of sortal terms. The real issue for the phenomenalist concerns the identity of a collection of sensible qualities over time. A phenomenalist's account of body must provide an analysis of such a common statement as, 'This (brown stem) is the same gardenia that was green last spring.' Since some of the qualities of the gardenia have changed over the months, the phenomenalist must employ notions of identity and continuity that do not depend upon the invariableness of an object. Yet Hume explicitly claimed that the identity of an object, and by implication its continuity, presupposes its invariableness and uninterruptedness through time (*T* 201). Thus, the strictness of his criteria of identity and continuity is incompatible with a phenomenalistic interpretation.

Second, one might claim that Hume's assertion that "tis impossible for us so much as to conceive or form an idea of anything specifically different from ideas and impressions', that is, perceptions (*T* 67), indicates that he accepted *R* and perhaps even *N*. The argument based on this passage presumably is that if only perceptions or combinations of perceptions can be conceived, then minds and bodies, if construed as categorially different from perceptions, are inconceivable, and so must be construed *as* combinations of perceptions. Even if one accepts an ontological reading of this passage,[11] Hume's assertion of this position concerning the limits of the conceivable cannot be considered strong evidence that he held either *R* or *N*. Consider it, first, as evidence for *HN*. The mere fact that we conceive nothing but impressions or impressions and ideas (copies of impressions) does not in any way show that impressions, and hence ideas, cannot be systematically divided into two kinds, immaterial and material. Now for *HR*. Hume maintained that to conceive a world beyond impressions is and must be to conceive a realm of entities causally related to one's impressions. He did not deny the existence or possibility of such a realm. He merely held (a) that we have no independent evidence for the existence of such a realm and (b) that consequently, a philosopher's (and Hume's?) belief in it is parasitic upon one's native belief that some impressions of sense are external objects. He could confidently maintain this because, unlike Berkeley, he allowed that perceptions might exist unperceived (*T* 207). Hence, Hume's doctrine of the limits of the conceivable cannot be said to establish *HR*.

A third argument for *HR* concerns the variety of theories one may propose to justify one's belief in the external world. There are three common candidates for such a theory: naive realism, representationalism and phenomenalism. Since Hume rejected both naive realism (the position of the vulgar) and representationalism (the philosophical theory), it follows that he was a phenomenalist, that is, that he reduced bodies to impressions. So goes the argument. There are several problems here. While it is true that Hume was critical of both naive realism and representationalism, his primary concern in 'Of Scepticism with Regard to the Senses' was not with the justification of one's belief in the external world. His task was to inquire into 'the *causes* which induce us to believe in the existence of body' (*T* 187-8). In line with this, he provided an account of the causes of the common person's naive realism and the philosopher's representationalism. He also argued that the common person's belief is contrary to the facts of the case and that the philosopher's representationalist hypothesis cannot be substantiated by the evidence. As we have seen, his conclusions were, first, that Pyrrhonism and only Pyrrhonism is a philosophically justifiable position regarding the material world, but, second, that such extreme scepticism cannot be sustained psychologically (*T* 218; cf. *EHU* 151-4, 158-60). Hence, unlike the phenomenalist, Hume was not primarily concerned with the justification of one's belief in bodies, and in so far as he concerned himself with that issue, he argued that any belief is ultimately unjustifiable.

There is a further problem with a phenomenalistic interpretation of Hume. Phenomenalism is an attractive theory in so far as it provides a justification for one's native belief in the material world by providing an explanation that is largely immune from sceptical doubt. To avoid the pitfalls of scepticism, the phenomenalist must take sense data to be fundamental and primitive. Although he or she might adhere to the general claim that sense data are caused, to propose specific physical causes of sense data is to reintroduce uncertainty. Yet Hume repeatedly claimed that impressions of sensation are caused by the interaction of material bodies with a living human body (*T* 247-8 and 275-6). Not only does this constitute a causal claim regarding impressions that is too specific for a reductionistic phenomenalist, but it also suggests that bodies are causally prior to impressions of sensation (sense data), a position that is clearly incompatible with phenomenalism. Hence, there is no substantive evidence that Hume was a phenomenalist, that is, there is no evidence for *HR*.

Perhaps not all this argumentation is necessary. Should anyone claim that my criteria for a phenomenalistic reduction are too strict and there is still evidence for *HR* in 'Of Scepticism with Regard to the Senses', I am willing to concede the point so long as the critic does not also hold that *R* entails *N*.[12] So long as one holds either that *R* does not entail *N* or that Hume did not accept *R*, there must be independent evidence for *HN* to establish *HM*. This raises the third difficulty, namely, that there is no independent evidence for *HN*.

There are several passages that might be cited to establish *HN*. The first is a passage in which Hume seems to claim that one ought not take seriously the distinction between perceptions and objects. He wrote:

> I shall at first suppose; that there is only a single existence, which I shall call indifferently *object* or *perception*, according as it shall seem best to suit my purpose, understanding by both of them what any common man means by hat, or shoe, or any other impression, convey'd to him by his senses (*T* 202; cf. *T* 213).

Surely this cannot establish *HN*. The mere fact that Hume used two contrasting terms for a single set of entities does not establish that he drew no categorial distinction with respect to those entities. At most the passage provides evidence for *HR*. He used the examples of a hat and a shoe to illustrate what he meant by the word 'object'. If a hat or a shoe is nothing other than a perception or group of perceptions, one might be inclined to use 'object' and 'perception' indifferently. The neutrality of perceptions, however, remains an open question. It is possible that Hume drew a categorial distinction between material and immaterial perceptions even if he accepted *R*.

Others have found Hume's claim that it is possible for a perception to exist unperceived, that is, without being a component of a mind, to provide telling evidence for *HN* (Laird 1932: 151; Price 1940: 105). The crucial passage follows Hume's famous assertion that the mind is nothing but a collection of related perceptions. It reads:

> Now as every perception is distinguishable from another, and may be consider'd as separately existent; it evidently follows, that there is no absurdity in separating any particular perception from the mind; that is, in breaking off all its relations, with that connected mass of perceptions, which constitute a thinking being. (*T* 207)

If to be mental is to be a mind or something dependent upon a mind, this passage shows that for Hume perceptions are not inherently mental. But did Hume so define the mental? After all, he held that the mind is nothing but a collection of related though logically independent perceptions. The above passage, therefore, does not preclude the possibility that he held a categorial distinction among perceptions that is incompatible with *N*.

The passage cited above is only half of Hume's argument, and if one considers it in conjunction with its complement, a stronger argument for *HN* might be developed. Hume's argument continues:

> If the name *perception* renders not this separation from a mind absurd and contradictory, the name *object*, standing for the very same thing, can never render their conjunction impossible. External objects are seen, and felt, and become present to the mind; that is, they acquire such a relation to a connected heap of perceptions, as to influence them very considerably in augmenting their number by present reflexions and passions, and in storing the memory with ideas. The same continu'd and uninterrupted Being may, therefore, be sometimes present to the mind, and sometimes absent from it, without any real or essential change in the Being itself. (*T* 207)

Whether one refers to any particular entity as a perception or as an object is, it seems, merely a function of the relations that obtain between it and other entities. If the entity is part of a 'bundle' constituting a mind, one refers to it as a perception. If its existence is independent of such a bundle, one refers to it as an object. This seems to suggest that the difference between minds and bodies rests upon the relations among their components and that the entities themselves are fundamentally neutral, that is, it seems to indicate that Hume accepted *N*.

If one looks at these passages within their context, however, one finds that Hume was concerned with a different issue. The argument was presented as a refutation of dependence-idealism, a position such as Berkeley's. This is apparent from the way Hume raised the issue to which his argument is a response. As we have seen, Hume was in the process of offering a causal explanation of the common person's belief that an object of sensible awareness (an impression) is identical with a previous impression, and therefore is capable of independent existence. He paused to consider an objection:

> [A]s the *appearance* of a perception in the mind and its *existence* seem at first sight entirely the same, it may be doubted, whether we can ever assent to so palpable a contradiction, and suppose a perception to exist without being present to the mind. (*T* 206)

If it is possible for an entity to exist independently of a mind, dependence-idealism is refuted, and the common person's belief that certain impressions are external objects is at least consistent (cf. *T* 208). Consequently, the argument cannot preclude the possibility that Hume drew a material/immaterial distinction among perceptions, as long as that distinction is so drawn as not to preclude the separate existence (mind-independence) of both material and immaterial perceptions.

Thus, the question whether Hume accepted *N* remains open. Although it has been shown that the alleged evidence for *HN* will not withstand careful scrutiny, no explicit evidence has been provided that he rejected *N*. However, in turning to the question whether Hume was a dualist, it will be seen that the rejection of *N* is a consequence of his discussion of the nature of perceptions.

The Material/Immaterial Distinction

To determine whether or not Hume was a dualist, it will be necessary to draw several distinctions among dualistic theories. Traditionally, dualism was construed in terms of a dualism of substances. If dualism is understood in this way, it is clear that Hume was *not* a dualist. The substance theorist holds that substance is ontologically fundamental.

This fundamentality often is marked by the independence of substance (cf. Descartes, *Principles*, I, 51; Spinoza 1985: 408; Arnauld 1964: 39). But according to Hume, to make independence the defining characteristic of substance is to allow that even perceptions are substances (*T* 233). Since 'A substance is entirely different from a perception' (*T* 234), it is clear that Hume rejected the doctrine of substance, and therefore was not a substance dualist (cf. *Letters*, I, 94, and *EHU* 155.)

Nonetheless, substance dualism provides one with certain insights regarding dualistic theories. A dualism of substances is a dualism of fundamental entities. Such a theory is a form of what might be called 'entity-dualism'. If Hume was an entity-dualist, he drew a distinction among *his* fundamental entities, impressions. As will be seen, he provided a criterion for such a distinction, a distinction I call the material/immaterial distinction.

Hume's statement of his criterion for a material/immaterial distinction occurs in Book I, Part IV, Section 5 of the *Treatise*. It is part of a reformulation and critical discussion of a commonplace argument for the existence of immaterial substance. It is an argument against the position that a bodily creature that thinks is, or could be, a single substance, namely, a thinking extended substance. The critical premise is that an extension (an item with dimensions) is inherently divisible, whereas thoughts and feelings are not. It is agreed that if an extended thing thinks, the thought is somehow connected with the body. It is further agreed that if a thought is conjoined with the body, it must be at some place or location in the body. From these premises a dilemma is generated. Either the thought must be at some particular place within the body, which makes the place indivisible and therefore not an extended part of the body, or the thought must be in every part of the body, which makes the thought extended, contrary to the original hypothesis. Hence, the supposition of a thinking extended substance is absurd. Thus, there must be both an immaterial thinking substance and an extended material substance (*T* 234-5).

Hume recognized that if the conclusion is to follow from the premises there must be a suppressed substance-requirement premise, a premise he clearly rejected. Nonetheless, apart from this suppressed premise the argument points to an important conclusion: there is a class of objects that is incapable of local conjunction with extended objects. This provided the basis for his material/immaterial distinction. Hume proposed that impressions are to be divided into two mutually exclusive classes: (a) those that are incapable of standing in spatial relations (being directly locatable) and do not generate by combination an extension, and (b) those that are capable of standing in spatial relations (being directly locatable) and do generate extensions. The former cannot be spatially conjoined with the latter. They may be deemed immaterial entities, while the latter may be deemed material entities.

Hume prefaced the statement of his criterion with a discussion of the origin of the ideas of space and extension. The origin of those ideas implies that not all impressions are extended or capable of generating extensions in combination. He wrote:

> The first notion of space and extension is deriv'd solely from the senses of sight and feeling; nor is there any thing, but what is colour'd or tangible, that has parts dispos'd after such a manner, as to convey that idea . . . . Whatever marks the place of its existence either must be extended, or must be a mathematical point, without parts or composition. What is extended must have a particular figure, as square, round, triangular; none of these agree to a desire, or indeed to any impression or idea, except of these two senses above-mentioned. (*T* 235)

The ideas of space and extension are derived solely from the senses of sight and touch. An entity that is available to sight or touch is either extended or a Humean mathematical point, that is, a minimum visible color point or a minimum tactile point (*T* 38-9). Impressions derived from the other senses, as well as impressions of reflection, cannot give rise to the ideas of space and extension, since none of them is locatable relative to a figured impression.

Having indicated that impressions naturally divide themselves into two mutually exclusive classes, those that can give rise to the idea of extension and those that cannot, Hume proceeded to state that spatiality (spatial locatability) constitutes the criterion upon which a material/immaterial distinction rests. In his words:

> 'Twill not be surprising after this, if I deliver a maxim, which is condemn'd by several metaphysicians, and is esteem'd contrary to the most certain principles of human reason. This maxim is *that an object may exist, and yet be no where*: and I assert, that this is not only possible, but that the greatest part of beings do and must exist after this manner. An object may be said to be no where, when its parts are not so situated with respect to each other, as to form any figure or quantity; nor the whole with respect to other bodies as to answer to our notions of contiguity and distance. Now this is evidently the case with all our perceptions and objects, except those of sight and feeling. (*T* 235-6, cf. *T* 504n)

Hume's position was that there is a class of impressions, visible points of color and tactile points of 'feeling', that can be contiguous to or locally conjoined with other points of the same type such that classes of them can compose an extension--a being with magnitude. With this class he contrasted all other impressions which (a) cannot be locally conjoined with one another, (b) cannot comprise a being with magnitude, and (c) cannot be locally conjoined to an extension or any point capable of composing an extension. No impression is a member of both classes. Among the impressions of the second class are sounds, odors, savors, feelings of pleasure and pain, and passions--such as anger or fear. A sound, for example, has no size: it makes no sense to say how long or how wide it is. The ultimate elements of experience and so the ultimate objects are to be divided into two groups, which may be called *material* and *immaterial*.[13]

In drawing the material/immaterial distinction on the basis of the spatiality of impressions, Hume's entity dualism extends to his secondary entities, ideas. Ideas are copies of impressions and possess the same spatial characteristics as the impressions from which they are copied. Hence, the distinction among impressions yields the same distinction among ideas: ideas copied from impressions of sight or touch are material, all others are immaterial entities (*T* 239-40).

The material/immaterial distinction is a categorial distinction drawn among perceptions (impressions and ideas). This establishes that for Hume not all perceptions are entities of the same sort. But if not all perceptions are of the same sort, it follows that Hume rejected *N*, and therefore *HM* is false.

Minds, Bodies, and Interaction

Although Hume drew a material/immaterial distinction among perceptions, his fundamental entities, two further questions remain to be answered. Did Hume consider his systematic distinction between immaterial and material entities to constitute a systematic distinction between minds and bodies? If not, did he draw any systematic distinction between minds and bodies? Before attempting to answer these questions, I must explain what they are asking.

Consider two substance theorists who subscribe to an irreducible systematic distinction between immaterial and material properties. Suppose they agree that a substance is a mind if it has at least one immaterial property and a body is a substance with at least one material property. One of them might hold that no substance can be both a mind and a body, and that the mind/body distinction is correlated with the systematic distinction between immaterial and material properties. (Descartes was such a philosopher.) The other substance theorist might insist or at least allow the possibility that some substances have both material and immaterial features. (Recall Locke's suggestion that matter might think (Locke, *Essay* 4.3.6).) For such a substance theorist the two systematic distinctions (immaterial/material and mind/body) do not exactly correlate. Given these considerations, the first question with respect to Hume is whether he defined minds and bodies as immaterial perceptions and material impressions respectively, that is, whether he had two correlating systematic distinctions. The second question is whether he held any systematic distinction between minds and bodies, and if so, what type of distinction it was.

If for Hume the immaterial/material distinction correlates with the mind/body distinction, bodies are composed of spatial perceptions, that is, perceptions that are extended or capable of generating extensions, while minds are composed of nonspatial perceptions. But this does not fit with the evidence. Surely for Hume ideas are constituents of minds. They also are images (copies) of impressions. But some ideas are of spatial objects or impressions. Since presumably every idea that copies a spatial object is in some sense itself a spatial object (*T* 239-40), it follows that when I remember or reason about the table in my kitchen, one of the ideas composing my mind is spatial, that is, material. What is one to conclude from this? That Hume drew no systematic distinction between minds and bodies? Or that he drew it but in no way related it to his distinction between spatial (material) and nonspatial (immaterial) entities? These conclusions are too extreme. There is some evidence, admittedly less than complete and conclusive, that Hume did utilize spatiality in his attempt to set boundaries between minds and bodies. Let us consider that attempt.

I begin by defining a body as a physical system and defining a physical system as a class of entities each member of which is contiguous with or at a distance from every other member. I define a mind as a mental system and define a mental system as a class of entities such that either spatial relations do not obtain among all its members or whose unity as a system does not depend on the spatial interrelatedness of its members, that is, a system that is not a part of or spatially related to the physical realm.[14] For example, the stream of consciousness constituting a mental system is composed, in part, of visual (material) and auditory (immaterial) impressions. Since visual impressions are, while auditory impressions are not, spatial entities, it is impossible that spatial relations obtain among all members of a mental system. On the other hand, if there is a realm of objects that exist unperceived, this realm would be physical, that is, it would consist of a system or systems of entities unified by spatial relations. My contention is that Hume could and did hold a systematic distinction between minds and bodies, implicitly defining them along the lines just sketched.

It is quite clear that Hume considered the realm of bodies to be one or more physical systems. This is reflected not only in his claim that one's belief in body involves the belief in externality (*T* 190-1), but also in his considerations of causation. One of Hume's paradigms of a causal relation is stated in terms of billiard balls, that is, bodies (*T* 164; *EHU* 29; cf. *T* 12 and 76-7). Indeed, in the *Treatise* his first definition of causation is couched in terms of the relation of spatial contiguity, which indicates that those entities in terms of which he defined causation are in a spatial system (*T* 170, 172, and 173).[15] Thus, even though Hume considered the epistemic question of the existence of bodies irresolvable (*T* 188-218), he held that if bodies exist, they are systems in a spatial realm.[16]

On the other hand, spatial relations do not obtain among all the entities in a mental system, nor is a mental system spatially related to a physical system. Hume briefly discussed these points in 'Of Personal Identity'. He claimed that a mind (mental system) consists of nothing but related perceptions (*T* 207, 252). In spelling out the relations that obtain among the perceptions in a mental system, he indicated that contiguity has 'little or no influence' in such a system. He wrote:

> The only question, therefore, which remains, is by what relations this uninterrupted progress of our thought is produc'd, when we consider the successive existence of a mind or thinking person. And there 'tis evident we must confine ourselves to resemblance and causation, and must drop contiguity, which has little or no influence in the present case. (*T* 260)

At first blush this appears to be a rather curious assertion. After all, Hume's definition of causation was, 'An object precedent and contiguous to another, where all the objects resembling the former are plac'd in like relations of precedency and contiguity to those that resemble the latter' (*T* 170, 172). How is it that Hume came to claim that causation is a relation among perceptions in a mental system, while contiguity is not, even though contiguity is one of the relations that define a cause? Hume had two notions of contiguity: spatial and temporal contiguity (*T* 14). Clearly, spatial contiguity cannot be a factor involved in causal relations among perceptions if not all perceptions are spatial entities. Since it has been shown that Hume drew a material/immaterial distinction on the basis of the spatiality of impressions, it is clear that not all perceptions are susceptible to the relation of spatial contiguity. Thus, it is in keeping with a systematic distinction between mental and physical systems of entities to hold that spatial contiguity has little or no influence in a mental system.[17]

Nor does the absence of spatial contiguity in a mental system preclude causal relations among perceptions. In his initial argument for the essentiality of spatial and temporal contiguity to the causal relation, Hume indicated that there are cases in which contiguity is not essential. There he wrote:

> We may therefore consider the relation of CONTIGUITY as essential to that of causation; at least we may suppose it such, according to the general opinion, till we find a more proper occasion to clear up this matter, by examining what objects are or are not susceptible of position and conjunction. (*T* 75)

In a footnote to this passage, Hume indicates the place where he was to discuss this issue further. The footnote reads, 'Part IV. sect. 5' (*T* 75n), the very passage in which he discussed the material/immaterial distinction. This provides further evidence that a mental system is a system in which not all objects are susceptible to spatial relations.

Furthermore, Hume indicated that no spatial relations obtain between mental and physical systems, that is, that a mental system is not locatable in a physical system. This is clear from the limits to the analogy between a mind and a theater:

> The mind is a kind of theatre, where several perceptions successively make their appearance; pass, re-pass, glide away, and mingle in an infinite variety of postures and situations. . . . They are the successive perceptions only, that constitute the mind; *nor have we the most distant notion of the place, where these scenes are represented*, or the materials, of which it is compos'd. (*T* 253; emphasis added)

A mental system is like a theater in so far as the perceptions of which it is composed appear and disappear, just as actors move to and from a stage. But here the analogy ends. Although all the actors in a theater stand in spatial relations with each other and all the other objects on the stage, spatial relations do not obtain among all the perceptions constituting a mental system. Further, whereas a theater itself stands in spatial relations with other physical objects, Hume's claim that one does not have 'the most distant notion of the place, where these scenes are represented' implies that no spatial relations obtain between a mental system and the physical realm.[18]

But it is not sufficient merely to indicate that Hume drew a distinction between mental and physical systems of entities if one is to demonstrate that he was a mind-body dualist. If mental and physical systems are distinct, one must be able to account for the phenomenon of interaction, a perennial problem for the substance dualist. In Hume's case this is not difficult to do. He held that there is no problem of interaction provided one understands causation in the proper sense. If causation is understood merely in terms of a constant conjunction of objects, anything can be the cause of anything else, and the so-called problem of interaction disappears. As Hume wrote:

> We need only reflect on what has been prov'd at large, that we are never sensible of any connexion betwixt causes and effects, and that 'tis only by our experience of their constant conjunction, we can arrive at any knowledge of this relation. Now as all objects, which are not contrary, are susceptible of a constant conjunction, and as no real objects are contrary; I have inferr'd from these principles, that to consider the matter *a priori*, any thing may produce any thing, and that we shall never discover a reason, why an object may or may not be the cause of any other, however great, or however little the resemblance may be betwixt them. (*T* 247)

Since only experience can discover causal relations, and since there can be no *a priori* reason why there cannot be a causal relation between a mental and a physical system, one's experience of such a relation is sufficient to establish that there is such a relation. (Or, if you wish, if any evidence can establish a causal relationship, it is experience of constant conjunction which is that evidence.) Since Hume went on to claim that ''tis certain we have [such experience]' (*T* 248), it is clear that he held there is causal interaction between mental and physical systems. Hence, his concern with mental-physical interaction together with his considerations of spatiality are sufficient to establish that he held mental and physical systems to be distinct systems of entities.

Conclusions

In this chapter we have examined Hume's discussion of the belief in the external world. I have shown that the discussion in 'Of Scepticism with Regard to the Senses' is a study in doxastic pathology: Hume criticizes the common belief in the existence of material objects (naive realism) and the philosophical account (representationalism) and explains both beliefs on the basis of the principles of the association of ideas. Asking what Hume's own views were regarding the problem of perception and the existence of the external world, I argued that he favored a form of indirect realism, taking external objects to be whatever it is that is described by the laws of Newtonian mechanics and causes one's impressions. This is *suggested* by Hume's discussions of constancy and coherence in conjunction with his meta-theoretical principles. But since many commentators have argued that Hume was a phenomenalist, indeed, a neutral monist, I argued that the case for Hume's phenomenalism cannot be substantiated on the basis of the textual evidence and that the categorial distinctions Hume draws among perceptions are inconsistent with the doctrine of neutral monism. I argued that Hume adhered to a sophisticated form of dualism, a dualism of both entities and systems. He drew a distinction among his fundamental entities, impressions, on the basis of their susceptibility to spatial relations. He drew a further distinction between mental and physical systems of entities on the basis of the susceptibility to spatial relations of *all* the entities in each system. And his theory of causation allowed him to provide a consistent account the interaction between mental and physical systems.

Notes

[1] This is not to say that either critical thinking or philosophical invention is in some sense extraordinary, rather the ordinary mode of thinking is that in which all human beings engage, even philosophers when not doing philosophy. Cf. *T* 98-106, 218, and *EHU* 23-4, 40-7.

[2] Hume's argument at *T* 191 is more complicated than this, indicating that one has no notion of distance on the basis of sense alone, and it is one of the first places where Hume introduces a distinction among perceptions on the basis of their susceptibility to spatial relations. We will examine the importance of susceptibility of an object to spatial relations below.

[3] This is a very general characterization of objects and is consistent with even Berkeley's phenomenalistic account of real objects. (See Berkeley, *PHK* I, 29-34.) This should not be taken to imply, however, that the external objects to which Hume alludes are to be understood phenomenalistically. As we shall see, there is no place in 'Of Scepticism with Regard to the Senses' where Hume claims that an external object is identical with a collection of perceptions, and his characterization of the belief in external objects--particularly his account of the belief in the kind of identity germane to external objects--is, in fact, inconsistent with the requirements of phenomenalism.

[4] This is not surprising, since 'philosophical decisions are nothing but the reflections of common life, methodized and corrected' (*EHU* 162; cf. *D* 134).

[5]This, of course, does not entail that perceptions are *logically* dependent upon perceivers.

[6]Notice what Hume wrote about this in the final paragraph of the section: 'This sceptical doubt, both with respect to reason and the senses, is a malady, which can never be radically cur'd, but must turn upon us every moment, however we may chace it away, and sometimes may seem entirely free from it' (*T* 218).

[7]Fred Wilson recently has defended a similar interpretation, although Wilson seems to put less stock in the role of Hume's sceptical arguments. See Wilson 1989.

[8]If I am correct that Hume's objection to the primary/secondary qualities distinction is an objection based upon theoretical inadequacies, one need not conclude, as Bricke does, that 'the very belief in physical objects can be shown, by causal reasoning, to be false' (Bricke 1980: 11). Physical objects might exist, even if one can say little about their positive nature. The theme that little can be known regarding the positive nature of a thing is common throughout Hume's works. Cf. *D* 142ff.

[9]Hammond 1964: 209-26; Laird 1932: 151; Price 1940: 105-6; Shaffer 1967: 340; Chappell 1972: 88-98.

[10]See Russell 1921: 11, 17-18, 35-6, and 141-2. Several prominent Hume scholars, notably H. H. Price and John Laird, have accepted as their paradigms of neutral monism and reductionistic phenomenalism the discussions Russell developed in *The Analysis of Mind* (Russell 1921), *Our Knowledge of the External World* (Russell 1922), and a pair of essays in *Mysticism and Logic* (Russell 1963: 94-107 and 108-31). (See Price 1940: 105ff, and Laird 1932: 146-56, especially pp. 151-2.) These scholars, therefore, hold that the second definition of neutral monism more properly captures the essence of the doctrine.

[11]I have argued for an alternative reading of the passage in Chapter 1, note 3.

[12]My concession here is merely to demonstrate that even if Hume accepted *R*, *independent evidence would be needed to establish HN*. Were anyone to seriously argue for Hume's phenomenalism, it would be necessary either to discount his repeated claims that certain sensible qualities are incapable of being components of material objects and are merely 'projected' into objects by the mind (*T* 167, 236-7, and 504n), or to establish that the projection thesis is compatible with phenomenalism. Neither alternative is plausible.

[13]At this point someone might object that it is inappropriate to label the distinction between spatial and nonspatial entities the 'material/immaterial distinction', for Hume never refers to it by that name. Nonetheless, since his discussion of the spatial/nonspatial distinction among perceptions occurs within the context of his criticism and reformulation of an argument for the existence of immaterial substances, it seems appropriate to employ these terms in referring to his distinction. On the other hand, some might suggest that the spatial/nonspatial distinction is more readily mapped on to the terms 'physical' and 'mental', since physical objects are extended and many early modern philosophers used the words 'extended' and 'physical' coextensively. I shall

grant this, noting only that Humean mathematical points (minimum visibles or tactile points) are spatially locatable but indivisible and unextended. When I discuss the views of such philosophers as Descartes and Locke in the next section of this chapter and refer to certain properties as material and immaterial, one might well read 'physical' for 'material' and 'mental' for 'immaterial', since those philosophers employed the mental-physical terminology. Nonetheless, I have reserved the terms 'mental' and 'physical' for my discussion of Hume's distinction between mind and body to avoid any confusion with the dualism of perceptions.

Yolton also has acknowledged that Hume drew such a distinction among perceptions (Yolton 1983: 51-2), but, finding it within the context of what he takes to be a purely satirical 'Of the Immateriality of the Soul', he fails to acknowledge the significance of the distinction. As Hume introduces it, the distinction is drawn among characteristics of perceptions, and, as such, has nothing to do with a resemblance account of ideas (cf. Yolton 1983: 51). Further, it is a distinction to which Hume alludes at various other points in the *Treatise* (cf. *T* 76n, 504n), and consequently, it seems unreasonable to suggest that it is introduced purely for satirical purposes.

[14]The fulfillment of either of these conditions is sufficient for a system of entities to be a mental system. Consequently, even if there were a person whose impressions of sensation were limited to sight and to whom impressions of reflection were unavailable, Hume would claim that his or her mind would be a mental system, since, as will be seen below, Hume held that no mind is locatable in the physical realm (realm of bodies).

[15]The paradigms Hume employed played a significant role in the definitions of causation he offered. In the *Treatise* his paradigm was billiard balls, that is, bodies, and as a consequence he employed the notion of spatial contiguity in his first definition. When he came to define causation in the first *Enquiry*, his discussion focused on volition, and no reference to spatial contiguity was made in his definitions (*EHU* 76-7). Should this be considered inconsistent, one should note that 'Where objects are not contrary, nothing hinders them from having that constant conjunction, on which the relation of cause and effect totally depends' (*T* 173). Since no existent objects are contrary (*T* 173), anything can be the cause of anything else. As will be seen below, when Hume departed from his paradigm of causation in the *Treatise*, that is, causation among bodies, he held that there are certain cases in which spatial contiguity is inessential to causation.

[16]Nonetheless, it is clear that he accepted the existence of bodies as a working assumption. Note that at *T* 187 he wrote, 'We may well ask, *What causes induce us to believe in the existence of bodies?* but 'tis in vain to ask, *Whether there be body or not?* That is a point, which we must take for granted in all our reasonings'. Further, as we saw above, the physicalist hypothesis provides the best explanation of the cause of impressions.

[17]The perceptive reader will have noticed that the passage quoted above is from 'Of Personal Identity'. Since one can reasonably suggest that Hume's task in that section was to examine the causes of one's belief in personal

identity, it could be suggested that the passage says nothing regarding the relations that obtain among perceptions in a mental system. Nonetheless, since Hume explicitly stated that perceptions in a mental system are united by the relations of association, that is, resemblance, spatial and temporal contiguity, and causation (*T* 10-11), it is reasonable to take this passage to indicate that spatial contiguity is the least significant of the relations of association.

[18]Some may claim that the evidence is inconsistent in this regard. At *T* 60-1, Hume wrote as if ideas are literally in the brain. If ideas are literally in the brain they are spatial entities, and if ideas are spatial entities this is inconsistent with claiming that Hume held to dualisms of entities and systems along the lines I have proposed. Nonetheless, two things are worthy of notice. First, when Hume wrote as if ideas are literally in the brain, he was presenting a 'specious and plausible' account of why the principles of association lead one into error (*T* 60). Since the account was labeled 'specious', this suggests that one ought not take it as a literal indication of Hume's position. Second, at one point Hume also spoke as if impressions literally strike on the organs of sense (*T* 7-8). Taken literally, such a claim is inconsistent with his repeated assertions that impressions of sensation are caused by the interaction of external objects with a functioning human body (*T* 247-8, 275-6). However, if one keeps in mind that the meaning Hume attached to the word 'impression' differed from both the common and the philosophical usage of his time (*T* 2n; *EHU* 18; see also Cummins 1973b: 297-301), the reference to impressions striking upon the senses is best understood as a metaphorical means of referring to the causes of impressions. Similarly, the passage that speaks of ideas in the brain is consistent with Hume's discussion of perceptions only if one understand the phrase 'ideas in the brain' to refer to the neural mechanism that causes ideas.

7
Personal Identity

Any adequate interpretation of Hume's discussions of personal identity must explain why he considered the discussion in the body of the *Treatise* a veritable 'labyrinth of contradictions' (cf. *T* 633). In this chapter I argue that if 'Of Personal Identity' is part of a more general theoretical enterprise, an explanation of Hume's lamentations in the Appendix can be provided. I begin by showing that the discussion in 'Of Personal Identity' is primarily an application and amplification of the explanation of the belief in the identity and simplicity of substance found in 'Of the Antient Philosophy' (cf. Brett 1972; Wolfram 1974; Penelhum 1975a: 75-9; Penelhum 1975b; Penelhum 1976: 10-11). But the explanation fails, for even if Hume can explain why one believes in the perfect numerical identity of the mind on the basis of a conflation of several kinds of identity, he cannot apply the same considerations *mutatis mutandis* to the belief in simplicity. The result is a series of seemingly irresolvable paradoxes, paradoxes that call into doubt the most fundamental aspects of his theory of mind. This explains why, at the end of the Appendix, Hume can do no more than 'plead the privilege of a sceptic' (*T* 636).

'Of Personal Identity'

Hume begins his discussion 'Of Personal Identity' by noting that 'There are some philosophers, who imagine we are every moment intimately conscious of what we call our SELF; that we feel its existence and continuance in existence; and are certain, beyond the evidence of demonstration, both of its perfect identity and simplicity' (*T* 251). As we have seen, Hume commonly characterizes the belief in substance as the belief in the simplicity and identity of an object (*T* 219-21), and it is certainly to the belief in a substantial self that Hume here alludes. This belief, of course, Hume takes to be unwarranted, and in the second paragraph of the section he presents an argument or series of arguments to show that it is impossible to have an idea of a simple and perfectly identical self. He wrote:

> Unluckily all these positive assertions are contrary to that very experience, which is pleaded for them, nor have we any idea of the *self*, after the manner it is here explain'd. For from what impression cou'd this idea be deriv'd? This question 'tis impossible to answer without a manifest contradiction and absurdity; and yet 'tis a question, which must necessarily be answer'd, if we wou'd have the idea of self pass for clear and intelligible. It must be some one impression, that gives rise to every real idea. But self or person is not any one impression, but that to which our several impressions and ideas are suppos'd to have reference. If any impression gives rise to the idea of self, that impression must continue invariably the same, thro' the whole course of our lives; since self is suppos'd to exist after that manner. But there is no impression constant and invariable. Pain and pleasure, grief and joy, passions and sensations succeed each other, and never all exist at the same time. It cannot, therefore, be from any of these impressions, or from any other, that the idea of self is deriv'd; and consequently there is no such idea. (*T* 251-2)

While this paragraph is certainly not a paradigm of clarity (cf. Traiger 1985), when examined in the light of Hume's earlier attacks on the doctrine of substance, the intent of Hume's claims seems clear. First, since Hume raises the question of the impression from which the idea of self is copied, he must be taken to be concerned solely with positive ideas (images). Second, since one is concerned with an idea of a *simple* entity, the positive idea itself must be simple. Third, it must be taken to represent on the basis of resemblance, for simple ideas are 'copies' of simple impressions and it is on the basis of resemblance that things are divided into kinds. Hence, the idea in question must be a simple idea of an impression which is identical through time. But since 'all impressions are internal and perishing existences, and appear as such' (*T* 194), it is at least inconsistent with this *fact* about impressions to contend that there could be an idea of a thing that is perfectly identical through time. Further, the contents of one's impressions of sensation and reflection are not things of the sort needed to provide one with an idea of an entity that is identical through time. One's impressions are limited to sensible qualities and the 'feelings' peculiar to the several cognitive and emotional states. Hence, it is inconsistent with the *facts* regarding the contents of impressions to claim that there is an impression, and consequently an idea, of a simple and perfectly identical self. Finally, as we have noticed in discussing 'Of the Immateriality of the Soul', Hume argued that the only way an idea could represent a substance would be for it to have all the qualities of a substance, and therefore, to be derived from an impression that has all the qualities peculiar to a substance. However, such an impression itself would be a substance (*T* 232-3), a position any substance theorist would deem 'a manifest contradiction and absurdity' (*T* 251; cf. *T* 234). But since only ideas that are copied from impressions are clear (cf. *T* 72-3), if it is impossible to have an impression of a substantial self, it is also impossible to have a clear idea of it. Consequently, it is unintelligible to claim the self is simple and perfectly identical through time.

Hume continues by rehearsing the argument he had advanced against the Cartesian definition of substance in 'Of the Immateriality of the Soul' (*T* 233), arguing that since 'All [our particular perceptions] are different, and distinguishable, and separable from each other, and may be separately consider'd, and may exist separately, and have no need of any thing to support their existence', they cannot be connected with a 'self' that is distinct from them (*T* 252). He draws out the implications of the metaphysical independence and particularity of perceptions by commenting on what he learns on the basis of introspection, namely, that he no substantial self can be discovered and that experience provides grounds for claiming that there is no continuous self. In Hume's words:

For my part, when I enter most intimately into what I call *myself*, I always stumble on some particular perception or other, of heat or cold, light or shade, love or hatred, pain or pleasure. I never catch *myself* at any time without a particular perception, and never can observe any thing but the perception. When my perceptions are remov'd for any time, as by sound sleep; so long am I insensible of *myself*, and may be truly said not to exist. And were all my perceptions remov'd by death, and cou'd I neither think, nor feel, nor see, nor love, nor hate after the dissolution of my body, I shou'd be a perfect non-entity. If any one upon serious reflexion, thinks he has a different notion of *himself*, I must confess I can reason no longer with him. All I can allow him is, that he may be in the right as well as I, and that we are essentially different in this particular. He may, perhaps, perceive something simple and continu'd, which he calls *himself*; tho' I am certain there is no such principle in me.

In examining himself, Hume found nothing more than particular perceptions. Further, given that perfect identity presupposes uninterruptedness through time (*T* 201, 253), there are no experiential grounds for attributing identity to the self, for the self available to introspection is temporally discontinuous. Hume claims that when one is in a deep sleep, there is no awareness of perceptions, which is a sufficient condition for the nonexistence of the self. If all one's perceptions were removed upon death, this would be sufficient to constitute a complete annihilation of the self. Since perceptions are individual existents and are conditions *sine qua non* for the existence of the self, there is no reason to believe that the mind is composed of anything over and above perceptions. Nevertheless, Hume allowed--ironically, given his previous arguments regarding the limitations of one's perceptions--that others might be aware of a self that is distinct from perceptions.

Having provided grounds for calling the common belief in the substantiality of the mind into doubt, Hume provided a positive characterization of the mind as 'nothing but a bundle or collection of different perceptions, which succeed each other with an inconceivable rapidity, and are in a perpetual flux and movement' (*T* 252; cf. *T* 207). After indicating that the mind is analogous to a theater, and asserting that 'There is properly no *simplicity* in it at one time, nor *identity* in different; whatever natural propension we may have to imagine that simplicity and identity' (*T* 253), he proceeded to inquire into the causal basis for the natural tendency to ascribe identity to the mind. He wrote:

> What then gives us so great a propension to ascribe an identity to these successive perceptions, and to suppose ourselves possest of an invariable and uninterrupted existence, thro' the whole course of our lives? In order to answer this question, we must distinguish betwixt personal identity, as it regards our thought or imagination, and as it regards our passions or the concern we take with ourselves. The first is our present subject; and to explain it perfectly we must take the matter pretty deep, and account for that identity, which we attribute to plants and animals; there being a great analogy betwixt it, and the identity of a self or person. (*T* 253)

Hume proposed to examine the causes of one's belief in personal identity. He was concerned only with personal identity as it pertains to a thinking and sensible being, not as it pertains to a passionate being. Through analogies with the sort of identity one ascribes to plants and animals, indeed, through considerations of the criteria one employs in attributing identity to many kinds of things, Hume proposed to explain one's belief that the mind is identical through time.[1]

Hume proceeds to offer an explanation of the belief in the perfect identity of the mind along now familiar lines. Defining 'identity' in terms of the invariableness and uninterruptedness of an object 'thro' a suppos'd variation of time', and defining 'diversity' in terms of 'a distinct idea of several different objects existing in succession, and connected by a close relation' (*T* 253, cf. 201), Hume notes that the ideas of identity and diversity 'are generally confounded with each other' (*T* 253, cf. 202). He explains:

> That action of the imagination, by which we consider the uninter-rupted and invariable object, and that by which we reflect on the succession of related objects, are almost the same to the feeling, nor is there much more effort of thought requir'd in the latter case than in the former. The relation facilitates the transition of the mind from one object to another, and renders its passage as smooth as if it contemplated one continu'd object. This resemblance is the cause of the confusion and mistake, and makes us substitute the notion of identity, instead of that of related objects. (*T* 253-4)

Notice that Hume here explains the conflation of the ideas of identity and diversity in much the same way he had done in 'Of Scepticism with Regard to the Senses' (*T* 204-5), but the differences should be noted. In the earlier discussion, Hume claimed that the resemblance relation obtains among both the perceptions and acts of the mind; in this discussion he claims that the resemblance relation obtains *only* among the actions of the imagination, while an unspecified 'close relation' obtains among the perceptions (*T* 253). As we shall see, this 'close relation' is a combination of causal and resemblance relations; it cannot be resemblance relations alone, since the perceptions in the mind are of different kinds. Hence, in the case of the belief in mental identity, it is primarily on the basis of resemblances among 'actions of the imagination' that Hume explains the conflation of identity and diversity.

But the conflation of identity and diversity is unstable, and it is the conflict between the tendency to ascribe identity to the mind and diversity to the distinct perceptions that explains one's tendency to posit the existence of a mental substance. As Hume wrote:

> However at one instant we may consider the related succession as variable or interrupted, we are sure the next to ascribe to it a perfect identity, and regard it as invariable and uninterrupted. Our propensity to this mistake is so great from the resemblance above-mention'd, that we fall into it before we are aware; and tho' we

incessantly correct ourselves by reflexion, and return to a more accurate method of thinking, yet we cannot long sustain our philosophy, or take off this biass from the imagination. Our last resource is to yield to it, and boldly assert that these different related objects are in effect the same, however interrupted and variable. In order to justify ourselves this absurdity, we often feign some new and unintelligible principle, that connects the objects together, and prevents their interruption and variation. Thus we feign the continu'd existence of the perceptions of our senses, to remove the interruption; and run into the notion of a *soul*, and *self*, and *substance*, to disguise the variation. But we may farther observe, that where we do not give rise to such a fiction, our propension to confound identity with relation is so great, that we are apt to imagine something unknown and mysterious, connecting the parts, beside their relation; and this I take to be the case with regard to the identity we ascribe to plants and vegetables. And even when this does not take place, we still feel a propensity to confound these ideas, tho' we are not able fully to satisfy ourselves in that particular, nor find any thing invariable and uninterrupted to justify our notion of identity. (*T* 254-5)

In observing the mind, it is always possible to notice the individual perceptions, and thereby to notice that one's perceptions vary. But the smoothness of the transition from one perception to the next is so great that one typically will deem the mind one thing, that is, one will claim 'that these different related objects are in effect the same, however interrupted and variable'. Since there is a conflict between this and the 'more accurate method of thinking' of each of the perceptions as an individual, one generally posits either the existence of a substance in which perceptions inhere or the existence of necessary connections among objects. In the first case, the mind is taken to be something distinct from perceptions, and perceptions are taken to be essentially mind-dependent. In the second case, the mind is a whole composed of perceptions, but each perception is essentially connected with every other.[2] In either case, the mind is held to be unified into one thing, but only at the price of theoretical intelligibility and simplicity. It is because of this common propensity to posit either a substantial self or of necessary connections among the perceptions in a mind that Hume claimed 'the controversy concerning identity is not merely a dispute of words' (*T* 255).

One naturally believes in the strict identity of items which critical reflection discovers to be classes of distinct objects. Substances or real connections are invented to save one's natural beliefs from the ravages of critical reflection. If the belief in identity in general, and personal identity in particular, involves uncritical if not mistaken commitments, then Hume's position is plausible only if he can provide a plausible explanation of one's natural, though uncritical, belief in identity. In particular, to support his theory of mind, he must explain all improper ascriptions of identity on the basis of the principles of the association of ideas. To do this, he considered several cases in which one attributes identity to objects that are not perfectly identical through time. Let us examine the case of ascribing identity to an object in spite of minute changes in detail, since this provides the basis for understanding his accounts of identity claims in cases of more radical change.

If there is little change in an object, one overlooks the change and attributes identity to the properly distinct objects. As Hume wrote:

> In order to this, suppose any mass of matter, of which the parts are contiguous and connected, to be plac'd before us; 'tis plain we must attribute a perfect identity to this mass, provided all the parts continue uninterruptedly and invariably the same, whatever motion or change of place we may observe either in the whole or in any of its parts. But supposing some very *small* or *inconsiderable* part to be added to the mass, or substracted from it; tho' this absolutely destroys the identity of the whole, strictly speaking; yet as we seldom think so accurately, we scruple not to pronounce a mass of matter the same, where we find so trivial an alteration. The passage of the thought from the object before the change to the object after it, is so smooth and easy, that we scarce perceive the transition, and are apt to imagine, that 'tis nothing but a continu'd survey of the same object. (*T* 255-6; cf. Locke, *Essay* 2.27.3)

Consider a cube of wood with a two-inch side. The cube retains its identity so long as there is no change in the matter composing it. But by this strict criterion of identity, any change in the matter composing the cube, however minute, would destroy its identity over time.[3] But, in fact, one does not apply so strict a criterion of identity. Assume one hundredth of an inch of wood were shaved from each face of the cube. Would one, in fact, claim it is the same mass of matter? Hume suggested one would, since the amount of change is relatively insignificant.

This consideration led Hume to his first general conclusion: it is the proportion of the change, not change *per se*, that accounts for one's ascriptions of identity or diversity. As he wrote:

There is a very remarkable circumstance, that attends this experiment; which is, that tho' the change of any considerable part in a mass of matter destroys the identity of the whole, yet we must measure the greatness of the part, not absolutely, but by its *proportion* to the whole. The addition or diminution of a mountain wou'd not be sufficient to produce a diversity in a planet; tho' the change of a very few inches wou'd be able to destroy the identity of some bodies. 'Twill be impossible to account for this, but by reflecting that objects operate upon the mind, and break or interrupt the continuity of its actions not according to their real greatness, but according to their proportion or each other: And therefore, since this interruption makes an object cease to appear the same, it must be the uninterrupted progress of the thought, which constitutes the imperfect identity. (*T* 256; cf. Locke, *Essay* 2.27.3)

When an object changes slightly, one still will assert that there is a single object that is identical throughout the change. On the other hand, if there is a proportionately large change in an object, one might not claim identity. For example, it is sometimes such a proportionately large change in the amount or arrangement of matter that explains why it might be difficult to recognize one's former classmates at a reunion. Hume could account for these differences in one's ascriptions of identity on the basis of the effects these changes have on perceiving mind. If there is a slight change, one's flow of thought is not interrupted, and one claims that the original object is identical with the subsequent object. The interruption in one's thought when there is a major change in the object accounts for one's ascription of diversity.[4]

Hume's discussion of one's tendency to ascribe identity to an object in the face of quantitative change yields the first of two important distinctions regarding identity: the distinction between perfect and imperfect identity.[5] Perfect identity may be ascribed only to such objects as are invariable and uninterrupted through a period of time. Imperfect identity is the identity one in fact ascribes to an object that changes, but changes without interruption, and which, therefore, does not interrupt the progress of one's thought. Thus, since most of one's ascriptions of identity do not comply with the criteria for perfect identity, they can be only ascriptions of imperfect identity.

Hume continued by examining further factors that lead to improper ascriptions of identity. These factors included the gradual rate at which changes occur (*T* 256), the presumption that the parts of an object have a common end or purpose (*T* 257), and the presumption that there are reciprocal causal relations among the parts of an object such as a plant or an animal (a sympathy of parts) (*T* 257; cf. Locke, *Essay*, 2.27.3, and Shaftesbury 1964: 2:100). In each of these cases the general form of the argument is the same: if any particular change is proportionately small and one or more of these general factors obtain, then the mental transition involved in observing the changes is sufficiently smooth that one attributes identity to the object in spite of the changes.

Hume continued his discussion of the causes of mistaken but commonplace identity claims by presenting the second of his distinctions regarding identity. He wrote:

> We may also consider the two following phenomena, which are remarkable in their kind. The first is that tho' we commonly are able to distinguish pretty exactly betwixt numerical and specific identity, yet it sometimes happens, that we confound them, and in our thinking and reasoning employ the one for the other. Thus a man, who hears a noise, that is frequently interrupted and renew'd, says, it is still the same noise; tho' 'tis evident the sounds have only a specific identity or resemblance, and there is nothing numerically the same, but the cause, which produc'd them. (*T* 257-8)

The distinction between numerical and specific identity can be confused, and this can lead to an ascription of numerical identity where only specific identity obtains. To understand this claim one must differentiate what Hume meant by numerical and specific identity.

In 'Of Scepticism with Regard to the Senses', as here, Hume was concerned with misascriptions of numerical identity. In the earlier section, after defining 'identity' in terms of invariableness and uninterruptedness (*T* 201), he pointedly indicated that he was referring to numerical identity. He wrote:

> I now proceed to explain the *second* part of my system, and shew why the constancy of our perceptions makes us ascribe to them a *perfect numerical identity*, tho' there be very long intervals betwixt their appearance, and they have only one of the essential qualities of identity, *viz. invariableness*. (*T* 201-2, emphasis added).

In 'Of Scepticism with Regard to the Senses' Hume intended to demonstrate that the invariableness of one's perceptions of an object leads to the claim that the existence of an object is uninterrupted. Each time one sees the table in one's kitchen, one's visual impressions resemble all previous visual impressions of it (cf. *T* 209). The difference between this case and that of a discontinuous noise is that in the former case it is one's *experience* that is interrupted, while in the latter case the *noise* is interrupted within a segment of one's experience. Since an object's cessation in existence is contrary to the uninterruptedness essential to numerical identity, while its change is not (even though it is contrary to invariableness), the assertion of identity through change that is implicit in the notion of imperfect identity indicates that the distinction between perfect and imperfect identity was drawn on the side of numerical identity. On the other hand, specific identity or identity of kind is concerned only with resemblances among numerically distinct objects (cf. *T* 15, 20). Except in the trivial sense in which every object is of the same kind with itself, specific identity presupposes numerical distinctness.[6]

Hume's final example of a false claim of numerical identity concerns the identity of a river. In his words:

> Secondly, We may remark, that tho' in a succession of related objects, it be in a manner requisite that the change of parts be not sudden nor entire, in order to preserve the identity, yet where the objects are by their nature changeable and inconstant, we admit of a more sudden transition, than wou'd otherwise be consistent with the relation. Thus as the nature of a river consists in the motion and change of parts; tho' in less than four and twenty hours these be totally alter'd; this hinders not the river from continuing the same during several ages. What is natural and essential to any thing is, in a manner, expected; and what is expected makes less impression, and appears of less moment, than what is unusual and extraordinary. A considerable change of the former kind seems really less to the imagination, than the most trivial alteration of the latter; and by breaking less the continuity of the thought, has less influence in destroying the identity. (*T* 258; cf. Arnauld 1964: 145)

The slightest change is sufficient to destroy the numerical identity of an object, one would have to grant Heraclitus that one never can step in the same river twice. But, if one observes a flowing body of water from the same point on two distinct days, one will call it the same river, even though none of the water is the same on the second day. Unlike changes in many natural objects, the change of the water constituting a river is rapid. The basis for claiming the identity of the river over time lies not merely in a confusion of numerical with specific identity, it also rests upon the conformity of the changes in the river with one's expectations. It is essential to a river that the water of which it is composed be in a constant state of change. The realization of this expectation complies with the continuity of thought, and for that reason one declares the river numerically identical over time.

To this point Hume has concerned himself solely with false ascriptions of perfect numerical identity. Although a correct ascription of perfect numerical identity requires that an object exist without interruption and variation through a period of time, when there is a gradual change, one will attribute numerical identity to the series of objects. Such identity Hume calls 'imperfect identity'. If there is an interruption in the existence of an object, that object cannot be numerically identical with a subsequent object, although the subsequent object can be specifically identical (resembling, identical in kind). Nonetheless, one often conflates numerical and specific identity, and the propensity toward such a conflation is most pronounced when perpetual change is an essential characteristic of an object such as a river.

With his preliminary discussion of identity completed, Hume focused his attention on one's belief in personal identity. He wrote:

> We now proceed to explain the nature of *personal identity*, which has become so great a question in philosophy, especially of late years in *England*, where all the abstruser sciences are study'd with a peculiar ardour and application. And here 'tis evident, the same method of reasoning must be continu'd, which has so successfully explain'd the identity of plants, and animals, and ships, and houses, and of all the compounded and changeable productions either of art or nature. The identity which we ascribe to the mind of man, is only a fictitious one, and of a like kind with that which we ascribe to vegetables and animal bodies. It cannot, therefore, have a different origin, but must proceed from a like operation of the imagination upon like objects. (*T* 259)

This paragraph makes clear that Hume's previous discussions of false ascriptions of identity were merely a propaedeutic to his discussion of personal identity. If one understands why one improperly attributes identity to material objects, one has the basis for explaining one's belief that one's mind is perfectly identical over time. His assertion that the same method of reasoning is to be employed that was used to explain ascriptions of identity to '*all* the compounded and changeable productions either of art or nature' (*T* 259, my emphasis), indicates the complexity of the issue. To account for one's belief in the perfect identity of the mind, Hume appealed to the causes of one's ascription of perfect numerical identity to objects that are imperfectly identical, to those objects that are only specifically identical, and to those that are in a perpetual flux.[7]

Having stated his general thesis, that 'the identity, which we ascribe to the mind is only a fictitious one' (*T* 259), Hume defends the claim by reaffirming that perceptions are *essentially* individual entities, that 'every distinct perception, which enters into the composition of the mind, is a distinct existence, and is different, and distinguishable, and separable from every other perception either contemporary or successive' (*T* 259). Noting that, in spite of this, 'we suppose the whole train of perceptions to be united by identity', he asks whether there is 'something that really binds our several perceptions together, or only associates their ideas in the imagination' (*T* 259). The issue with which he is concerned is the Shaftesburian contention that there are real or necessary connections among the perceptions that constitute the mind. He argues that there are no such connections. Citing his earlier discussion of necessary connections (*T* 259-60; cf. *T* 155-72), he concludes that there are no good grounds for claiming necessary connections among perceptions. Hence, the perceptions in the mind are 'connected' by nothing stronger than the relations of the association of ideas. Because of this, the perceptions retain their status as independent existents, and the identity of the mind is properly a fiction.

Yet, given his enumeration of the several senses of 'identity', there is *some* sense in which the mind can be deemed identical through time, and it is 'on some of these three relations of resemblance, contiguity and causation, that identity depends' (*T* 260). Hume argued that of these relations, resemblance and contiguity alone play a role in providing a smooth transition between, and therefore in ascribing identity to, temporally separated perceptions: resemblance in memory and causation in a myriad of mental phenomena (*T* 260-1).[8] While discussing causal relations among perceptions, Hume provided an analogy between a mind and a commonwealth that is instructive regarding one's tendency to ascribe (perfect) identity to the mind. He wrote:

> In this respect, I cannot compare the soul more properly to any thing than a republic or commonwealth, in which the several members are united by the reciprocal ties of government and subordination, and give rise to other persons, who propagate the same republic in the incessant changes of its parts. And as the same individual republic may not only change its members, but also its laws and constitutions; in like manner the same person may vary his character and disposition, as well as his impressions and ideas, without losing his identity. Whatever changes he endures, his several parts are still connected by the relation of causation. And in this view our identity with regard to the passions serves to corroborate that with regard to the imagination, by making our distant perceptions influence each other, and by giving us a present concern for our past or future pains and pleasures. (*T* 261)

The mind, like a republic, consists of distinct but related parts. A republic consists of individuals who live for a period of time, interact together, bear or fail to bear children, and die. Similarly, the mind consists of a series of perceptions that cause other perceptions. The individuals composing a republic or commonwealth are regulated by the laws of that republic. Similarly, causal relations provide the regularity found among the perceptions in the mind. As a republic is capable of changing, so is a mind, and both retain an imperfect identity through change. It is due to the assumption that there is a common end and sympathy of (reciprocal causal relations among) parts through change that Hume could claim that the identity of both a republic and a mind are similar to the identity of a plant or animal body (cf. *T* 259).

The analogy, however, is imperfect, for there are two respects in which the mind is not analogous to a republic. By acknowledging the limits of the analogy, one discovers the roles played by specific identity and the sort of identity applicable to objects in perpetual flux in one's belief in personal identity. Consider the French Third Republic. The Third Republic existed without interruption between 1870 and 1940. The mind, on the other hand, exists only during one's periods of consciousness (cf. *T* 252). The discontinuous existence of a mind is the first respect in which a mind and a republic are disanalogous. The second lies in the rate of change involved in each. The mass of individuals that compose a republic changes slowly over a period of years. The perceptions constituting a mind, on the other hand, 'succeed each other with an inconceivable rapidity, and are in a perpetual flux and movement' (*T* 252). In the first case, the ascription of identity to a mind is like the ascription of identity to an interrupted sound, and in the second, it is like the ascription of numerical identity to a river. Since Hume had argued that such ascriptions of identity rest upon a conflation of numerical and specific identity, the ascription of identity to the mind must stem from the same root.

Having explained the false ascriptions of perfect numerical identity involved in one's belief in personal identity, Hume inquired into the source of that belief. He located it in memory. As he wrote:

> As memory alone acquaints us with the continuance and extent of this succession of perceptions, 'tis to be consider'd, upon that account chiefly, as the source of personal identity. Had we no memory, we never shou'd have any notion of causation, nor consequently of that chain of causes and effects, which constitute our self or person. But having once acquir'd this notion of causation from the memory, we can extend the same chain of causes, and consequently the identity of persons beyond our memory, and can comprehend times, and circumstances, and actions, which we

have entirely forgot, but suppose in general to have existed. For how few of our past actions are there, of which we have any memory? Who can tell me, for instance, where were his thought and actions on the first of *January* 1715, the 11th of *March* 1719, and the 3d of *August* 1733? Or will he affirm, because he has entirely forgot the incidents of these days, that the present self is not the same person with the self of that time; and by that means overturn all the most establish'd notions of personal identity? In this view, therefore, memory does not so much *produce* as *discover* personal identity, by shewing us the relations of cause and effect among our different perceptions. 'Twill be incumbent on those, who affirm that memory produces entirely our personal identity, to give reason why we can thus extend our identity beyond memory. (*T* 261-2)

Memory functions in two significant ways in causing a belief in the identity of the mind. First, it acquaints one with past perceptions, and thereby indicates the temporal reach of the perceptions constituting the mind. Second, memory is necessary for one to have a notion of causation. Causal reasoning allows one to fill in the gaps in one's memory. Further, in so far as each memory is itself caused, the memory makes one aware of the existence of relations among the perceptions in one's mind. Since these causal relations lead to the ascription of identity to the mind, it is fundamentally upon these relations that one's belief in personal identity depends. Since memory *discovers* causal relations, it more properly can be said to *discover* than to produce the belief in personal identity.

Hume concludes his discussion of personal identity by reaffirming that there is a sense in which disputes concerning personal identity are philosophically significant and indicating that there is another sense in which they are merely verbal. He wrote:

The whole of this doctrine leads us to a conclusion, which is of great importance in the present affair, *viz.*, that all the nice and subtle questions concerning personal identity can never be decided, and are to be regarded rather as grammatical than as philosophical disputes. Identity depends on the relations of ideas; and these relations produce identity, by means of that easy transition they occasion. But as the relations, and the easiness of the transition may diminish by insensible degrees, we have no just standard by which we can decide any dispute concerning the time, when they acquire or lose a title to the name of identity. All the disputes concerning the identity of connected objects are merely verbal, except so far as the relation of parts gives rise to some fiction or imaginary principle of union, as we have already observ'd. (*T* 262)

Disputes regarding the identity of the mind are, *as such*, verbal. Given a strict notion of perfect numerical identity, it is improper to declare the mind identical over time. On the other hand, if one uses the less stringent notions of imperfect numerical identity and specific identity, one can attribute identity to the mind. The issue is of philosophical significance only if in claiming the identity of the mind one posits either the existence of an imperceptible substance or real (necessary) connections among perceptions as a ground for claiming the perfect numerical identity of the mind. Such a philosophical theory lacks both the intelligibility and simplicity of a bundle theory constructed along the lines Hume proposed. Further, if his several explanations of problematic beliefs are adequate, Hume has gone some distance toward showing that his bundle theory of mind is preferable to a substance theory.

But Hume is not finished. He has examined the belief in the identity of the mind through time, found the belief wanting, and explained why one holds the belief in spite of its lack of evidence. But the belief in the *identity* of the mind is not the whole of the philosophical belief (and belief of the common person (*T* 253)) with which Hume began. Recall Hume reported that these philosophers 'are certain, beyond the evidence of a demonstration, both of [the] perfect identity and simplicity' of the mind (*T* 251). Having examined the belief in the identity of the mind at length, it was incumbent upon Hume to provide a similar examination of the belief in the simplicity of the mind: it is only if he could show that both beliefs are evidentially unwarranted but explainable on the basis of the principles of the association of ideas that he could account for the common belief in mental substance. Hume suggests that both the problems with and the explanation of the belief in the simplicity of the mind parallel his discussion of the belief in identity. As he wrote in the penultimate paragraph of the section:

What I have said concerning the first origin and uncertainty of our notion of identity, as apply'd to the human mind, may be extended with little or no variation to that of *simplicity*. An object, whose different co-existent parts are bound together by a close relation, operates upon the imagination after much the same manner as one perfectly simple and indivisible, and requires not a much greater stretch of thought in order to its conception. From this similarity of operation we attribute a simplicity to it, and feign a principle of union as the support of this simplicity, and the center of all the different parts and qualities of the objects. (*T* 263)

Why could Hume so confidently claim that the belief in the simplicity of the mind, the second aspect necessary to account for the belief in mental substance, is exactly parallel to the belief in the identity of the mind? The reason seems to be that he had already explained the belief in the existence of material substance, and in the former case the two explanations were parallel (cf. *T* 220-1). This would at least provide Hume with the *presumption* that in explaining the belief in the identity of the mind he had provided all the materials necessary to construct a parallel explanation of the belief in simplicity and that he could leave the detailed construction of this explanation as little more than an exercise for the reader.

With his explanation of the belief in personal identity (the belief in the substantiality of the mind) Hume's explanatory program comes to an end. We have seen that he critically examined the doctrine of material substance and the contention that there are real or necessary connections among perceptions. He critically examined both the common and the philosophical beliefs in the existence of material objects. And he critically examined the belief in personal identity (mental substance). In each case, the sceptical arguments 'admit of no answer and produce no conviction' (*EHU* 155n), that is, the beliefs in question are shown to be unwarranted but persist in spite of the arguments. Nonetheless, Hume has argued, and that one can explain each of the beliefs on the basis of the principles of the association of ideas. If his explanations are successful, they tend to support his general position that the mind is nothing but a collection of independent perceptions united together by the relations of resemblance, contiguity and causation. His theory has the further advantage of being superior to the substance theory on both the grounds of intelligibility and simplicity. Given the epistemic problems with the substance theory, and assuming that his explanations of the problematic beliefs are adequate, Hume has grounds for claiming that his theory provides the best explanation of mental phenomena and, therefore, should be accepted.

The Appendix

Although Hume seemed very optimistic that he had provided an adequate account of one's belief in personal identity when writing in the body of the *Treatise*, this optimism was reduced to gloom in the Appendix. There Hume begins his discussion:

> I HAD entertain'd some hopes, that however deficient our theory
> of the intellectual world might be, it wou'd be free from those

contradictions, and absurdities, which seem to attend every explication, that human reason can give of the material world. But upon a more strict review of the section concerning *personal identity*, I find myself involv'd in such a labyrinth, that, I must confess, I neither know how to correct my former opinions, nor how to render them consistent. If this be not a good *general* reason for scepticism, 'tis at least a sufficient one (if I were not already abundantly supplied) for me to entertain diffidence and modesty in all my decisions. I shall propose the arguments on both sides, beginning with those that induc'd me to deny the strict and proper identity and simplicity of a self or thinking being. (*T* 633)

While this paragraph shows that Hume found *some* problem with his discussion of personal identity, the precise reason for his dissatisfaction is anything but clear. The arguments he rehearses (*T* 633-5) differ little from those that had led him to repudiate the doctrine of substance in the body of the *Treatise*. The only clue he provides, his notorious appeal to the inconsistency of two principles, is cryptic at best. Nonetheless, if one examines those principles in light of the task he set for himself in 'Of Personal Identity' and what I take to be his general task in the first book of the *Treatise*, I believe it is possible to disentangle the web of difficulties Hume confronted. I shall show that if Hume recognized that his explanation of the belief in the simplicity of the mind was inadequate and knew of no way to reconstruct that explanation on the basis of the principles of the association of ideas, then he recognized that his bundle theory of mind failed to fulfill the requirement of explanatory completeness. This failure has consequences that call the most fundamental elements of his theory of mind into doubt. So let us begin by examining Hume's 'inconsistent' principles.

Hume summarized his problem as follows:

In short there are two principles, which I cannot render consistent; nor is it in my power to renounce either of them, viz., *that all our distinct perceptions are distinct existences*, and *that the mind never perceives any real connexion among distinct existences*. Did our perceptions either inhere in something simple and individual, or did the mind perceive some real connexion among them, there wou'd be no difficulty in the case. For my part, I must plead the privilege of a sceptic, and confess, that this difficulty is too hard for my understanding. I pretend not, however, to pronounce it absolutely insuperable. Others, perhaps, or myself, upon more mature reflection, may discover some hypothesis, that will reconcile those contradictions. (*T* 636)

Most scholars acknowledge that the principles are anything but inconsistent (cf. Smith 1941: 558-9; Passmore 1980: 83; Robison 1976: 188-93; Nathanson 1976: 36-46). By examining the principles, however, one discovers that each principle is inconsistent with the belief in the simplicity of the mind: the first is inconsistent with the content of the belief, and the second, given Hume's theories of belief and the origin of ideas, precludes the possibility of the belief.

Consider the first principle (*P1*). Hume's assertion that perceptions are distinct existences affirms that a perception neither (1) depends for its existence upon a substance nor (2) is essentially a part of some entity. Since any account of mind must recognize that a multiplicity of perceptions are in some way associated with a mind, to declare the distinctness and (metaphysical) independence of perceptions entails that a mind must be complex. Hence, (*P1*) is inconsistent with the belief that the mind is simple.

The second principle (*P2*), '*that the mind never perceives any real connexion among distinct existences*' (*T* 636), is nothing but an epistemic corollary of *P1*. If there are no essential connections among the perceptions constituting a mind, it is obviously impossible to discover any logical or empirical evidence that there are such connections. Consequently, it is in fact impossible to construct an idea of a Shaftesburian self. Further, if Hume construed the notion of a real connection in *P2* more broadly than he did in other contexts and allowed, consistent with the Cartesian theory of substance, that a substratum is a real connection, the consequences of *P2* are extremely significant. Since all ideas are copies of impressions, and since a belief must have an idea as its object, it appears impossible to believe in the simplicity of substance.[9] This, of course, conflicts with the fact that one holds such a belief (*T* 253).

The apparent impossibility of a belief in the simplicity of the mind is not in principle problematic. Hume's program of doxastic pathology was predicated upon the assumption that there are beliefs that are unevidenced or false, that these beliefs rest upon a conflation or misidentification of ideas, and that it is possible to causally explain these beliefs on the basis of the principles of the association of ideas. So long as such an explanation can be provided, there is no basis for ascribing truth to the belief.

In the case of the belief in personal identity, however, Hume found his causal account inadequate. On this point he was explicit:

> But having thus loosen'd all our particular perceptions, when I proceed to explain the principle of connexion, which binds them together, and makes us attribute to them a real simplicity and

identity; I am sensible that my account is very defective, and that nothing but the seeming evidence of the precedent reasonings cou'd have induc'd me to receive it. (*T* 635)

Remember, the *belief* in personal identity is the belief that the mind is simple and perfectly identical through time (*T* 251, 253; cf. 635), that is, the belief in a substantial mind. The inconsistency of *P1* and *P2* with the belief in the simplicity of the mind is symptomatic of the respect in which Hume considered his causal account to have failed.

Remember too, Hume's explanation of the belief in the simplicity of the mind was limited to the penultimate paragraph of 'Of Personal Identity' (*T* 263). There are two points that should be noticed. First, Hume considered the causal account of the belief in the simplicity of the mind to parallel exactly the account of the belief in the identity of the mind. Second, as his reference to 'co-existent parts' suggests, the belief in simplicity pertains to simplicity at a moment (cf. *T* 253). And, as I noted above, Hume's discussions of the ancient philosophers' belief in the simplicity of material substance exactly parallels the explanation of their belief in the identity of substance. The issues, then, are whether there is an explanation of the belief in mental simplicity that correlates with the explanation of the belief in identity, and whether that explanation is analogous to the explanation of the belief in the simplicity of material substance. As I shall show, although one can draw distinctions regarding simplicity that parallel those drawn regarding identity, the situation regarding the belief in the simplicity of the mind is fundamentally different from that pertaining to the simplicity of material substance.

Recall that in discussing one's belief in the identity of the mind, Hume distinguished among at least three senses of the term 'identity'.[10] Perfect identity presupposes 'the *invariableness* and *uninterruptedness* of any object, thro' a suppos'd variation in time' (*T* 201, 253). It is this sense of identity that is attributed to a substantial substratum. Imperfect identity is ascribed to objects whose changes are gradual and proportionately small, especially when the 'object' in question is actually a system of causally related parts. Both perfect and imperfect identity are species of numerical identity and are to be contrasted with specific identity (identity of kind).

Can one explain the belief in the simplicity of the mind along the same lines as the belief in identity? If one can, one should be able to draw distinctions regarding simplicity that are analogous to those regarding identity, that is, one should be able to distinguish between perfect and imperfect simplicity and to distinguish numerical simplicity from specific simplicity. While those distinctions can be drawn, we shall see that it is implausible to suggest that the belief in the simplicity of the mind involves the same kind of conflation of senses of 'simplicity' that Hume believed were involved in explaining the belief in the perfect numerical identity of a mind.

At bottom, the notion of simplicity presupposes the indivisibility of an object into parts (cf. *T* 2). Consequently, if an object possesses perfect numerical simplicity, it cannot be divided into numerically distinct parts. The notion of imperfect simplicity, then, is attributed to objects that are properly complex, but whose parts are so closely related to one another that one does not distinguish among the parts. One takes the complex object to be *one* thing and disregards its complexity (cf. *T* 221 and 263).

The notions of specific simplicity (simplicity of kind) and specific complexity are best understood as complying with the distinction between determinates and determinables. Recalling that Hume divided the world into kinds on the basis of resemblance (*T* 17-25), determinates of the same kind are those that resemble exactly, that is, those that are composed of the same qualities. The object itself may be numerically complex, that is, composed of several qualities, but in asserting specific simplicity to the object one asserts that most, if not all, of the qualities of the object are necessary for it to be the kind of thing it is: were any qualities added or removed, the object would be a different kind of thing (cf. *T* 15-17).

Having distinguished the various senses in which one can speak of simplicity, one must now ask whether it is possible to explain why one (falsely) attributes perfect simplicity to a mind. To do this, it will be beneficial to compare and contrast the attribution of simplicity and identity to a plant with the attribution of the same qualities to a mind.

Hume claimed that the sort of identity one attributes to a mind is the same sort of identity one attributes to a plant, namely, imperfect identity (*T* 259). Just as a mind is a system of causally related perceptions, so a plant is a system of causally related parts. Further, just as some perceptions in a mind resemble one another (are specifically identical), so momentary temporal phases of a plant are specifically identical. In both cases one takes an object to be simple at a time and identical through time. But if one examines the situations further, one finds that there is a respect in which the two cases are not analogous.

Consider a plant, for example, a tree. At any time, the various parts of the tree--the trunk, the leaves, the bark, and so forth--are taken to be parts of *one* thing, and one attributes simplicity to the tree. The causal relations among temporally successive phases of the tree provide the basis for ascribing (imperfect) identity to the tree, and when there is a temporal break in one's observation of the tree, the subsequent momentary phases one observes resemble (are specifically identical with) the phases one previously observed. But the case is not the same in the case of the mind. In the case of the tree, each temporal phase is specifically identical with (resembles) every other. Consequently, it is correct to suggest that a tree is specifically simple throughout its existence: a tree at one moment is a particular kind of thing, and at any other moment it is the same kind of thing. Since the idea of specific simplicity is an idea of simplicity, it is consistent with Hume's general appeal to the conflation of ideas to suggest that the idea of specific simplicity is confused with that of numerical simplicity and that this provides the basis for claiming that the tree is numerically simple.

In the case of the mind, an analogous situation is not available, at least not if *P1* and *P2* are true. In the system of perceptions that constitute a mind, a relation of specific identity does not obtain among *all* the perceptions constituting a mind. There are, after all, tree-perceptions, book-perceptions, pineapple-perceptions, anger-perceptions, and so forth. Although memory might allow one to claim that the relation of specific identity obtains among *some* perceptions in the mind, it is indubitable that not all perceptions are of a kind. Hence, even if one holds that the complex of perceptions constituting a mind at a moment is (imperfectly) numerically simple, the absence of the relation of specific identity among all the perceptions in the mind disallows the attribution of specific simplicity to the mind and undercuts the basis for claiming that there is a conflation of senses of simplicity in attributing *perfect* simplicity to the mind. Indeed, to claim that a complex momentary component of the mind is (imperfectly) simple enforces the notion of the complexity of the mind, for given the perpetual change of types of perceptions, the illusion of identity cannot be maintained. Even if the causal relations that obtain among perceptions in a mind unite these perceptions into a single system, so that one could claim that temporally separated perceptions are parts of the same system, the specific diversity of the parts suggests that the system is complex, not simple. Hence, it appears impossible to account for the belief in the simplicity of the mind on the basis of the relations of association, and Hume's explanatory program fails.

Is the problem insuperable? No, but the price Hume would have to pay is extremely high. Were Hume to allow that all perceptions are of the same kind, just as are all temporal phases of a plant, the causes of the attribution of simplicity to the mind would exactly parallel those involved in attributing identity to a plant. But to make such an allowance would demand the rejection of *P1*: it would demand that just as a momentary temporal phase of a plant is essentially a part of a plant, so a perception (a momentary temporal phase of a mind) must be deemed essentially a part of a mind. Furthermore, it seems there is no other way in which one could explain the belief. There is no non-natural philosophical relation that could augment the relations of association and provide an explanation of one's belief in simplicity.[11] Were one to suggest that there is a non-philosophical relation that could provide such an explanatory principle, two problems would be generated. First, if there were relations other than those Hume lists as philosophical relations, his claim that all relations can be subsumed under seven general headings would be false, and this would entail that he could not obtain the degree of theoretical simplicity for which he had striven. Second, and more significantly, it is unclear that any putative relation that is not included in the list of philosophical relations is empirically discoverable, and to introduce a theoretical term denoting such a relation would require that Hume renounce his empiricist theory of meaning. Hence, one can understand why Hume the theoretician expressed a certain amount of dismay.

Nonetheless, it would be an exaggeration to describe the problems we have considered to this point as a 'labyrinth of contradictions'. At worst the considerations to this point suggest one actually has an idea of a perfectly simple and identical mind, since every belief presupposes an idea. So long as Hume placed no constraints on what it is possible to believe, the fact that one has such an idea provides no strong basis for calling *P1* and *P2* into doubt. As I shall show, however, there is evidence that Hume placed constraints on belief and that these constraints are sufficient to generate a labyrinth.

One of Hume's most fundamental principles is the conceivability criterion of possibility, the maxim *'That whatever the mind clearly conceives includes the idea of possible existence, or in other words, that nothing we imagine is absolutely impossible'* (*T* 32). Since every belief must have an idea as its object, this principle has a doxastic corollary which I call the principle of the rationality of belief (*RB*). *RB* asserts that, where *p* is a proposition, if one can believe that *p*, *p* is internally consistent (not a necessary falsehood). Since Hume claimed that all real objects are consistent and ideas are real objects (*T* 173, 247), it seems to follow that at least all clear ideas are internally consistent.[12] While Hume's version of *RB* requires that the mind have a clear idea of a thing if one is to claim that it could exist, the failure of the explanatory program at least raises the specter that one has such a clear idea of the mind as a thing that is perfectly simple and identical through time. It is this specter that generates the labyrinth.

If there is a clear idea of a perfectly simple and identical mind, *P1* must be false, since *P1* is inconsistent with the belief in the simplicity of the mind. And if *P1* is false, the bundle theory cannot be the correct theory of the mind. Further, if one has a clear idea of a perfectly simple and identical self, then if the copy theory of simple ideas is correct, *P2* must also be false, that is, the mind must be capable of perceiving real connections among perceptions. Finally, if there are real connections among perceptions, there is little or no basis for claiming that there are no real connections among (physical) objects, which is sufficient to call Hume's analysis of causation into doubt.

These, however, are not the most serious problems Hume confronts on the presumption that one has a clear idea of a perfectly simple and identical self. The magnitude of the problem, the reason Hume found himself in a labyrinth of contradictions, becomes clear only if one assumes that both *P1* and *P2* are false and examines the idea of the self. Remember, if *P1* is false, the mind is either a whole composed of connected perceptions or a substance. As will be seen, both possibilities yield grave consequences.

Let us assume, first, that there are real connections among perceptions and that the mind is simple only as a whole (the Shaftesburian position). If it is one's idea of the mind as a whole that provides the basis for one's belief in personal identity, one must be simultaneously aware of all the perceptions constituting one's mind up to and including the moment of one's awareness. Further, since a (positive) idea represents by resemblance (*T* 233), an adequate idea of one's mind, an idea that includes all the relational properties of the perceptions in one's mind (cf. *T* 29), must consist of all the simultaneous awareness of all the perceptions constituting one's mind complete with the temporal properties of the mind. Leaving aside the factual problems posed by the fallibility of memory,[13] there are two major problems to be considered.

First, it is impossible to have an idea of all the perceptions constituting the mind that adequately represents one's mind. Since one's idea is a simultaneous awareness of these perceptions, that is, an awareness at a single moment of all the perceptions constituting the mind, the idea of the whole cannot represent the temporal duration of the whole. Hence, any idea one could have of one's mind as a whole would be an inadequate idea.

Second, even if one assumes that the temporal properties of the mind pose no problem in the formation of an idea of the whole, there is a difficulty that establishes the absolute impossibility of such an idea. Assume that at time *t* one has an idea of one's mind as a whole, that is, one is simultaneously aware of the temporally ordered sequence of perceptions constituting one's mind. Call this idea 'alpha'. Call the idea of all the perceptions constituting one's mind up to and including the moment before t 'beta'. How would one describe alpha? Would alpha be identical with beta? If alpha were identical with beta, it would be incomplete, for it would be only the idea of all the perceptions that *have* constituted the mind: it would not be an idea of all the perceptions constituting the mind up to and *including* time t. Since the holistic view takes each perception to be essentially a component of the particular mind of which it is a component, an incomplete idea of the mind would not be an adequate representation of it (cf. T 23). Nonetheless, beta must be a component of alpha. If one recalls that all ideas are copies of perceptions (impressions and ideas), it is clear that ideas are historical in their orientation: they represent what has occurred in the mind.[14] At time t, however, alpha must be an idea that represents all past perceptions (beta) and the present component of the mind, that is, to be a complete idea of the mind alpha must represent (be a copy of) itself. Since a copy or a representation must be distinct from its original (were this not the case, Hume's impression/idea distinction would make no sense), it is impossible to have an idea that is a copy of itself, and it is therefore impossible to have an idea of one's mind as a whole.[15]

Due to the problems Hume would confront upon assuming a Shaftesburian theory of the self, one might ask whether he would fare any better if the rejection of *P1* and *P2* presupposed that the mind is a substance in which perceptions inhere. Taking a substance to be a real connection among perceptions, assume one has an impression of substance. By hypothesis, *P1* is false, and all perceptions are dependent upon a substance. As we noticed above, Hume claimed that an impression could represent a substance only on the basis of resemblance (T 233, cf. T 251). If an impression represents a substance and a substance is simple, the impression must have the property peculiar to substance, namely, metaphysical independence. But if an impression of a substance has the property of metaphysical independence, it could not be an impression, since all impressions are, by the present hypothesis, metaphysical dependents. Hence, if *P1* and *P2* are false, it follows that *P2* is true: it is impossible to have an impression of a substantial self (cf. T 232-3).[16]

Thus, it is impossible to hold a belief in personal identity, since it is impossible to form the requisite idea for such a belief even if one assumes the falsehood of *P1* and *P2*. Yet one has this belief. Since every belief presupposes an idea, the type of idea that grounds the belief in the perfect simplicity and identity of the mind must differ radically from the type of idea that is the object of most beliefs. It can neither represent by resemblance nor be a copy of an impression. The idea grounding the belief in personal identity must be transcendental.[17]

The discovery of a transcendental idea lays to waste the foundations of Hume's philosophy, for it entails the falsehood of his most fundamental principle, the copy theory of simple ideas. Thus, recalling that Hume was unable to discover the respect in which his arguments for *P1* and *P2* were defective, indeed, since he found most of his arguments for the principles 'attended with sufficient evidence' and 'promising' (*T* 634-5), this alone would explain why he pleaded the privilege of a sceptic. Yet there is another path in the maze that remains to be explored.

Hume's attempt to explain the belief in the simplicity of the mind failed. I have argued that it is this failure in conjunction with *RB* that calls *P1* and *P2* into doubt. But *RB* presupposes the copy theory of ideas. An idea is clear if and only if it is a copy of an impression (*T* 32). But if it is a transcendental idea that provides the basis for one's belief in the simplicity and identity of the mind, *RB* will not show that the belief is internally consistent. Hence, there is no basis for claiming that *P1* and *P2* are false. But since the explanatory program of which *P1* and *P2* are a part also had failed, there is no basis for claiming that those principles are true. So Hume could do little more than plead the privilege of a sceptic.

Conclusions

In this chapter I have shown that 'Of Personal Identity' is another study in doxastic pathology. After arguing that the belief in personal identity, that is, the belief in the perfect simplicity of a mind at a time and the perfect identity of a mind over time, is unsupported by the evidence, he attempts to explain the belief on the basis of the principles of the association of ideas. His explanation focuses primarily on the belief in the identity of the mind, devoting only the penultimate paragraph of the section to the belief in simplicity. In the Appendix Hume lamented the failure of his discussion of personal identity, claiming that his discussion involved a veritable labyrinth of contradictions. I have shown that Hume could not explain the belief in the simplicity of the mind along the same lines he had used to explain the belief in identity, and I sketched the conceptual labyrinth that this explanatory failure carried in its wake.

'Of Personal Identity' is a unique discussion. It is one of the few discussions in the first book of the *Treatise* that has no counterpart, however brief, in the *Enquiry concerning Human Understanding*. In turning to the latter work we shall see that while Hume was still concerned with 'giving an account of the mind', the nature of the account differs significantly from that in the *Treatise*.

Notes

[1]This is one of several respects in which Hume's discussion follows Locke's discussion in *Essay* 2.27 (cf. Hall 1974). As we proceed, I shall cite several of the Lockean texts that parallel Hume's discussion.

[2]As we saw in Chapter 5, this is Shaftesbury's position, and Hume cites Shaftesbury as a proponent of such a position (*T* 254n).

[3]Locke put the point this way. Assuming that masses of matter are composed of atoms, 'if one of these Atoms be taken away, or one new one added, it is no longer the same mass' (Locke, *Essay* 2.27.3).

[4]Hume's discussion at this point continues to build upon Locke's considerations of quantitative change (*Essay* 2.27.3), but the strictly quantitative origination is too simplistic. Certainly there are qualitative changes in objects which, though quantitatively insignificant, lead to a denial of the identity claim. Recall that in the case considered above, the removal of a hundredth inch of wood from each face of the cube probably would not be noticed; that is, so long as one did not observe the change, one would claim it is the same amount of matter and the same cube after the change. On the other hand, if the same volume of wood were removed from a single corner of the cube, and one were asked, 'Is this the same cube you saw three minutes ago?' one probably would answer in the negative, for it no longer would be a cube. Nonetheless, so long as there were no noticeable quantitative change or the qualitative similarity outweighed the qualitative change, we may assume Hume's account is acceptable.

[5]W. von Leyden has argued that the word 'imperfect' at *T* 256 is probably a printing error and should read 'improper' (Leyden 1957: 340-52). For my purposes, such a possible printing error is of no consequence.

[6]This understanding of 'specific identity' is substantiated by Hume's statement that in cases where one ascribes numerical identity to objects that are only specifically identical, the first ceases to exist before the second comes into existence. See the case of the church at *T* 258.

[7]Various commentators have argued that an understanding of the kind of identity Hume attributed to the mind demands a recognition of the distinction between perfect and imperfect identity. They claim that although the mind is not perfectly identical throughout the course of one's life, Hume would allow that it is imperfectly identical (Brett 1972: 118-21; Wolfram 1974: 586-93; Ashley and Stack 1974: 244-52). On the other hand, Noxon has argued that

the ascription of identity to the mind rests fundamentally on ascribing numerical identity where only specific identity is warranted (Noxon 1969: 370-5). I shall show that Hume *explains* the belief in the perfect numerical identity of the mind on the basis of a natural blurring of these distinctions.

[8]If the reader finds it puzzling that Hume here discounts contiguity, two reasons might be cited. First, as we saw in the last chapter, in 'Of the Immateriality of the Soul' Hume argued that *spatial* contiguity does not pertain to all perceptions (*T* 239-40), and consequently, spatial contiguity could play no role in relating *all* the perceptions in the mind. Second, Hume is concerned with the belief in identity through time. Of the relations of association, only the relations of resemblance and causation can obtain between temporally separated perceptions: temporally contiguous perceptions are by definition not separated.

[9]Even if one does not so construe 'real connexion' in this context, the same consequence follows, for Hume had argued at *T* 232-3 and, more obliquely, at *T* 251 that it is impossible to have an impression of substance.

[10]For the present purposes I assume that the identity one attributes to rivers can be subsumed under 'specific identity'.

[11]The only viable candidate would be the relation of identity, but if all perceptions in a mind were identical in any sense of that ambiguous term, this would entail a rejection of *P1*.

[12]As we saw in Chapter 3, Hume construed ideas primarily in terms of images. Hence, his claim is that any idea *qua* image is internally consistent. The idea (image) '2 + 2 = 5' is internally consistent, although the proposition expressed by it is necessarily false. The ideas '2 + 2', '5' and '=' are themselves symbols to be understood in terms of other ideas, and it is taking the idea represented by the symbol '2 + 2' to be the same as that represented by '5' that is inconsistent. Consequently, so long as one is able to frame an idea (picture something to oneself), the idea is internally consistent.

[13]The fallibility of memory poses a dilemma. Either it is a fact that one can never have an idea of the mind as a whole, or, if one allows an incomplete idea of the mind to stand for the whole, one confronts the type of paradox posed by the case of Reid's gallant officer (Reid 1969b: 357-8).

[14]Even in the case of ideas of the imagination, the simple components of these complex ideas represent qualities that have been perceived.

[15]The paradox arises due to the temporal nature of the situation. Were it possible to step outside time and view the mind from such a nontemporal context, it would be possible to construct a complete idea of a mind at *t*. Since it is not, in fact, possible to withdraw oneself from the temporal context, and since the idea one would form outside a temporal context could not provide the basis for a belief in personal identity that occurs within time, the paradox remains.

[16]It is quite clear that the labyrinth involves issues other than personal identity. Remember *RB* together with the belief in the simplicity of the mind provide the basis for calling *P1* into doubt. If *P1* is false, the common person's belief in external objects is false, since the common person believes that

impressions are identical with material objects and exist independently of the mind. (Cf. Hume's argument that this belief is consistent, *T* 207.) But *RB* cuts the other way as well. Given that the common person actually believes that impressions (that is, objects) exist independently of the mind, the belief must be internally consistent. But the common person's belief can be consistent only if *P1* is true. And if *P1* is true, the belief in the substantiality of the mind is false. This is another path in the maze.

[17]By 'transcendental idea' I mean an idea that is capable of providing the foundation for a belief, but which is inexplicable on the basis of the copy theory of ideas and does not represent by resemblance.

8
The *Enquiries*

Hume's attempt to develop a theory of mind in the *Treatise* failed on grounds of explanatory completeness. Although the Appendix suggests that he agonized over the inadequacies of his theory (*T* 633-6; cf. *Letters* 1:38-9), and even though late in his life he still seemed to prefer something like the theory of the *Treatise* to a substance theory of mind (cf. *D* 159-60), there is no evidence that he was able to refurbish his bundle theory or to provide an alternative theory that would meet his meta-theoretical requirements. In this chapter I briefly examine the 'account of mind' Hume developed in the first *Enquiry*. I show that that account reflects a shift away from the theoretical reduction of the *Treatise* to merely a lawful description of the operations of the mind. This shift is manifest in four ways. (1) The Hume of the *Enquiries* makes no positive statement regarding the nature of the mind: his account is consistent with either a substance or a bundle theory of mind. (2) The evidence for the copy theory of ideas is independent of the principles of the association of ideas. (3) Explanations and predictions are made strictly at the level of phenomena. (4) Finally, there is an increased emphasis on natural laws. I conclude the chapter by arguing that this shift in his account of mind provides a nonstylistic ground for Hume's disavowal of the *Treatise* (cf. GG 3:v; *EHU* 2).

The Science of Human Nature

As a proponent of the accurate and abstruse method for doing moral philosophy, Hume's task in the *Enquiries* was to 'find those principles, which regulate our understanding, excite our sentiments, and make us approve or blame any particular object, action, or behaviour' (*EHU* 6). Hume appears to be concerned solely with the discovery of the laws governing thought, rather than to discover the 'essence of the mind' (cf. *T* xvii). Further, given his reduction of the notion of 'force' to lawful regularity (*EHU* 69-70), Hume's extolment of Newton's success in 'determin[ing] the laws and forces, by which the revolutions of the planets are governed and directed' and his hope for similar success with respect to the mind (*EHU* 14) suggest he was searching for the laws governing thought. Hume's statement of his objectives in the first section of the second *Enquiry* also supports my contention that he was searching for nothing more than a lawful description of the activities of the mind. In stating his objectives, he contrasts his own method with an alternative scientific method. He wrote:

> The only object of reasoning [in morals] is to discover the circumstances on both sides, which are common to these qualities; to observe that particular in which the estimable qualities agree on the one hand, and the blameable on the other; and thence to reach the foundation of ethics, and find those universal principles, from which all censure or approbation are ultimately derived. As this is a question of fact, not of abstract science, we can only expect success, by following the experimental method, and deducing general maxims from a comparison of particular instances. The other scientific method, where a general abstract principle is first established, and is afterwards branched out into a variety of inferences and conclusions, may be more perfect in itself, but suits less the imperfection of human nature, and is a common source of illusion and mistake. (*EPM* 174)

The objective of the second *Enquiry* is to discover those principles that describe the situations in which one actually approves or disapproves of an action or motive. It is nothing more than an attempt to construct inductive generalizations that describe experience, and in the body of the second *Enquiry* one finds little more than an extensive case study showing that, as a matter of fact, human beings approve of those actions and motives that are useful to themselves or others.[1] Hume contrasts this 'experimental method' with one in which 'a general principle is first established, and is afterwards branched out into a variety of inferences and conclusions' (*EPM* 174). As we have seen, the second method is the method Hume himself employed in the *Treatise*, a method of establishing general principles (the principles of the association of ideas) and then explaining other phenomena (beliefs in the external world and substance) in an attempt to confirm the theory. Hume's distinction between the 'experimental method' in the *Enquiries* and the 'other scientific method', the method he himself had employed in the *Treatise*, suggests that he had consciously changed his philosophical objectives from giving an account of the nature of the mind to merely giving a lawful description of the operations of the mind.

If this is correct, then one should find that the several laws of thought proposed in the *Enquiries*, including the copy theory of ideas, are supported solely on the basis of inductive generalizations from experience. This is what one finds. Recall that in the *Treatise* Hume claimed a 'full examination' of the adequacy of the copy theory of simple ideas 'is the subject of the present treatise' (*T* 4). No such claim is made in the first *Enquiry*. If the copy theory were a part of a more general theory, then, although one might provide inductive evidence for the truth of the copy theory, the copy theory of ideas would be deemed adequate if and only if the theory of which it is a part were adequate. The inadequacy of the theory of mind in the *Treatise* raises doubts regarding the copy theory of ideas. As in the *Treatise*, the Hume of the first *Enquiry* provides inductive evidence for the truth of the copy theory (*EHU* 19-20), but in the *Enquiry* this is the only evidence he provides for the truth of the copy theory. The fact that he claimed no theoretical connection between the copy theory of ideas and any other aspect of his account of mind suggests that there is a shift away from an account of the nature of the mind to a lawful description of thought.

One finds a similar shift with respect to the laws of the association of ideas. In the 1777 edition of the first *Enquiry*, Hume's evidence for the principles of the association of ideas is two-fold. First, he contends that 'It is evident that there is a principle of connexion between the different thoughts or ideas of the mind, and that, in their appearance to the memory or imagination, they introduce each other with a certain degree of method and regularity' (*EHU* 23). His evidence for this is drawn from observations of various kinds of thinking and discourse. Second, he contends that 'there appear to be only three principles of connexion among ideas, namely, Resemblance, Contiguity in time and place, and Cause or Effect' (*EHU* 24). The evidence for this claim is given in a single paragraph. Hume wrote:

> That these principles serve to connect ideas will not, I believe, be much doubted. A picture naturally leads our thoughts to the original [resemblance]: the mention of one apartment in a building naturally introduces an enquiry or discourse concerning the others [contiguity]: and if we think of a wound, we can scarce forbear reflecting on the pain which follows [cause and effect]. But that this enumeration is complete, and that there are no other principles of association, except these, may be difficult to prove to the satisfaction of the reader, or even to a man's own satisfaction.

All we can do, in such cases, is to run over several instances, and examine carefully the principle which binds the different thoughts to each other, never stopping till we render the principle as general as possible. The more instances we examine, and the more care we employ, the more assurance we shall acquire, that the enumeration, which we form from the whole, is complete and entire. (*EHU* 24)

Hume's evidence for the principles of association is limited to a few instances plus a promissory note that further instances will bear out his hypothesis. Further, all the instances Hume provides are all drawn from one's immediate observations. While in the pre-1777 editions of the first *Enquiry* Hume provided a more detailed examination of cases by examining the role of the association of ideas in narrative compositions, those cases also are based strictly upon observation: the evidence for the acceptance of the rules of association consists of nothing more than inductions from observable phenomena (cf. GG, 4:19n-23n).[2]

It is one thing to discover general rules. It is another thing to apply them and to ask what inferences can be drawn on the basis of a lawful description of a phenomenon. The issues we should consider are: Does the Hume of the *Enquiries* use the principles of the association of ideas to explain phenomena? If he does, are all the phenomena explained purely observable phenomena? And does he use these explanations to draw any inferences regarding the nature of the mind?

In the first *Enquiry*, Hume's sole use of the principles of the association of ideas is to explain the 'transfer of force and vivacity' from impressions to ideas in belief contexts. Much of his evidence for this is drawn verbatim from the *Treatise* (*EHU* 51-3; cf. *T* 99-101), and even those portions that differ in detail remain the same in spirit: there is an observable increase in the force and vivacity of an idea that follows an impression in a belief context. On the other hand, the use of the principles of association to explain empirically problematic beliefs is markedly absent in the *Enquiries*.

Is this absence of an attempt to explain problematic beliefs symptomatic of a more general change in the *Enquiries*, or does it merely mark an attempt on Hume's part to popularize his writings? I believe they reasonably can be taken to mark a change in his philosophical objectives. It was on the basis of the putative success of the explanations of these problematic beliefs that Hume could claim that his theory of mind provides the best explanation of mental phenomena and could infer that the mind is a bundle of perceptions. In the first *Enquiry*, no inference is made from the propriety of the principles of association to the nature of the mind. Allusions to the bundle theory of mind, which were so prominent in the *Treatise* (cf. T 207, 251, 264, 277), are strikingly absent in both the *Enquiries* and the *Dissertation on the Passions*. Further, Hume's invectives against the doctrine of substance, his metaphysical considerations regarding the nature of perceptions, and the discussion of mind-body interaction (*T* 232-50) have few counterparts in the *Enquiries*. Although he claimed that the doctrine of material substance as 'only a certain unknown, inexplicable something as the cause of our perceptions; [is] a notion so imperfect, that no sceptic will think it worth while to contend against it' (*EHU* 155), in 'Of the Idea of Necessary Connexion' he referred to both mind and body as substances (*EHU* 65, 68-9). Hume's noncritical use of the term 'substance' in that context is, by itself, unimportant. But together with the absence of any positive account of the nature of the mind, it suggests that Hume considered his account of mind in the *Enquiries* to be nothing more than a lawful description of observable mental phenomena. Such an account leaves open the question of the nature of the mind. If this is correct, then it is plausible to suggest that Hume changed his philosophical objectives between the time he completed the first book of the *Treatise* and the time he wrote the *Enquiries*.[3]

The Disavowal of the *Treatise*

So far we have seen that there seems to be a shift in Hume's philosophical objectives in going from the *Treatise* to the *Enquiries*. While the Hume of the *Treatise* attempted to infer the nature of the mind from observational and explanatory claims, the Hume of the *Enquiries* attempted to provide nothing more than a lawful description of the mind. In what remains I argue that in this shift from a theory of mind to merely a lawful description one finds a plausible nonstylistic reason for Hume's disavowal of the *Treatise*.

The *Treatise* was an anonymous work. Although his authorship was fairly well known in intellectual circles, Hume acknowledged it only in his posthumous works, first in 'My Own Life' and later in an Advertisement added to the 1777 edition of *Essays and Treatises on Several Subjects*. In the latter, he acknowledged his authorship only to disavow the work. The Advertisement reads:

Most of the principles, and reasonings, contained in this volume, were published in a work in three volumes, called *A Treatise of Human Nature:* A work which the Author had projected before he left College, and which he wrote and published not long after. But not finding it successful, he was sensible of his error in going to the press too early, and he cast the whole anew in the following pieces, where some negligences in his former reasoning and more in the expression, are, he hopes, corrected. Yet several writers, who have honoured the Author's Philosophy with answers, have taken care to direct all their batteries against the juvenile work, which the Author never acknowledged, and have affected to triumph in any advantages, which, they imagined, they had obtained over it: A practice very contrary to all the rules of candour and fair-dealing, and a strong instance of those polemical artifices, which a bigotted zeal thinks itself authorized to employ. Henceforth, the Author desires, that the following Pieces may alone be regarded as containing his philosophical sentiments and principles. (GG 3:5; *EHU* 2)

If Hume disavowed the *Treatise*, at least in part, on philosophical grounds, there is a subtle shift in one of the central issues of concern in both the *Treatise* and the *Enquiries*. Providing an account of mind was a fundamental objective in both works. If Hume recognized that his bundle theory of mind lacked explanatory completeness and, as a consequence, he rejected it in favor of a mere lawful description of the operations of the mind, this constitutes such a subtle shift. But if this was Hume's reason for disavowing the *Treatise*, we should find some evidence in his several accounts of the failings of that work. It is to these that we shall now turn.

Even before the third book was published, Hume considered the *Treatise* a failure. In a letter to Hutcheson on 16 March 1740, where he expressed 'some Impatience for a second Edition [of the *Treatise*] principally on Account of Alterations I intend to make in my Performance' (*Letters* 1:38), Hume wrote:

I wish I cou'd discover more fully the particulars wherein I have fail'd. I admire so much the Candour I have observd in Mr Locke, Yourself, & very few more, that I woud be extremely ambitious of imitating it, by confessing my Errors: If I do not imitate it, it must proceed neither from my being free of Errors, nor from want of Inclination; but from my real unaffected Ignorance. (*Letters* 1:39)

The 'Errors' to which Hume refers can only be understood as substantive errors, and his concern with the 'particulars wherein I have fail'd' reminds one of the worries ultimately found in the Appendix on personal identity. In so far as Hume recognized and desired to correct certain errors in the *Treatise* as early as 1740, one would expect him to correct them in any subsequent writings on the same subject. Since there was no second edition of the *Treatise*, if the errors struck at the heart of his theory of mind, it should not be surprising that he would disavow the earlier work.

Hume's more famous comments on the *Enquiries vis-à-vis* the *Treatise* are more ambiguous. His comment in 'My Own Life' that 'I had always entertained a notion, that my want of success in publishing the *Treatise* of Human Nature, had proceeded more from the manner than the matter' (GG, 3:3) is often taken to be a comment on the stylistic shortcomings of the *Treatise*. As Nelson has suggested, however, the 'manner' involved might be philosophic, rather than literary, manner (Nelson 1972: 335). If my argument that Hume changed his philosophical objectives is sound, this would constitute a change in philosophic 'manner'.

A similar ambiguity is found in his letter to Gilbert Elliot of March or April 1751. There Hume wrote:

> I believe the philosophical Essays contain every thing of Consequence relating to the Understanding, which you woud meet with in the *Treatise*; & I give you my advice against reading the latter. By shortening & simplifying the Questions, I really render them much more complete. *Addo dum minuo.* The philosophical Principles are the same in both: But I was carry'd away by the Heat of Youth & Invention to publish too precipitately. So vast an Undertaking, plan'd before I was one and twenty, & compos'd before twenty five, must necessarily be very defective. I have repented my Haste a hundred, & a hundred times. (*Letters* 1:158)

The ambiguous term here is 'philosophical Principles'. If by this term Hume means the content is the same in both the *Treatise* and the *Enquiries*, the claim is false. Although many of the issues Hume considered, and many of his positions regarding those issues, are the same in both works, we have seen that there is a significant difference regarding his account of mind. Further, there are a number of issues discussed in the *Treatise* that are passed over without comment in the *Enquiries*, for example, Hume's discussions of space and time (*T* 27-65) as well as personal identity. If 'philosophical Principles' refers to nothing more than his empiricist presuppositions, and not to his methodological presuppositions, they remain approximately the same, although, given the methodological shift, Hume's empiricism might be deemed even stronger in the *Enquiries* than it was in the *Treatise*. But the term 'philosophical Principles' also might denote his principles of the association of ideas--or those principles together with his general principles regarding those properties, objects, or actions one deems good--which are exactly the same in both the *Treatise* and the

Enquiries. It is worthy of notice that Hume often refers to general rules as principles, and even in the Introduction to the *Treatise* he indicated that he was attempting to 'explain the *principles* of human nature' (*T* xvi, emphasis added). If my account of Hume's shift in objectives is correct, one can understand why he would claim that 'By shortening & simplifying the Questions, I really render them much more complete', namely, the lawful description in the *Enquiries* provides as adequate an account of the mind as he believed to be available to human understanding (cf. *EPM* 174). Therefore, the evidence from these two well-known passages is consistent with my contention that Hume's disavowal of the *Treatise* rests upon a change in his account of mind.

But Hume's disavowal was also intended to constitute an answer to those critics 'who . . . have taken care to direct all their batteries against the juvenile work, . . . and have affected to triumph in their advantages, which, they imagined, they had obtained over it' (GG, 3:v, *EHU* 2). Hume identified those 'several writers' in a letter to William Strahan, suggesting that the Advertisement 'is a complete Answer to Dr Reid and to that bigotted silly Fellow, Beattie' (*Letters* 2:301). This seems to imply that by disavowing the *Treatise*, Hume undercut the basis for all of Reid's and Beattie's criticisms. Such a claim seems incredible for two reasons. First, some aspects of Hume's philosophy that were criticized in both Reid's *Inquiry into the Human Mind* and Beattie's *Essay on the Nature and Immutability of Truth*--the only critical works they had published by 1776--are doctrines common to both the *Treatise* and the first *Enquiry*. For example, Reid was critical of Hume's account of belief and his inductive scepticism (Reid 1970: 244-6), views that seem not to have changed appreciably in the transition from the *Treatise* to the first *Enquiry*. Second, while most of Reid's criticisms were directed against the 'author of the *Treatise* of Human Nature', Beattie took issue with 'Mr HUME'S Essay on a particular providence and a future state' (Beattie 1770: 115, cf. 487n-488n), 'Of National Characters' (Beattie 1770: 479-82), 'Of Liberty and Necessity' (Beattie 1770: 308-26), the views of the second *Enquiry* (Beattie 1770: 422-35) as well as virtually everything Hume said in the first book of the *Treatise*. Beattie, at least, did not 'direct all [his] batteries against the juvenile work.'

Does this imply that either Hume was confused or simply attempting to save face in disavowing the *Treatise*? Perhaps. But there is a more sympathetic interpretation of Hume's disavowal. If one takes seriously Hume's contention that the disavowal of the *Treatise* is an answer to Reid and Beattie, that 'answer' was limited to views that are peculiar to the *Treatise*.[4] Further, it seems reasonable to limit considerations to those issues in the *Treatise* that were discussed both in Reid's *Inquiry* and in Beattie's *Essay*. The one issue that fits both of these conditions is the bundle theory of mind. It is particularly with respect to this issue that both of those philosophers might be charged with 'bigotted zeal' (GG, 3:v, *EHU* 2).

In his *Inquiry*, Reid's criticisms of Hume's theory of mind are directed solely at the bundle theory. Although Reid sets the tone of his criticisms in the 'Introduction' (Reid 1970:   14-15), the bulk of criticisms are found in Section VI of Chapter 2. There Reid focuses on the theory of ideas in general and Hume's contention that perceptions are independent existents in particular. Beginning with the plea that 'no offence may be taken in charging [Hume's bundle theory] or any other metaphysical notions with absurdity, or being contrary to the common sense of mankind' (Reid 1970:   31-2), he proceeds to argue that 'Ideas seem to have something in their nature unfriendly to other existences' (Reid 1970: 33). Tracing the history of the 'way of ideas', he indicates initially that ideas were taken to be mental images of nonmental objects, but as reasoning regarding the nature of ideas became more acute, ideas played larger and larger roles in philosophical systems. Reid wrote, 'But the triumph of ideas was completed by the *Treatise* of Human Nature, which discards spirits also, and leaves ideas and impressions as the sole existences in the universe' (Reid 1970: 33; cf. Reid 1970: 34 and Beattie 1770:   266-7). Even if this were an accurate statement of Hume's position in the *Treatise*, we have seen that the denial of material or immaterial substance plays little or no role in the account of mind Hume offers in the first *Enquiry*. Given the shift in Hume's account of mind in the *Enquiries vis-à-vis* the *Treatise* and the centrality of that account to those works, Reid's contentions that Hume's theory of mind is inconsistent with common sense (Reid 1970:   34-5) and capable of being believed only while in one's philosophical closet (Reid 1970: 35 and 36), and Beattie's contention that Hume's theory of mind is nonsense, impious, and based upon a misrepresentation of common facts and a misuse of common words (Beattie 1770: 263-7) might well have provoked Hume to repudiate the *Treatise*.

Conclusions

In this chapter we have seen that Hume's recognition that his bundle theory of mind failed on explanatory grounds led to a shift in his philosophical objectives in the *Enquiries*. While the *Treatise* provides a theory of the nature of the mind, the *Enquiries* provides merely a lawful description of the operations of the mind. Even though there is little question that Hume considered a bundle theory of mind more plausible than a doctrine of substance throughout his philosophical career (cf. *D*, 159), the explanatory failure of his own account resulted in a shift away from theoretical reduction to mere description. Given Reid's and Beattie's criticisms of the bundle theory of mind, I argued that this shift in his account of mind provides nonstylistic grounds for Hume's disavowal of the *Treatise*.

Notes

[1] It is worthy of notice that Hume apparently considered the inductive program in the second Enquiry very successful, since he considered it, 'of all my writings, historical, philosophical, or literary, incomparably the best' (GG, 3:4, *Letters* 1:4; cf. *Letters* 1:227).

[2] It should be acknowledged that the language of the pre-1777 *Enquiry* is somewhat ambiguous, and it is possible that it was only late in his life, that Hume concluded that a lawful description of the mind was the most for which one could reasonably hope. Note that the section begins as follows: 'Instead of entering into detail of this kind, which would lead into many subtilties, we shall consider some of the effects of this connexion upon the passions and imagination; where we may open a field of speculation more entertaining, and perhaps more instructive, than the other' (GG, 4:19n; cf. GG, 23n). This might suggest that the kind of explanatory program in which he had engaged in the *Treatise* was viable in principle. His removal of the section from the final edition of the work suggests that he had concluded that it is improbable that an adequate theory of the nature of the mind could be discovered.

[3] Nelson recently has argued that Hume's philosophical position underwent a more significant change, viz., the Hume of the *Enquiries* rejected metaphysics (Nelson 1972). This seems too strong. If metaphysical inquiries concern the nature of objects, then the later Hume should make no claims regarding the nature or probable nature of objects. But in the *Natural History of Religion* Hume referred to the corpuscular hypothesis as 'the most probable, at least the most intelligible philosophy' (*NHR* 29), and, as Cummins has shown, there are few differences in the metaphysical positions of the first *Enquiry* vis-à-vis the *Treatise* (Cummins 1973a). My interpretation provides an account of a change in Hume's philosophy that allows for the continued acceptance of much of the metaphysics of the *Treatise* while explaining the absence of an account of the nature of the mind.

[4] This requires that one not assume the disavowal is a 'complete' answer to Reid and Beattie, in the sense that it is an answer to all their criticisms, but only that it is a sufficient answer.

Appendix:
Force and Vivacity

In Chapter 2 I argued that Hume's attempt to distinguish impressions from ideas on the basis of the greater force and vivacity of an impression *vis-à-vis* its corresponding idea failed, since he was quite willing to acknowledge that there are cases in which the force and vivacity of an impression and idea are indistinguishable (cf. *T* 2, 86; pp. 20-2 above). While in an attempt to set out Hume's general program in the *Treatise* I did not dwell on the problems with force and vivacity, more should be said regarding these notions since they play a prominent role in distinguishing not only impressions from ideas (*T* 1-2), but ideas of the memory from those of the imagination (*T* 9, 85)[1] and beliefs from conceptions (*T* 96). Yet, the notions of force and vivacity have received relatively little scholarly attention,[2] and it is not widely recognized that Hume himself was dissatisfied with his claim in the *Treatise* that it is the force and vivacity of the idea which is the object of belief that distinguishes a belief from a mere conception (cf. *T* 636).

I believe there are serious problems with the account of force and vivacity in the *Treatise*. In what follows I argue (a) that given Hume's general principles, it is unintelligible to claim that 'force and vivacity' are perceivable characteristics of impressions and ideas *as such*, and (b) that although the Hume of the *Treatise* generally treated force and vivacity as characteristics of perceptions as such, there is some evidence that the Hume of the first *Enquiry* took force and vivacity to be impressions of reflection.

Hume claimed that impressions and ideas differ phenomenally in their degrees of 'force and liveliness' (*T* 1), or 'force and violence' (*T* 1), or 'force and vivacity' (*T* 2). An idea is 'fainter' than its corresponding impression (*T* 1). The greater degree of force and vivacity is commonly taken to be an inherent characteristic of impressions that distinguishes them from ideas,[3] and such an understanding seems to be supported by Hume's subsequent remark that 'in sleep, in a fever, in

madness, or in any very violent emotions of soul, our ideas approach to
our impressions' (*T* 2; cf. *EHU* 17). But what can Hume mean by such
expressions as 'force and vivacity'? And how are these alleged
phenomenal differences between impressions and ideas to be known?

Consider the claim that an idea of sensation is a 'faint image' of an
impression (a sensible quality). Since impressions are sense-specific,
let us consider an impression of a spot of a specific shade of red and the
idea that corresponds to it. What does it mean to claim that one's idea
of the shade of color is fainter than the impression from which it is
copied? If this 'faintness' is an aspect of an idea corresponding to a
visual impression, it must be something one could visually perceive if it
were possible visually to compare an idea to its corresponding impression. Is there any such aspect? It would seem there is not. Hume held
that colors come in discrete shades each of which, on a color line, is the
least discernible difference from those flanking it on either side (*T* 5-6;
EHU 20-1). Shades of color are distinguished on the basis of hue,
saturation and brightness: if any one of these is varied, there is a
discernible difference in the shade of the color.[4] The most natural way
to understand the notion of 'faintness' with respect to an idea of color
is in terms of the brightness of color. On this scheme, the idea of a
certain shade of color would be 'lighter' than the impression from
which it is derived, just as a photocopy often is 'lighter' than its
original. But shades of color are paradigms of simple ideas (*T* 6; *EHU*
21). Any variation in the brightness of the idea of a color with respect
to its corresponding impression would entail that the idea does *not*
exactly represent (resemble) the simple impression, in violation of
Hume's most fundamental philosophical principle (*T* 4). And, of
course, if 'faintness' is construed in terms of variation in hue or saturation, the same conclusion follows.[5] Thus, it seems that a simple idea of
sight could not differ visually from the impression from which it was
derived, and given that sensible perceptions are sense-specific, there
could be no non-visual differences between a simple impression and its
corresponding idea.[6]

Nor does one do any better if one attempts to state this difference in
terms of 'force' or 'liveliness' or 'vivacity' or 'strength' or 'steadiness'.
What is the difference? If all impressions and ideas possess a certain
degree of force and vivacity, then some degree of force and vivacity
must be a 'characteristic' or an 'aspect' of every impression and idea of
sensation. But, for the reasons we have already examined, this characteristic or aspect of a perception cannot be a sensible quality: if it were
a sensible quality, then it would vary in going from an impression to an
idea and, consequently, a simple idea would not exactly resemble the

impression from which it was derived. Further, Hume seems committed to the view that, although impressions of sensation are sense-specific, a certain degree or range of degrees of force and vivacity is found in all impressions of sensation, that is, that the force and vivacity of an impression are sense-independent. And, of course, one would need to make the same kind of claim regarding memories of any kind of impressions, beliefs of any kind, and so forth: each must have a certain degree of force and vivacity or range of degrees regardless what the object of the belief or memory might be. What are 'degrees of force and vivacity'? How can they be known?

While throughout the body of the *Treatise* Hume treats the notions of 'force and vivacity' as if they were primitive and unproblematic, he eventually realized that more needed to be said. In the Appendix, he sheds some light on the nature of force and vivacity. Commenting on belief, Hume wrote:

> I conclude, by an induction which seems to me very evident, that an opinion or belief is nothing but an idea, that is different from a fiction, not in the nature, or the order of its parts, but in the *manner* of its being conceiv'd. But when I wou'd explain this *manner*, I scarce find any word that fully answers the case, but am oblig'd to have recourse to every one's feeling, in order to give him a perfect notion of this operation of the mind. An idea assented to *feels* different from a fictitious idea, that the fancy alone presents to us: And this different feeling I endeavour to explain by calling it a superior *force*, or *vivacity*, or *solidity*, or *firmness*, or *steadiness*. This variety of terms, which may seem so unphilosophical, is intended only to express that act of the mind, which renders realities more present to us than fictions, causes them to weigh more in the thought, and gives them a superior influence on the passions and imagination. (*T* 629; cf. *T* 636; *Abstract*, *T* 653-7; *EHU* 49)

In this passage Hume uses force and vivacity to distinguish belief from conception, and characterizes 'force and vivacity' in terms of a 'feeling'. It is differences in 'feeling' that provide the basis for distinguishing between states or operations of the mind and, presumably, between impressions and ideas.

Is it significant that Hume describes 'force and vivacity' as a 'feeling'? Perhaps. Hume drew a distinction between perceptions of sensation and perceptions of reflection (*T* 7-8). Although Hume seems to be concerned primarily with impressions of reflection as marks or characteristics of emotional states, the Lockean tradition takes ideas of reflection to be the distinguishing marks of mental faculties in general.

In introducing his discussion '*Of Simple* Ideas *of Reflection*', Locke wrote:

§1. The Mind receiving the *Ideas*, mentioned in the foregoing Chapters, from without [ideas of sensation], when it turns its view inward upon it self, and observes its own Actions about those *Ideas* it has, takes from thence other *Ideas*, which are as capable to be the Objects of its Contemplation, as any of those it received from foreign things.

§2. The two great and principal Actions of the Mind, which are most frequently considered, and which are so frequent, that every one that pleases, may take notice of 'em in himself, are these two:

Perception, or *Thinking*, and
Volition, or *Willing*

The Power of Thinking is called the *Understanding*, and the Power of Volition is called the *Will*, and these two Powers or Abilities in the Mind are denominated *Faculties*. Of some of the Modes of these simple *Ideas* of Reflection, such as are *Remembrance*, *Discerning*, *Reasoning*, *Judging*, *Knowledge*, *Faith*, etc. I shall have occasion to speak hereafter. (Locke, *Essay*, 2.6.1-2)

Locke held that the actions and powers or faculties of one's mind are known on the basis of ideas of reflection. His comments seem to suggest that one becomes aware of ideas of reflection only when the mind 'turns its view inward upon it self, and observes its own Actions about those *Ideas* it has', although one might reasonably take this to mean that it is only when one focuses on the actions of the mind that one attends to the ideas of reflection that are peculiar to various kinds of cognitive states. After all, the question of how cognitive states are differentiated is one that a philosopher can be expected to ask, even though it is not an issue that would be of interest to the common person. The ideas of reflection peculiar to a state of memory might be present whenever one remembers, although one might 'notice' them only when one inquires into the actions of the mind.[7] Thus, one discovers that there are ideas of reflection that are peculiar to one's several cognitive states, and such ideas of reflection might reasonably be construed as 'feelings'.

If Hume followed Locke in suggesting that there are impressions of reflection that are peculiar to each of one's cognitive states--not merely to emotional states--then the various degrees of force and vivacity might be taken to be such impressions of reflection. If this were the case, then, just as colors come in shades that resemble one another to a limited extent, one also could suggest that the locution 'degrees of force and vivacity' denotes a class of impressions of reflection that imperfectly resemble one another. Indeed, one might go further and suggest (a) that there are several distinct impressions of reflection that are peculiar to a certain general kind of cognitive state--thereby allowing one to distinguish between, for example, sense perception in a wholly wakeful state and sense perception immediately upon waking from a deep sleep, or to distinguish lucid dreams from nonlucid dreams--and (b) that the degrees of force and vivacity might be arranged in something like the following descending order: (1) sense perception, (2) madness-dreaming, (3) memory and other belief states, (4) imagining, and (5) simple conceiving.[8] This would have the advantage of allowing Hume to explain, for example, why a person suffering from a mirage seems to perceive an oasis in the distance, or why a person suffering from paranoia seems to believe that he or she is being persecuted. In the first case, there would be a confusion between the impression of reflection found in a weak perceptual state and that in a peculiar type of psychological delusion, while in the second there would be confusion of a state of madness and a state of belief. Both kinds of confusion would then be explainable on the basis of resemblance, 'the most fertile source of error' (*T* 61).

But does the Hume of the *Treatise* construe 'degrees of force and vivacity' in terms of impressions of reflection? Although the evidence is inconclusive, it seems to show that he did not. I begin by considering a pair of objections to my general claim that Hume could construe the notion of force and vivacity in terms of impressions of reflection. Next, I examine Hume's several discussions of belief. I show that while the Hume of the *Treatise* seems not to have taken an impression of reflection to be the mark of belief, the road from the *Treatise* to the first *Enquiry suggests* that Hume eventually came to hold that an impression of reflection is the mark of belief.

Someone might object to my general claim that it is possible to construe the notions of force and vivacity in terms of impressions of reflection by citing Hume's discussion of original and secondary impressions at the beginning of Book II of the *Treatise*. The passage in question reads as follows:

> All the perceptions of the mind may be divided into *impressions* and *ideas*, so the impressions admit of another division into *original* and *secondary*. This division of the impressions is the same with that which I formerly made use of when I distinguish'd them into impressions of *sensation* and *reflexion*.

Original impressions or impressions of sensation are such as without any antecedent perception arise in the soul, from the constitution of the body, from the animal spirits, or from the application of objects to the external organs. Secondary, or reflective impressions, are such as proceed from some of these original ones, either immediately or by the imposition of its idea. Of the first kind are all the impressions of the senses, and all bodily pains and pleasures: Of the second are the passions, and other emotions resembling them. (*T* 275)[9]

The critic would note (1) that Hume considers impressions of reflection secondary in the sense that they are causally dependent upon impressions of sensation and (2) that he seems to limit impressions of reflection to emotional states. Because Hume held that a cause must be temporally prior to its effect (*T* 75, 175; cf. *EHU* 76), my account implies that cognitive states cannot be distinguished at the moment of their occurrence, a position that seems contrary to the tone of most of Hume's remarks on the distinguishability of cognitive states. Furthermore, the critic would continue, here, and virtually everywhere else, Hume identifies 'impressions of reflection' with passions and emotions, and whatever force and vivacity might be, they are not emotions. Such are the objections.

Can they be answered? I believe they can. Let us begin by considering the claim that impressions of reflection are limited to emotive states.

If Hume provided no examples of nonemotive states that are marked by impressions of reflection, then it might be plausible to claim that impressions of reflection pertain solely to emotive states. But there are at least two passages in the *Treatise* that show that there are nonemotive impressions of reflection. The first, and most famous, of these is Hume's discussion of the idea of a necessary connection in a causal relation. After arguing that the idea of necessity arises from the constant conjunction of resembling objects but that there is 'nothing new either discover'd or produc'd in any objects by their constant conjunction' (*T* 164), Hume argues that the impression that gives rise to the idea of necessity must be 'internal', that is, an impression of reflection. In his words:

Tho' the several resembling instances, which give rise to the idea of power, have no influence on each other, and can never produce any new quality *in the object*, which can be the model of that idea, yet the *observation* of this resemblance produces a new impression *in the mind*, which is its real model. . . . These instances are in themselves totally distinct from each other, and

173

have no union but in the mind, which observes them, and collects them, and collects their ideas. Necessity, then, is the effect of this observation, and is nothing but an internal impression of the mind, or determination to carry our thoughts from one object to another. Without considering it in this view, we can never arrive at the most distant notion of it, or be able to attribute it either to external or internal objects, to spirit or body, to causes or effects. (*T* 164-5)

The idea of necessity arises from an impression of necessity, and since there is no sensible impression of necessity, 'It must, therefore, be deriv'd from some internal impression, or impression of reflection' (*T* 165). This idea of reflection is the *feeling* of 'an easy Transition from one Idea to the other' (*Letters*, 1:155). It is the feeling of a particular kind of certainty (cf. *Letters* 1:187). As an idea of reflection, the idea of a necessary connection is nonspatial (cf. *T* 165, 235-6), but as Hume goes on to indicate, it is quite common for the mind to 'project' non-spatial qualities into spatially located objects (*T* 167; *Letters* 1:155-6; cf. *T* 217, 237, 504n), that is, one takes the spatially related objects of one's thought to be necessarily connected.[10] Thus, it is clear that Hume took the impression of a necessary connection to be an impression of reflection; and he even explained why one does not take it to be such.

The second case may be mentioned briefly. In discussing the will, Hume said that 'by the *will*, I mean nothing but *the internal impression we feel and are conscious of, when we knowingly give rise to any new motion of our body, or new perception of our mind*' (*T* 399). All we need notice here is (1) that the mark of the will is a certain 'internal impression', and (2) that the will is not an emotive state. This shows that, for Hume, not all impressions of reflection are impressions of emotional states.

Turning to the question of the temporal priority of impressions of sensation to impressions of reflection, remember that if the account I am developing is correct, then there is a correlation between impressions of sensation and those impressions of reflection that are peculiar to states of sense perception. The problem is that these two kinds of impressions seem to occur simultaneously, and consequently, the critic maintains, it makes little sense to suggest that an impression of sensation is the cause of the impression of reflection that is correlated with it. Two points should be made. First, if force and vivacity are construed strictly as impressions of reflection, it would be impossible to know that the impression itself occurred prior to and was the cause of the impression of reflection that is peculiar to sense perception. At the phenomenal level, it is solely on the basis of 'degrees of force and vivacity'--however that is construed--that allows one to distinguish an impression from an idea. Second, if there were grounds for claiming that the force and vivacity of an impression must be simultaneous with the impression itself, it might be plausible to claim that there is one cause of both a particular impression of sensation and its correlative impression of reflection, while granting Hume that the 'ultimate cause [of impressions of sensation] is . . . perfectly inexplicable' (*T* 84; but cf. *T* 275-6). In the case of other cognitive or emotive states, it is quite reasonable to suggest that an impression of sensation causes an impression of reflection: I might claim, for example, that seeing Jones was the cause (or a partial cause) of my subsequent feeling of anger. Similarly, one might claim that seeing a red sky in the morning was the cause of my belief that it will rain, and if belief is also marked by a peculiar kind of impression of reflection, then one might reasonably claim that an impression of sensation was the cause of both an impression of reflection that is peculiar to belief and an idea of sensation. We must now ask whether there is any textual evidence that Hume understood the notions of 'force and vivacity' in terms of impressions of reflection and therefore used impressions of reflection as the sole basis for differentiating cognitive states. To do this, I shall examine the evolution of Hume's discussion of belief, since Hume discusses belief more than any other cognitive state.[11] If there is evidence that Hume used impressions of reflection to distinguish belief states from other cognitive states, then there will be grounds for contending that Hume generally used impressions of reflection for differentiating cognitive states.[12]

At several points in the body of the *Treatise* Hume attempts to differentiate belief from mere conception on the basis of the greater force and vivacity of a belief with respect to a bare conception. As is generally acknowledged, Hume's several accounts are not equivalent, and arguably they are not consistent with one another (cf. Passmore 1980: 61-2). *Generally*, Hume limits belief to the domain of ideas, although in his initial remark on belief he included impressions of sensation among the objects of belief: 'the *belief* or *assent*, which always attends the memory and senses, is nothing but the vivacity of those perceptions they present' (*T* 86). In his discussion 'Of the Nature of Belief', however, Hume limits himself to ideas as the objects of belief, and he lays stress on the *manner* in which ideas are conceived (*T* 95, 96). In his words:

> When you wou'd any way vary the idea of a particular object, you can only encrease or diminish its force and vivacity. If you make any other change on it, it represents a different impression. . . . So

that as belief does nothing but vary the manner, in which we conceive any object, it can only bestow on our ideas an additional force and vivacity. An opinion, therefore, or belief may be most accurately defin'd, A LIVELY IDEA RELATED TO OR ASSOCIATED WITH A PRESENT IMPRESSION. (*T* 96; cf. *T* 97, 105-6)

In his official definition of 'belief', Hume is concerned with the 'manner' in which belief differs from the simple conception of an idea, and this difference is stated in terms of the 'force and vivacity' of the believed idea, 'that certain *je-ne-scai-quoi*, of which it 'tis impossible to give any definition or description, but which everyone sufficiently understands' (*T* 106). Here, as in most places in the *Treatise*, Hume talks of a 'lively idea', a phrase which suggests that the 'liveliness' is a characteristic of the idea itself. And his allusions to the 'communication' of force and vivacity from an impression to an idea (cf. *T* 98) tend to support such a reading.

But Hume's descriptions of belief in the *Treatise* are not completed with the claim that the undefined and undefinable characteristics of 'force and vivacity' are the distinguishing marks of belief. In 'Of the Influence of Belief', Hume makes a remark that is consistent with construing 'force and vivacity' as an impression of reflection. He wrote, 'Belief, therefore, *since it causes an idea to imitate the effects of the impressions* [my emphasis], must make it resemble them in these qualities, and is nothing but *a more vivid and intense conception of an idea*' (*T* 119-20). Here Hume says that belief 'causes an idea to imitate the effects of the impressions'. Given what we noticed above regarding impressions of reflection, namely, that Hume claimed they are the effects of impressions or ideas of sensation (*T* 275), and given that Hume here identifies the 'effects of impressions' with degrees of force and vivacity, or vividness and intensity, it is consistent with this text to suggest that the 'force and vivacity' of a belief is an impression of reflection that 'imitates' (resembles) the impression(s) of reflection that are peculiar to perceptual states.[13]

In attempting to provide an account of the nature of belief, Hume was sailing on uncharted philosophical waters,[14] and his remarks in the Appendix to the *Treatise* indicate that he was not long satisfied with the account of belief he had provided (cf. *T* 624-7, 628-9, 636). Part of this dissatisfaction rested upon ambiguities in the role he had assigned to 'force and vivacity'. In the Appendix he devotes more space to discussions of belief than to any other topic and acknowledges he had erred in claiming that 'two ideas of the same object can only be different by their different degrees of force and vivacity', adding, 'had I said, that two ideas of the same object can only be different by their different *feeling*, I shou'd have been nearer the truth' (*T* 636). In turning to the Appendix, the *Abstract*, and the first *Enquiry*, we shall see that Hume consistently explicates the notions of 'force and vivacity' in terms of 'feeling' or 'sentiment'--terms that Hume generally reserves for discussing impressions of reflection.

Hume begins the Appendix with an extensive discussion of belief. He wrote:

> We can never be induc'd to believe any matter of fact, except where its cause, or its effect, is present to us; but what the nature is of that belief, which arises from the relation of cause and effect, few have had the curiosity to ask themselves. In my opinion, this dilemma is inevitable. Either the belief is some new idea, such as that of *reality* or *existence*, which we join to the simple conception of an object, or there is merely a peculiar *feeling* or *sentiment*. That it is not a new idea, annex'd to the simple conception, may be evinc'd from these two arguments. *First*, We have no abstract idea of existence, distinguishable and separable from the idea of particular objects. 'Tis impossible, therefore, that this idea of existence can be annex'd to the idea of any object, or form the difference betwixt a simple conception and belief. *Secondly*, The mind has the command over all its ideas, and can separate, unite, mix, and vary them, as it pleases; so that if belief consisted merely in a new idea, annex'd to the conception, it wou'd be in a man's power to believe what he pleas'd. We may therefore, conclude, that belief consists merely in a certain feeling or sentiment; in something, that depends not on the will, but must arise from certain determinate causes and principles, of which we are not masters. When we are convinc'd of any matter of fact, we do nothing but conceive it, along with a certain feeling, different form what attends the mere *reveries* of the imagination. And when we express our incredulity concerning any fact, we mean that the arguments for the fact produce not that feeling. Did not the belief consist in a sentiment different from our mere conception, whatever objects were presented by the wildest imagination, wou'd be on an equal footing with the most establish'd truths founded on history and experience. There is nothing but the feeling, or sentiment, to distinguish the one from the other. (*T* 623-4)

This passage is ambiguous, although *taken by itself* one could argue that it is consistent with taking the mark of belief to be an impression of reflection. Suggesting belief is obtained either by adding the idea of existence or reality to one's idea of an object or 'there is merely a peculiar *feeling* or *sentiment*' that is the mark of belief, Hume argues for the latter on two grounds: (1) there is no idea of existence, and (2) if beliefs were formed by adding a peculiar kind of idea to an idea of an object, then one could choose what to believe, but one cannot choose what to believe. Thus, belief is to be understood in terms of a 'feeling' or 'sentiment', and since these terms are commonly used with respect to impressions of reflection, this *suggests* that there is an impression of reflection that is the mark of a belief. This suggestion *seems* to be supported by Hume's claim that, in a belief, one conceives of an object *'along with* [my emphasis] a certain feeling, different from what *attends* [my emphasis] the mere *reveries of the imagination.'* This language seems to suggest that the feeling is distinct from the idea that is the object of the belief and that since the feeling cannot be an idea, it must be an impression. But Hume denies that the feeling is an impression.

Stressing that there is a feeling peculiar to belief, Hume asks whether there are analogies between it and any other mental states. He wrote: 'This, therefore, being regarded as an undoubted truth, *that belief is nothing but a peculiar feeling, different from the simple conception*, the next question that naturally occurs, is, *what is the nature of this feeling, or sentiment, and whether it be analogous to any other sentiment of the human mind*?' (*T* 624). He then emphasizes that in beliefs there is 'a greater firmness and solidity in the conceptions' (*T* 624), that beliefs 'strike us with more force' (*T* 624), and 'approach nearer to the impressions, which are immediately present to us; and are therefore analogous to many other operations of the mind' (*T* 624-5). This leaves open the question whether 'force and vivacity' are characteristics of perceptions or impressions of reflection.

But Hume makes it clear in the following paragraph that he construed 'force and vivacity' as characteristics of the idea that is believed. In his words:

> There is not, in my opinion, any possibility of evading this conclusion, but by asserting, that belief, beside some simple conception, consists in some impression or feeling, distinguishable from the conception. It does not modify the conception, and render it more present and intense: It is only annex'd to it, after the same manner that *will* and *desire* are annex'd to particular conceptions of good and pleasure. (*T* 625)

This passage leaves little doubt that, at this point in his philosophical development, Hume considered 'force and vivacity' to be characteristics of the idea that is the object of the belief. If the degree of force and vivacity that is peculiar to belief were an impression of reflection, then it would be joined with the idea that is the object of belief, but it would not modify the idea itself. In this respect, it would be comparable to the direct passions of volition and desire, which, as effects of the pleasure one derives from the consideration of an object, add a certain emotional 'flavor' to the thought and can cause additional emotional responses, but do not modify the character of the impression or idea that is the object of the thought (cf. *T* 439). Hume here seems to believe that the modification of the idea itself that is the object of thought is what is essential to belief. And this is a theme that is stressed throughout Hume's four subsequent arguments that the feeling peculiar to belief is not an impression (cf. *T* 625-7).

The arguments Hume provides, however, are peculiar. The first focuses on impressions of sensation, and takes as its pivotal premise that 'no distinct impression attends every distinct idea, or conception of matter of fact. This is the subject of plain experience' (*T* 625). The kind of impression with which Hume must be concerned here is an impression of existence. But one might grant that, while there are no impressions of existence, there might be impressions of reflection that are peculiar to belief, although these would make no modification in the idea that is the object of belief. The second argument simply affirms that 'the mind has a firmer hold, or more steady conception of what it takes to be matter of fact, than of fictions' (*T* 626), and this is taken to be sufficient to show that there is no need to appeal to an impression. If this argument is at all plausible, the kind of impression Hume is denying to be peculiar to belief must be an impression of existence or reality. The third and fourth arguments are based upon explanatory principles (*T* 626-7), and by examining the third argument we shall be able to see why Hume denied that there is an impression that is peculiar to belief and why his argument fails.[15]

Hume's third argument reads:

> *Thirdly*, We can explain the *causes* of the firm conception but not those of any separate impression. And not only so, but the causes of the firm conception exhaust the whole subject, and nothing is left to produce any other effect. An inference concerning a matter of fact is nothing but the idea of an object, that has been frequently conjoin'd, or associated with a present impression. This is the whole of it. Every part is requisite to explain, from analogy, the more steady conception; and nothing remains capable of producing any distinct impression. (*T* 626)

To make sense of Hume's claim that 'We can explain the *causes* of the firm conception' one should notice that in the body of the *Treatise* Hume explains the causes of belief in terms of an impression's 'communication' of '*a share of its force and vivacity*' to an idea (*T* 98), and the conditions under which such a 'communication' occurs are specified by the principles of the association of ideas (*T* 98). Given Hume's account of causation, the notion of 'communication' of force and vivacity must be understood as metaphorical. While it might happen that an impression causes belief, one can no more claim that there is literally a communication or transfer of force and vivacity from an impression to an idea than one can claim that there is literally a transfer of momentum from one billiard ball to another: all that is warranted in claiming is that, in all cases of belief, a 'forceful and vivacious' impression is followed by a 'forceful and vivacious' idea (cf. *T* 174, the first 'definition' of cause and effect).

There are three shortcomings in Hume's third argument. First, Hume begs the question. He takes 'force and vivacity' to be qualities of an impression, but whether or not this is the case is the issue to be decided by the argument. His explanation of belief is germane to the question of the nature of 'force and vivacity' only if 'force and vivacity' are qualities of perceptions and are *literally* transferred from an impression to an idea in forming a belief. Second, he blurs the distinction between his two 'definitions' of causation. While Hume concerns himself with the question of inference, inference is irrelevant to explaining the causal relation between an impression (*qua* object) and the idea (*qua* object) that is 'enlivened' in the belief. Certainly, there *could* be a constant conjunction between two impressions of reflection, α and β, if α were peculiar to states of sense perception and β were peculiar to beliefs. In this case α would be the cause of β, but there would be no literal transfer of 'force and vivacity'. Finally, on his own principles, the claim that 'We can explain the *causes* of the firm conception but not those of any separate impression' is false, unless it is limited to impressions of sensation (cf. *T* 84). Giving such explanations is precisely what he does throughout his discussion of impressions of reflection. Thus, there is little reason to accept his conclusion that 'force and vivacity' are properties of impressions and ideas rather than impressions of reflection that are merely 'annex'd' to impressions and ideas. At best, his arguments show that 'force and vivacity' cannot be deemed impressions of sensation.

Did Hume come to recognize that his arguments in the Appendix were defective? There is some reason to believe he did. While in the *Abstract* Hume says little new regarding belief--continuing to talk of it, on the one hand, in terms of the 'strength' or 'vividness' of 'liveliness' of an idea (*Abstract*, *T* 654), and, on the other hand, in terms of 'a peculiar feeling or sentiment' (*Abstract*, *T* 655)--the language of the first *Enquiry* suggests a shift to the position that 'force and vivacity' is to be construed as an impression of reflection. After rehearsing his argument that belief cannot consist 'in any peculiar idea, which is annexed to such a conception as commands our assent' (*EHU* 47-8), he argues that it is marked by a particular 'sentiment or feeling, which is annexed' to a believed idea but not to a mere conception. In his words:

It follows, therefore, that the difference between *fiction* and *belief* lies in some sentiment or feeling, which is annexed to the latter, not to the former, and which depends not on the will, nor can be commanded at pleasure. It must be excited by nature, like all other sentiments; and must arise from the particular situation, in which the mind is placed at any particular juncture. Whenever any object is presented to the memory or senses, it immediately, by the force of custom, carries the imagination to conceive that object, which is usually conjoined to it; and this conception is attended with a feeling or sentiment, different from the loose reveries of the fancy. In this consists the whole nature of belief.

Notice that Hume here uses the word 'annexed'. The feeling peculiar to belief is not described as a characteristic of the idea which is the object of belief, rather, it is 'annexed' to it. Recall that in the Appendix Hume claimed that if the 'force and vivacity' peculiar to belief were not a characteristic of the idea which is the object of belief, then 'beside the simple conception, [there is] some impression or feeling . . . annex'd to it, after the same manner that *will* and *desire* are annex'd to particular conceptions of good and pleasure' (*T* 625). Hume's claims that the feeling is 'annexed' to the idea of the object of belief and that 'this conception is *attended with* [my emphasis] a feeling or sentiment' suggest that there is an impression of reflection that is contemporary with the idea believed, as does his analogy to 'all other sentiments'. Although Hume continues to use the terms 'force and vivacity' in describing belief, he gives an apology for the use of these terms (*EHU* 49; cf. *T* 629) and claims that 'Belief is the true and proper name of this feeling' (*EHU* 48-9). And the denial that 'force and vivacity' are to be construed as impressions and the contention that the claim that, in a state of belief, the force and vivacity of an impression is 'communicated to' an idea are conspicuously *missing* from the *Enquiry*.

Thus, I consider it plausible to suggest that by the time of the first *Enquiry* Hume had come to realize that 'force and vivacity' are to be explicated in terms of impressions of reflection that 'attend' or 'are annexed to' the object of belief. And since Hume was wont to stress that this makes belief analogous to 'other operations of the mind' (*EHU* 50), it is also reasonable to suggest that he acknowledged that the terms 'degrees of force and vivacity' and their presumptive synonyms denote a class of impressions of reflection that resemble one another in much the same way that shades of a color resemble one another. This implies that, at the phenomenal level, impressions are to be distinguished from ideas, not on the basis of any of their inherent characteristics, but on the basis of the impressions of reflection that are 'annexed' to them, that is, as impressions of reflection 'force and vivacity' function fundamentally as the basis for the differentiation of cognitive states.

If I am correct in suggesting that there are impressions of reflection that are peculiar to one's several cognitive states, this allows one to construct a coherent account of remembering a case of imagining. On the standard interpretation of 'force and vivacity' it is, at best, difficult to understand how it is possible to have a forceful and vivacious idea-- as is required in memory (*T* 9, 85)--of an idea that is inherently less forceful and vivacious. On my interpretation, this problem is easily resolved: one's current cognitive state includes a certain impression of reflection that is peculiar to states of memory, and the object of one's thought is *both* a certain idea of sensation and a certain idea of reflection that marks the previous cognitive state as a state of imagination.[16] Such an account also requires that cognitive states (thoughts, Humean intentional acts) are inherently even more complex than I suggested in Chapter 3: in addition to an impression of sensation, a causal relation and an idea of sensation, there must be an cognitive impression of reflection that 'accompanies' the impression of sensation. Like the impressions of sensation, these cognitive impressions of reflection might (or might not) cause an idea of a word (such as 'perception') which, in turn, might cause a cognitive idea of reflection.

Before concluding there is a further point that needs to be considered. I have been concerned solely with impressions of sensation and the impressions of reflection peculiar to cognitive states that accompany them. Since Hume also claimed that perceptions of reflection vary in degrees of 'force and vivacity', we must consider whether the account I have given also will allow one to distinguish between impressions and ideas of reflection. The answer to this question seems to be mixed. In the case of emotive impressions and ideas of reflection it seems that the distinction can be drawn, and if so, it is drawn on the basis of the kind of cognitive states in which impressions of reflection arise. In the case of cognitive impressions and ideas of reflection, however, it seems less promising. Consider the following examples.

Assume Sherlock Holmes is walking the streets of London and recognizes Moriarty standing near a street lamp. Since Holmes perceives Moriarty, there is a cognitive impression of reflection peculiar to states of perception that accompanies the Moriarty-impression of sensation. Recognizing Moriarty causes impressions of anger and hatred. How does one explain the 'force and vivacity' of those emotive impressions of reflection? It seems plausible to suggest that the 'force and vivacity' of those impressions of reflection is to be explained on the basis of the cognitive impression of reflection peculiar to the perceptual state in which Holmes is found. This cognitive impression of reflection would 'do double duty': it would mark both the impression of sensation and impression of reflection as an impression. I consider this plausible for the following reason. It seems that there are only a limited number of cognitive states in which an impression of reflection could be caused, and each of those is a state that, according to the standard way of interpreting Hume, contains a perception of sensation with a high degree of 'force and vivacity'. Holmes might become angry if he *sees* Moriarty. He might become angry if he *remembers* Moriarty. He might become angry if he thinks about Moriarty and *believes* that Moriarty is the master-mind behind the crime wave in London. And, perhaps, Holmes might become angry if Moriarty were the object of a dream. In each of these cases, it is the *fact* that Holmes *believes* Moriarty to be a master-criminal that is a partial cause of the impression of anger, and it seems reasonable to suggest that the 'force and vivacity' of the emotive impression of reflection is a function of the cognitive impression of reflection that is peculiar to that cognitive state. Were Holmes to discover that Moriarty actually has no criminal connections, the emotive impressions of anger and hatred would not occur.

Thus, it seems that one could explain the 'force and vivacity' of an emotive impression of reflection on the basis of the cognitive impression of reflection that is peculiar to the cognitive state in which the emotive impression is caused. However, there seems to be no similar phenomenal basis for distinguishing between cognitive impressions and ideas. The only way one could account for the greater 'force and vivacity' of a cognitive impression of reflection *vis-à-vis* its corresponding idea is by suggesting that each kind of cognitive impression of reflection itself causes another kind of cognitive impression of reflection, and such a move would generate an infinite hierarchy. While Hume might suggest that, after noting a certain number of the cognitive impressions of reflection in the hierarchy, 'the action of the mind becomes forc'd and unnatural' (*T* 185) and one simply ignores them, the very suggestion that there is an infinite hierarchy seems very unHumean. It seems more plausible to suggest that, if the account of Humean intentional acts that I developed in Chapter 3 is correct, a

183

cognitive idea of reflection is simply something that can be an *object* of thought, while a cognitive impression of reflection cannot be such. If this is correct and my argument that there is a shift in the account of 'force and vivacity' from the *Treatise* to the *Enquiry* is sound, then, while the copy theory of ideas in the *Treatise* was a causal hypothesis (*T* 4), in the *Enquiry* the copy theory of ideas can retain the status of a hypothesis only with respect to perceptions of sensation and emotive perceptions of reflection: with respect to cognitive impressions and ideas of reflection the contention that an impression is more 'forceful and vivacious' is simply stipulated. Perhaps this is why Hume could confidently write, 'The most lively thought is still inferior to the dullest sensation' (*EHU* 17).

Notes

[1]Noxon refers to this as the 'phenomenal criterion' for distinguishing between ideas of the memory and ideas of the imagination (Noxon 1976: 270-95; cf. Flage 1985b: 168-88). While most commentators take seriously Hume's two criteria for distinguishing between ideas of the memory and ideas of the imagination, Oliver Johnson recently has argued that 'force and vivacity' *alone* distinguish between ideas of the memory and ideas of the imagination (see Johnson 1987: 343-59). While Johnson almost certainly errs in attempting to reduce memory solely to feelings of force and vivacity, thereby ignoring all the epistemic considerations Hume seemed to consider essential to actual cases of memory, as will become clear below, I believe his thesis would have been more plausible if he had suggested that there is *a certain* feeling or *a certain range* of feelings of force and vivacity that are peculiar to states of memory. Unfortunately, Johnson leaves 'force and vivacity' undefined and does not even suggest that there is a particular 'degree of force and vivacity' that is peculiar to memory.

[2]One of the few explicit discussions of force and vivacity is Govier 1972. Govier attempts to explicate the terms 'force' and 'vivacity', and their Humean synonyms, in terms of the 'staying power' or influence of an idea and its clarity or amount of detail. She does not raise the kind of issue with which I shall be concerned. This is not to say that the kinds of problems with which I shall be concerned have gone unnoticed (cf. Stroud 1977: 27-33).

[3]R. J. Butler, for example, maintains that the degree of force and vivacity found of an impression, what he calls the 'feeling-tone' of an impression, can be distinguished from its content only on the basis of a distinction of reason (Butler 1976: 128-9; cf. Livingston 1984: 55).

[4]To facilitate a discussion of color, I pose my discussion in terms of the three-dimensional Munsell system.

[5]Some might take exception to this claim on the basis of the following passage: 'When you wou'd any way vary the idea of a particular object, you can only encrease or diminish its force and vivacity. If you make any other change on it, it represents a different object or impression. The case is the same as in colours. A particular shade of any colour may acquire a new degree of *liveliness or brightness* [my emphasis] without any other variation. But when you produce any other variation, 'tis no longer the same shade of colour' (*T* 96). Here Hume seems to say that variations in the degree of brightness do not change the idea. But here Hume's sense of 'brightness' must be different from that used in the Munsell system of color classification, for shades of the same hue that have the same saturation but differ in brightness are visibly distinguishable. Presumably, Hume used 'brightness' here in a further attempt to elucidate that characteristic--whatever it might be--that distinguishes impressions from ideas. This seems to be borne out by the fact that when Hume wrote the Appendix he cited this passage as containing an error. There he wrote, 'The second error may be found in Book I. page 96. where I say that two ideas of the same object can only be different by their different degrees of force and vivacity. I believe there are other differences among ideas, which cannot properly be comprehended under these terms. Had I said, that two ideas of the same object can only be different by their different *feeling*, I shou'd have been nearer the truth' (*T* 636). We shall examine below what can be made of this 'feeling'.

[6]Herbert Hochberg has taken exception to this argument, contending that I have not shown that force and vivacity cannot be a higher-level property of an impression, that is, a property of a state of affairs that is not itself a property of any component of that state of affairs. Such a property is comparable to a moral or an esthetic property. Since a moral or esthetic property can be an objective component of an object or situation (cf. Hochberg 1958: 2-19), there is no reason why degrees of force and vivacity could not be objective higher-level properties of impressions and ideas. For the sake of the argument, I shall grant the philosophical point that moral qualities might be objective. Further, the Hume of the *Treatise* generally treats degrees of force and vivacity as if they are properties of perceptions as such, and one of his remarks in the Appendix might lend some weight to a Hochbergian reading (cf. *T* 636). But two problems remain. First, even if one would grant that degrees of force and vivacity are higher-level properties of perceptions, such properties cannot be known directly. As Hume indicates in his discussion of morals, virtue is *known* only on the basis of a 'sentiment' (*T* 455-76), that is, an impression of reflection. This is consistent with the position I believe Hume ultimately favored. Second, as I argue below, to identify degrees of force and vivacity with characteristics of impressions and ideas *as such* will not do all the work Hume sets for force and vivacity, namely, the general differentiation of cognitive states.

[7]This is somewhat analogous to Locke's example of forming an idea of the nominal essence of gold. Malleability might be a property of gold, but one will 'notice' this property only under certain conditions (cf. Locke, *Essay*, 4.12.9).

[8]This scheme is almost certainly too simplistic, since it suggests a purely linear arrangement of impressions of reflection. If it is reasonable that 'degrees of force and vivacity' are impressions of reflection, it seems more plausible to suggest that, as in the three-dimensional Munsell system of color classification, there would be several aspects of impressions of reflection that would be involved. If this were the case, then, just as there are shades of different hues that resemble each other, so there might be 'shades' of sense perception that resemble both 'shades' of madness and 'shades' of belief.

[9]It seems clear that impressions of bodily pain or pleasure are a kind of impression of the touch, in so far as such impressions would seem to include kinesthetic sensations. Although Hume does not discuss kinesthetic sensations, it might be helpful to compare Berkeley (1948-57: 1:176-7).

[10]If my contention is correct that degrees of force and vivacity are to be construed as impressions of reflection, then they, like other nonspatial impressions, are not 'only co-existent in general' with impressions or ideas of sensation, 'but also co-temporary in the appearance in the mind' (*T* 237), and, just as in the case of the impression of necessity, there would be a tendency for the mind to 'project' the impression of reflection into the impression of sensation. Given Hume's fairly extensive commentary on the tendency of the mind to project nonspatial ideas into spatial entities (*T* 167, 217, 237, 504n), it might be ironic that the Hume of the *Treatise* does not announce with the appropriate fanfare, or even seem to have recognized, that a projection of impressions of reflection occurs in every case of sensible perception.

[11]For a more general discussion of the evolution of Hume's account of belief, see Hansen (1988).

[12]If the general case is plausible, this implies that Hume did not distinguish impressions of sensation from ideas of sensation on the basis of the characteristics of the respective perceptions, rather, he held that impressions of sensation are those perceptions found in states of sense perception while ideas of sensation are those found in all other cognitive states.

[13]As far as I know, this is the only place in the body of the *Treatise* where Hume provides anything that might be considered an elucidation of the notion of 'force and vivacity'.

[14]As he remarks in a footnote, 'This act of mind [belief] has never yet been explain'd by any philosopher; and therefore I am at liberty to propose my hypothesis concerning it; which is, that 'tis only a strong and steady conception of any idea, and such as approaches in some measure to an impression' (*T* 97n).

[15]The fourth argument reads: 'The *effects* of belief, in influencing the passions and imagination, can all be explain'd from the firm conception; and there is no occasion to have recourse to any other principle' (*T* 626). Most of the difficulties with the third argument also apply with regard to the fourth, and consequently, we may pass over the fourth argument without further comment.

[16]This is merely a phenomenal description. Hume also requires that the ideas that are the object of one's memory are 'restrain'd to the same order and form with the original impressions' (*T* 9). On memory, see Chapter 3 above.

Bibliography

A. (B.) C. (1727) *The Theory, or Rationale of Ideas, in a Letter to a Friend*, London: Thomas Howlatt.

Ammerman, R. (1965) 'Our Knowledge of Substance According to Locke', *Theoria* 31: 1-8.

Anderson, R. F. (1966) *Hume's First Principles*, Lincoln: University of Nebraska Press.

_____ (1975) 'Hume's Account of Knowledge of External Objects', *Journal of the History of Philosophy* 13: 471-80.

_____ (1976) 'The Location, Extension, Shape, and Size of Hume's Perceptions', in Livingston and King (1975), pp. 153-71.

Annas, J. and Barnes, J. (1985) *The Modes of Scepticism: Ancient Texts and Modern Interpretations*, London: Cambridge University Press.

Aristotle, (1941) *The Basic Works of Aristotle*, ed. Richard McKeon, New York: Random House.

Armstrong, D. M. (1968) *A Materialist Theory of the Mind*, London: Routledge & Kegan Paul.

Arnauld, A. (1964) *The Art of Thinking: Port-Royal Logic*, trans. James Dickoff and Patricia James, Indianapolis: Bobbs-Merrill, Library of Liberal Arts.

Ashley, L. and Stack, M. (1974) 'Hume's Theory of the Self and Its Identity', *Dialogue* 13: 239-54.

Ayer, A. J. (1980) *Hume*, Past Masters, New York: Hill & Wang.

Bacon, F. (1960) *The New Organon*, ed. Fulton H. Anderson, Indianapolis: Bobbs-Merrill, Library of Liberal Arts.

Basson, A. H. (1958) *David Hume*, Pelican History of Philosophy, Baltimore: Penguin.

Bayle, P. (1964) *Historical and Critical Dictionary*, trans. Richard H. Popkin, Indianapolis: Bobbs-Merrill, Library of Liberal Arts.

Beattie, J. (1770) *An Essay on the Nature and Immutability of Truth*, Edinburgh; rep. edn, New York: Garland, 1983.

Bennett, J. (1971) *Locke, Berkeley, Hume: Central Themes*, Oxford: Clarendon Press.

Bergmann, G. (1957) *Philosophy of Science*, Madison: University of Wisconsin Press.

Bibliography

____ (1959) 'Intentionality', in his *Meaning and Existence*, Madison: University of Wisconsin Press, pp. 3-38.

____ (1964) 'Acts', in his *Logic and Reality*, Madison: University of Wisconsin Press, pp. 3-44.

____ (1967) *Realism*, Madison: University of Wisconsin Press.

Berkeley, G. (1948-57) *The Works of George Berkeley, Bishop of Cloyne*, 9 vols, ed. by A. A. Luce and T. E. Jessop, London: Thomas Nelson.

Blundevile, T. (1599) *The Arte of Logicke*, London; rep. edn, New York and Amsterdam: De Capo Press and Theatrum Orbis Terrum, 1969.

Boër, S. E. and Lycan, W. G. (1986) *Knowing Who*, Cambridge, Mass.: MIT Press.

Bolingbroke, H. St.-J., Lord (1844) *The Works of Lord Bolingbroke*, 4 vols, London; rep. edn, New York: A. M. Kelly.

Boring, E. G. (1950) *A History of Experimental Psychology*, 2nd edn, New York: Appleton-Century-Crofts.

Braithwaite, R. B. (1959) *Scientific Explanation: A Study of the Function of Theory, Probability and Law in Science*, London: Cambridge University Press.

Brett, N. (1972) 'Substance and Mental Identity in Hume's *Treatise*', *Philosophical Quarterly* 22: 110-25.

Bricke, J. (1980) *Hume's Philosophy of Mind*, Princeton: Princeton University Press.

Broad, C. D. (1925) *The Mind and Its Place in Nature*, London: Kegan Paul.

____ (1961) 'Hume's Doctrine of Space', Dawes Hicks Lecture on Philosophy, *Proceedings of the British Academy* 47: 161-76.

Broughton, J. (1987) 'Hume's Ideas about Necessary Connection', *Hume Studies* 13: 217-44.

Butchvarov, P. (1959) 'The Self and Perceptions: A Study in Humean Philosophy', *Philosophical Quarterly* 9: 97-115.

Butler, J. (1906) *The Analogy of Religion*, intro. by Ronald Bayne, New York: Dutton.

Butler, R. J. (1976) 'Hume's Impressions', in Vesey 1976: 122-36.

Capaldi, N. (1975) *David Hume: The Newtonian Philosopher*, Boston: Twayne.

Chappell, V. C., (ed.) (1966) *Hume: A Collection of Critical Essays*, Garden City, New York: Doubleday.

____ (1972) 'Hume on What There Is', in *Reason and Reality*, Royal Institute of Philosophy Lectures V, London: Macmillan, pp. 88-98.

Colie, R. L. (1959) 'Spinoza and the Early English Deists', *Journal of the History of Ideas* 20: 23-46.

Copleston, F. (1959) *Modern Philosophy: The British Philosophers*, vol. 5, part 2 of *A History of Philosophy*, Garden City, New York: Doubleday Image Books.

Crousaz, J. P. (1724) *A New Treatise of the Art of Thinking; Or, A Compleat System of Reflections concerning the Conduct and Improvement of the Mind, Done into English*, 2 vols, London: Tho. Woodward.

Bibliography

Cummins, P. D. (1973a) 'Hume's Disavowal of the *Treatise*', *Philosophical Review* 82: 371-9.

_____ (1973b) 'Locke's Anticipation of Hume's Use of "Impression"', *Modern Schoolman* 50: 297-301.

Cummins, R. (1978) 'The Missing Shade of Blue', *Philosophical Review* 87: 548-65.

Descartes, R. (1970) *Philosophical Letters*, trans. and ed. Anthony Kenny, Minneapolis: University of Minnesota Press.

_____ (1976) *Descartes' Conversation with Burman*, trans. John Cottingham, Oxford: Clarendon Press.

_____ (1984-5) *The Philosophical Writings of Descartes*, 2 vols, trans. by John Cottingham, Robert Stroothoff, and Dugald Murdoch, Cambridge: Cambridge University Press.

Edwards, P. (1967) *The Encyclopedia of Philosophy*, 8 vols, New York: Macmillan.

Fang, W.-C. (1984) 'Hume on Identity', *Hume Studies* 10: 59-68.

Ferreira, M. J. (1986) 'Locke's "Constructive Skepticism"--A Reappraisal', *Journal of the History of Philosophy* 24: 211-22.

Flage, D. E. (1980) 'Hume's Identity Crisis', *Modern Schoolman* 55: 21-35.

_____ (1981a) 'Hume's Relative Ideas', *Hume Studies* 7: 55-73.

_____ (1981b) 'Locke's Relative Ideas', *Theoria* 47: 144-59.

_____ (1982a) 'Hume's Dualism', *Nous* 16: 527-41.

_____ (1982b) 'Relative Ideas Revisited: A Reply to Thomas', *Hume Studies* 8: 158-71.

_____ (1985a) 'Berkeley's Notions', *Philosophy and Phenomenological Research* 45: 407-25.

_____ (1985b) 'Hume on Memory and Causation', *Hume Studies*, 10th Anniversary Issue: 168-88.

_____ (1986a) 'Berkeley on Abstraction', *Journal of the History of Philosophy* 24: 483-501.

_____ (1986b) 'Hume on Denotation and Connotation', *Southern Journal of Philosophy* 24: 451-61.

_____ (1987a) *Berkeley's Doctrine of Notions: A Reconstruction based on his Theory of Meaning*, London: Croom Helm.

_____ (1987b) 'The Minds of David Hume', *Hume Studies* 13: 245-74.

Flage, D. E. and Glass, R. J. (1984) 'Hume on the Cartesian Theory of Substance', *Southern Journal of Philosophy* 22: 497-508.

Flew, A. (1961) *Hume's First Principles: A Study of His First 'Inquiry'*, International Library of Philosophy and Scientific Method, London: Routledge & Kegan Paul.

_____ (1986) *David Hume: Philosopher of Moral Science*, London: Blackwell.

Fogelin, R. J. (1985) *Hume's Scepticism in the Treatise of Human Nature*, London: Routledge & Kegan Paul.

Force, J. E. (1987) 'Hume's Interest in Newton and Science', *Hume Studies* 13: 166-216.

Bibliography

Gale, G. (1979) *Theory of Science: An Introduction to the History, Logic, and Philosophy of Science*, New York: McGraw-Hill.

Gardiner, P. L. (1963) 'Hume's Theory of the Passions', in Pears 1963: 31-42.

Garrett, D. (1981) 'Hume's Self-Doubts about Personal Identity', *Philosophical Review* 90: 337-58.

Glymour, C. (1980) *Theory and Evidence*, Princeton: Princeton University Press.

Govier, T. (1972) 'Variations on *Force* and *Vivacity* in Hume', *Philosophical Quarterly* 22: 44-52.

Hall, R. (1974) 'Hume's Use of Locke on Identity', *Locke Newsletter* 5: 56-75.

Hammond, W. S. (1964) 'Hume's Phenomenalism', *Modern Schoolman* 41: 209-26.

Hansen, S. J. (1988) 'Hume's Impressions of Belief', *Hume Studies* 14: 277-304.

Hanson, N. R. (1958) 'The Logic of Discovery', *Journal of Philosophy* 55: 1079-89.

____ (1961) *Patterns of Discovery*, London: Cambridge University Press.

____ (1971) *Observation and Explanation: A Guide to Philosophy of Science*, New York: Harper Torchbooks.

Harman, G. (1973) *Thought*, Princeton: Princeton University Press.

Hearn, T. K., Jr. (1969) 'Norman Kemp Smith on "Natural Belief"', *Southern Journal of Philosophy* 7: 3-7.

Hendel, C. (1963) *Studies in the Philosophy of David Hume*, new edn, Indianapolis: Bobbs-Merrill, Library of Liberal Arts.

Hickman, L. (1980) *Modern Theories of Higher Level Predication: Second Intentions in the Neuzeit*, Munich: Philosophia.

Hochberg, H. (1958) 'Phenomena, Value, and Objectivity', *Philosophical Quarterly* 8: 2-19.

____ (1978) *Thought, Fact and Reference: The Origins and Ontology of Logical Atomism*, Minneapolis: University of Minnesota Press.

Hume, D. (1886) *The Philosophical Works*, ed. Thomas Hill Green and Thomas Hodge Grose, 4 vols, London; rep. edn, Darmstadt: Scientia Verlag Aalen, 1964.

____ (1932) *The Letters of David Hume*, ed. J. Y. T. Greig, 2 vols, Oxford: Clarendon Press.

____ (1947) *Dialogues concerning Natural Religion*, ed. Norman Kemp Smith, Indianapolis: Bobbs-Merrill.

____ (1956) *The Natural History of Religion*, ed. H. E. Root, Stanford: Stanford University Press.

____ (1967) *A Letter from a Gentleman to his Friend in Edinburgh*, ed. E. C. Mossner and J. V. Price, Edinburgh: Edinburgh University Press.

____ (1975) *Enquiries concerning the Human Understanding and concerning the Principles of Morals*, ed. L. A. Selby-Bigge, 3rd edn revised by P. H. Nidditch, Oxford: Clarendon Press.

____ (1978) *A Treatise of Human Nature*, ed. L. A. Selby-Bigge, 2nd edn revised by P. H. Nidditch, Oxford: Clarendon Press.

Bibliography

Jessop, T. E. (1952) 'Some Misunderstandings of Hume', reprinted in Chappell 1966: 35-52.

Johnson, O. (1987) '"Lively" Memory and "Past" Memory', *Hume Studies* 13: 343-59.

Jones, P. (1982) *Hume's Sentiments: Their Ciceronian and French Context*, Edinburgh: Edinburgh University Press.

Kames, H. Home, Lord (1751) *Essays of the Principles of Morality and Natural Religion*, Edinburgh: A. Kincaid and A. Donaldson.

Kripke, S. A. (1980) *Naming and Necessity*, Cambridge, Mass.: Harvard University Press.

Laing, B. M. (1932) *David Hume*, London: Ernest Benn.

Laird, J. (1932) *Hume's Philosophy of Human Nature*, London; rep. edn, Hamdem, Conn.: Archon Books, 1967.

Leyden, W. von (1957) 'Hume and "Imperfect Identity"', *Philosophical Quarterly* 7: 340-52.

Livingston, D. W. (1979) 'Time and Value in Hume's Social and Political Philosophy', in Norton, Capaldi, and Robison (1979), pp. 181-201.

____ (1984) *Hume's Philosophy of Common Life*, Chicago: University of Chicago Press.

Livingston, D. W. and King, J. T. (eds) (1976) *Hume: A Re-Evaluation*, New York: Fordham University Press.

Locke, J. (1823) *The Works of John Locke*, 10 vols, London; rep. edn, Darmstadt: Scientia Verlag Aalen, 1963.

____ (1975) *An Essay concerning Human Understanding*, ed. Peter H. Nidditch, Oxford: Clarendon Press.

McRae, R. (1985) 'Perceptions, Objects and the Nature of Mind', *Hume Studies*, 10th Anniversary Issue: 150-67.

Marras, A. (ed.) (1972) *Intentionality, Mind, and Language*, Urbana: University of Illinois Press.

Matson, W. I. (1987) *A New History of Philosophy*, 2 vols, New York: Harcourt, Brace, Jovanovich.

Merrill, K. R. and Shahan, R. W. (eds) (1976) *David Hume: Many-Sided Genius*, Norman: University of Oklahoma Press.

Montaigne, M. de (1976) *Apology for Raymond Sebond*, in *The Complete Essays of Montaigne*, trans. Donald M. Frame, Stanford: Stanford University Press, 1976, pp. 318-457.

Monteiro, J. P. (1981) 'Hume's Conception of Science', *Journal of the History of Philosophy* 19: 327-42.

Moore, G. E. (1922) *Philosophical Studies*, London: Routledge & Kegan Paul.

Mouton, D. L. (1974) 'Hume and Descartes on Self-Acquaintance', *Dialogue* 13: 255-69.

Nathanson, S. (1976) 'Hume's Second Thoughts on the Self', *Hume Studies* 2: 36-46.

Nelson, J. O. (1972) 'Two Main Questions concerning Hume's *Treatise* and *Enquiries*', *Philosophical Review* 81: 333-50.

191

Bibliography

Neujahr, P. J.(1978) 'Hume on Identity', *Hume Studies* 4: 18-28.

Newton, I. (1966) *Mathematical Principles of Natural Philosophy and His System of the World*, 2 vols, trans. Andrew Motte, trans. revised by Florian Cajori, Berkeley and Los Angeles: University of California Press.

Nicholas of Autrecourt (1986) *Letters to Bernard of Arezzo*, in *Philosophy in the Middle Ages*, ed. Arthur Hyman and James J. Walsh, 2nd edn, Indianapolis: Hackett, 1986.

Norton, D. F., Capaldi, N., and Robison, W. (1979) *McGill Hume Studies*, Studies in Hume and Scottish Philosophy, San Diego: Austin Hill Press.

Noxon, J. (1969) 'Senses Identity in Hume's *Treatise*', *Dialogue* 8: 367-84.

_____ (1973) *Hume's Philosophical Development: A Study of his Methods*, Oxford: Clarendon Press.

_____ (1976) 'Remembering and Imagining the Past', in Livingston and King 1976: 270-95.

Pappas, G. S. (ed.) (1979) *Justification and Knowledge*, Dordrecht: D. Reidel.

Passmore, J. (1980) *Hume's Intentions*, 3rd edn, London: Duckworth.

Pears, D. F. (ed.) (1963) *David Hume: A Symposium*, London: Macmillan.

_____ (1976) 'The Naturalism of Book I of Hume's *Treatise of Human Nature*', Dawes Hicks Lecture on Philosophy, *Proceedings of the British Academy* 62: 3-22.

Penelhum, T. (1975a) *David Hume*, Philosophers in Perspective, New York: St. Martin's Press.

_____ (1975b) 'Hume's Theory of the Self Revisited', *Dialogue* 14: 389-409.

_____ (1976) 'The Self in Hume's Philosophy', in Merrill and Shahan 1976: 9-23.

Popkin, R. H. (1979) 'Hume and Spinoza', *Hume Studies* 5: 66-9.

Price, H. H. (1940) *Hume's Theory of the External World*, Oxford: Clarendon Press.

_____ (1969) *Thinking and Experience*, London: Hutchison University Library.

Reid, T. (1969a) *Essays on the Active Powers of the Human Mind*, intro. Baruch Brody, Cambridge, Mass.: MIT Press.

_____ (1969b) *Essays on the Intellectual Powers of Man*, intro. Baruch Brody, Cambridge, Mass.: MIT Press.

_____ (1970) *An Inquiry into the Human Mind*, ed. Timothy J. Duggan, Chicago: University of Chicago Press.

Robison, W. L. (1976) 'Hume's Ontological Commitments', *Philosophical Quarterly* 26: 39-47.

Russell, B. (1912) *The Problems of Philosophy*, London: Oxford University Press.

_____ (1918) 'The Philosophy of Logical Atomism', in *Logic and Knowledge: Essays 1901-1950*. ed. R. C. Marsh, New York: Capricorn Books, 1956, pp. 175-281.

_____ (1921) *The Analysis of Mind*, London: Allen & Unwin.

_____ (1922) *Our Knowledge of the External World*, 2nd edn, London: Allen & Unwin.

____ (1963) *Mysticism and Logic*, London: Unwin Books.

Schlereth, T. J. (1977) *The Cosmopolitan Ideal in Enlightenment Thought*, Notre Dame: University of Notre Dame Press.

Searle, J. R. (1983) *Intentionality: An Essay in the Philosophy of Mind*, London: Cambridge University Press.

Segerstedt, Torgny T. (1935) *The Problem of Knowledge in Scottish Philosophy*, Lund: C. W. K. Gleerup.

[Sergeant, J.] J.S. (1696) *Method to Science*, London: W. Redamayne.

____ (1697) *Solid Philosophy Asserted, Against the Fancies of the Ideists: Or, The Method to Science Farther Illustrated*, London: Roger Clevil.

Sextus Empiricus (1985) *Selections from the Major Writings on Scepticism, Man, and God*, ed. P. H. Hallie, trans. S. G. Etheridge, Indianapolis: Hackett.

Shaffer, J. (1967) 'Mind-Body Problem', in Edwards 1967: 336-46.

Shaftesbury, A. A. Cooper, Third Earl, (1964) *Characteristics of Men, Manners, Opinions, Times*, 2 vols, ed. J. M. Robertson, intro. S. Grean, Indianapolis: Bobbs-Merrill, Library of Liberal Arts.

Sisson, C. H. (1976) *David Hume*, Edinburgh: Ramsay Head Press.

Smith, N. K. (1905) 'The Naturalism of Hume', *Mind* 14: 149-73 and 335-47.

____ (1941) *The Philosophy of David Hume: A Critical Study of Its Origins and Central Doctrines*, London: Macmillan.

Spinoza, B. (1985) *The Collected Works of Spinoza*, trans. and ed. Edwin Curley, Princeton: Princeton University Press.

Stephen, L. (1949) *History of English Thought in the Eighteenth Century*, 3rd edn, 2 vols, New York: Peter Smith.

Stroud, B. (1977) *Hume*, The Arguments of the Philosophers, London: Routledge & Kegan Paul.

Swain, M. (1979) 'Justification and the Basis of Belief', in Pappas 1979: 25-49.

Thagard, P. R. (1978) 'The Best Explanation: Criteria for Theory Choice', *Journal of Philosophy* 75: 76-92.

Traiger, S. (1985) 'Hume on Finding an Impression of the Self', *Hume Studies* 11: 47-68.

Tweyman, S. (1974a) 'Hume on Separating the Inseparable', in W. E. Todd, (ed.) *Hume and the Enlightenment: Essays Presented to Ernest Campbell Mossner*, Edinburgh: Edinburgh University Press, pp. 30-42.

____ (1974b) *Reason and Conduct in Hume and His Predecessors*, The Hague: Martinus Nijhoff.

____ (1986) *Skepticism and Belief in Hume's Dialogues Concerning Natural Religion*, International Archives of the History of Ideas, Dordrecht: Martinus Nijhoff.

Urbach, P. (1987) *Francis Bacon's Philosophy of Science*, La Salle: Open Court.

Vesey, G. (1976) *Impressions of Empiricism*, Royal Institute of Philosophy Lectures, vol. 9 (1974-5), New York: St. Martin's Press.

Bibliography

Watts, Isaac (1806) *Logic, or the Right Use of Reason, in the Inquiry after Truth*, 3rd American edn, Boston: Ranlett & Norris.

Wilson, F. (1989) 'Is Hume a Sceptic with Regard to the Senses?' *Journal of the History of Philosophy* 27: 49-73.

Wolfram, S. (1974) 'Hume on Personal Identity', *Mind* 83: 586-93.

Wright, J. P. (1983) *The Sceptical Realism of David Hume*, Minneapolis: University of Minnesota Press.

Yolton, J. W. (1956) *John Locke and the Way of Ideas*, Oxford: Clarendon Press.

—— (1980) 'Hume's Ideas', *Hume Studies* 6: 1-25.

—— (1983) *Thinking Matter: Materialism in Eighteenth-Century Britain*, Minneapolis: University of Minnesota Press.

—— (1984) *Perceptual Acquaintance from Descartes to Reid*, Minneapolis: University of Minnesota Press.

Zabeeh, F. (1960) *Hume: Precursor of Modern Empiricism: An analysis of his opinions on Meaning, Metaphysics, Logic and Mathematics*, The Hague: Martinus Nijhoff.

Index